FORM A
EIGHTH EDITION

The Least You Should Know about English

Writing Skills

Paige Wilson

Pasadena City College

Teresa Ferster Glazier

THOMSON
WADSWORTH

Australia   Canada   Mexico   Singapore   Spain   United Kingdom   United States

THOMSON

WADSWORTH

The Least You Should Know about English, Form A, Eighth Edition
Writing Skills

Wilson • Glazier

Publisher: *Michael Rosenberg*
Acquisitions Editor: *Stephen Dalphin*
Development Editor: *Michell Phifer*
Production Editor: *Matt Drapeau*
Executive Marketing Manager: *Ken Kasee*
Marketing Manager: *Katrina Byrd*

Manufacturing Coordinator: *Marcia Locke*
Compositor: *Modern Graphics*
Project Manager: *Colophon*
Cover Designer: *Dutton and Sherman Design*
Printer: *Phoenix Book*

Printed in the United States of America
3 4 5 6 7 8 9 10   06 05 04

For more information contact Wadsworth, 25 Thomson Place, Boston, Massachusetts 02210 USA, or you can visit our Internet site at http://www.wadsworth.com

For permission to use material from this text or product contact us:
Tel   1-800-730-2214
Fax   1-800-730-2215
Web   www.thomsonrights.com

**Library of Congress
Cataloging-in-Publication Data**

Wilson, Paige.
    The least you should know about English : writing skills : form A / Paige Wilson, Teresa Ferster Glazier.— 8th ed.
        p. cm.
    Includes bibliographical references and index.
    ISBN 0-15-506225-5 (alk. paper)
    1. English language—Rhetoric—Problems, exercises, etc. 2. English language—Grammer—Problems, exercises, etc. 3. Report writing—Problems, exercises, etc. I. Glazier, Teresa Ferster. II. Title.

PE1413 .G57 2003
808'.042—dc21

2003017197

This book is for students who need to review basic English skills and who may profit from a simplified "least you should know" approach. Parts 1 to 3 cover the essentials of word choice and spelling, sentence structure, punctuation and capitalization. Part 4 on writing teaches students the basic structures of the paragraph and the essay, along with the writing skills necessary to produce them.

Throughout the book, we try to avoid the use of linguistic terminology whenever possible. Students work with words they know instead of learning a vocabulary they may never use again.

There are abundant exercises, including practice with writing sentences and proofreading paragraphs—enough so that students learn to use the rules automatically and thus *carry their new skills over into their writing*. Exercises consist of sets of ten thematically related, informative sentences on such subjects as earthquake art, a wedding of elephants in Thailand, a pair of Levi's jeans worth nearly $50,000, the first tourist in outer space, and so on. Such exercises reinforce the need for coherence and details in student writing. With answers provided at the back of the book, students can correct their own work and progress at their own pace.

For the eighth edition, we have added a section on Parts of Speech to Part 1 and have continued to enhance Part 4 on writing. Part 4 introduces students to the writing process and stresses the development of the student's written "voice." Writing assignments follow each discussion, and there are samples by both student and professional writers. Part 4 ends with a section designed to help students with writing assignments based on readings. It includes articles to read, react to, and summarize. Students improve their reading by learning to spot main ideas and their writing by learning to write meaningful reactions and concise summaries.

The Least You Should Know about English functions equally well in the classroom and at home as a self-tutoring text. The simple explanations, ample exercises, and answers at the back of the book provide students with everything they need to progress on their own. Students who have previously been overwhelmed by the complexities of English should, through mastering simple rules and through writing and rewriting simple papers, gain enough competence to succeed in further composition courses.

For their thoughtful commentary on the book, we would like to thank the following reviewers: Brenda Freaney, Bakersfield College; Ann George, Northwestern Michigan College; Bronwyn Jones, Northwestern Michigan College; Kaye Kolkmann, Modesto Junior College; Rosella Miller, North Idaho College; Carol Miter, Riverside Community College; Brigid Murphy, Pima Community College; Barbara Perry, Northwest Indian College; and Jane Wilson, Modesto Junior College.

In addition, we would like to thank our publishing team for their expertise and hard work: Steve Dalphin, Acquisitions Editor; Michell Phifer, Developmental Editor; Matt Drapeau, Production Editor; Peg Latham of Colophon, Project Manager; and the staff of Modern Graphics, especially Michael Byers.

As always, we are indebted to Herb and Moss Rabbin, Kenneth Glazier, and the rest of our families and friends for their support and encouragement.

Paige Wilson and Teresa Ferster Glazier

A **Test Packet** with additional exercises and ready-to-photocopy tests accompanies this text and is available to instructors.

Contents

3. PUNCTUATION AND CAPITAL LETTERS   175

What Is the Least You Should Know?

Most English textbooks try to teach you more than you need to know. This book will teach you the least you should know—and still help you learn to write clearly and acceptably. You won't have to deal with grammatical terms like *gerund, modal auxiliary verb,* or *demonstrative pronoun.* You can get along without knowing such technical labels if you learn a few key concepts. You *should* know about the parts of speech and how to use and spell common words; you *should* be able to recognize subjects and verbs; you *should* know the basics of sentence structure and punctuation—but rules, as such, will be kept to a minimum.

The English you'll learn in this book is sometimes called Standard Written English, and it may differ slightly or greatly from the spoken English you use. Standard Written English is the form of writing accepted in business and the professions. So no matter how you speak, you will communicate better in writing when you use Standard Written English. You might *say* something like "That's a whole nother problem," and everyone will understand, but you would probably want to *write,* "That's a completely different problem." Knowing the difference between spoken English and Standard Written English is essential in college, in business, and in life.

Until you learn the least you should know, you'll probably have difficulty communicating in writing. Take this sentence for example:

Since I easily past my driving test, I deserve a car of my own.

We assume that the writer used the *sound,* not the meaning, of the word *past* to choose it and in so doing used the wrong word. If the sentence had read

Since I easily *passed* my driving test, I deserve a car of my own.

then the writer would have communicated clearly. Or take this sentence:

The tigers clawed each other and their trainer and I watched from outside the cage.

This sentence includes two statements and therefore needs punctuation, a comma in this case:

> The tigers clawed each other, and their trainer and I watched from outside the cage.

But perhaps the writer meant

> The tigers clawed each other and their trainer, and I watched from outside the cage.

Punctuation makes all the difference, especially for the trainer. With the help of this text, we hope you'll learn to make your writing so clear that no one will misunderstand it.

As you make your way through the book, it's important to remember information after you learn it because many concepts and structures build upon others. For example, once you can identify subjects and verbs, you'll be able to recognize fragments, understand subject-verb agreement, and use correct punctuation. Explanations and examples are brief and clear, and it shouldn't be difficult to learn from them—*if you want to*. But you have to want to!

How to Learn the Least You Should Know

1. Read each explanatory section carefully (aloud, if possible).

2. Do the first exercise. Compare your answers with those at the back of the book. If they don't match, study the explanation again to find out why.

3. Do the second exercise and correct it. If you miss a single answer, go back once more to the explanation. You must have missed something. Be tough on yourself. Don't just think, "Maybe I'll get it right next time." Reread the examples, and *then* try the next exercise. It's important to correct each group of ten sentences before moving on so that you'll discover your mistakes early.

4. You may be tempted to quit after you do one or two exercises perfectly. Instead, make yourself finish another exercise. It's not enough to *understand* a concept or structure. You have to *practice* using it.

5. If you're positive, however, after doing several exercises, that you've learned a concept or structure, take the next exercise as a test. If you miss even one answer, you should do all the rest of the questions. Then move on to the proofreading and sentence composing exercises so that your understanding carries over into your writing.

Learning the basics of word choice and spelling, sentence structure, and punctuation does take time. Generally, college students spend a couple of hours outside of class for each hour in class. You may need more. Undoubtedly, the more time you spend, the more your writing will improve.

Word Choice and Spelling

Anyone can learn to use words more effectively and become a better speller. You can eliminate most of your word choice and spelling errors if you want to. It's just a matter of deciding you're going to do it. If you really intend to improve your word choice and spelling, study each of the following eight sections until you make no mistakes in the exercises.

Your Own List of Misspelled Words
Words Often Confused (Sets 1 and 2)
The Eight Parts of Speech
Contractions
Possessives
Words That Can Be Broken into Parts
Rule for Doubling the Final Letter
Using a Dictionary

Your Own List of Misspelled Words

On the inside cover of your English notebook or in some other obvious place, write correctly all the misspelled words from your previously graded papers. Review the correct spellings until you're sure of them, and edit your papers to find and correct repeated errors.

Words Often Confused (Set 1)

Learning the differences between these often-confused words will help you overcome many of your spelling problems. Study the words carefully, with their examples, before trying the exercises.

a, an

Use *an* before a word that begins with a vowel *sound* (*a, e, i,* and *o,* plus *u* when it sounds like *uh*) or silent *h.* Note that it's not the letter but the *sound* of the letter that matters.

> an apple, an essay, an inch, an onion
>
> an umpire, an ugly design (the *u*'s sound like *uh*)
>
> an hour, an honest person (silent *h*)

Use *a* before a word that begins with a consonant sound (all the sounds except the vowels, plus *u* or *eu* when they sound like *you*).

> a chart, a pie, a history book (the *h* is not silent in *history*)
>
> a union, a uniform, a unit (the *u*'s sound like *you*)
>
> a European vacation, a euphemism (*eu* sounds like *you*)

accept, except

Accept means "to receive willingly."

> I *accept* your apology.

Except means "excluding" or "but."

> Everyone arrived on time *except* him.

advise, advice

Advise is a verb (pronounce the *s* like a *z*).

> I *advise* you to take your time finding the right job.

Advice is a noun (it rhymes with *rice*).

> My counselor gave me good *advice.*

affect, effect

Affect is a verb and means "to alter or influence."

> All quizzes will *affect* the final grade.
>
> The happy ending *affected* the mood of the audience.

Effect is most commonly used as a noun and means "a result." If *a, an,* or *the* is in front of the word, then you'll know it isn't a verb and will use *effect.*

The strong coffee had a powerful *effect* on me.

We studied the *effects* of sleep deprivation in my psychology class.

all ready, already

If you can leave out the *all* and the sentence still makes sense, then *all ready* is the form to use. (In that form, *all* is a separate word and could be left out.)

We're *all ready* for our trip. (*We're ready for our trip* makes sense.)

The banquet is *all ready*. (*The banquet is ready* makes sense.)

But if you can't leave out the *all* and still have the sentence make sense, then use *already* (the form in which the *al* has to stay in the word).

They've *already* eaten. (*They've ready eaten* doesn't make sense.)

We have seen that movie *already*.

are, our

Are is a verb.

We *are* going to Colorado Springs.

Our shows we possess something.

We painted *our* fence to match the house.

brake, break

Brake used as a verb means "to slow or stop motion." It's also the name of the device that slows or stops motion.

I had to *brake* quickly to avoid an accident.

Luckily I just had my *brakes* fixed.

Break used as a verb means "to shatter" or "to split." It's also the name of an interruption, as in "a coffee break."

She never thought she would *break* a world record.

Enjoy your spring *break*.

choose, chose

The difference here is one of time. Use *choose* for present and future; use *chose* for past.

I will *choose* a new major this semester.

We *chose* the wrong time of year to get married.

clothes, cloths

Clothes are something you wear; *cloths* are pieces of material you might clean or polish something with.

I love the *clothes* that characters wear in movies.

The car wash workers use special *cloths* to dry the cars.

coarse, course   *Coarse* describes a rough texture.

I used *coarse* sandpaper to smooth the surface of the board.

Course is used for all other meanings.

Of *course* we saw the golf *course* when we went to Pebble Beach.

complement, compliment   The one spelled with an *e* means to complete something or bring it to perfection.

Use a color wheel to find a *complement* for purple.

Juliet's personality *complements* Romeo's; she is practical, and he is a dreamer.

The one spelled with an *i* has to do with praise. Remember "*I* like compliments," and you'll remember to use the *i* spelling when you mean praise.

My evaluation included a really nice *compliment* from my coworkers.

We *complimented* them on their new home.

conscious, conscience   *Conscious* means "aware."

They weren't *conscious* of any problems before the accident.

Conscience means that inner voice of right and wrong. The extra *n* in *conscience* should remind you of *No*, which is what your conscience often says to you.

My *conscience* told me to turn in the expensive watch I found.

dessert, desert   *Dessert* is the sweet one, the one you like two helpings of. So give it two helpings of *s*.

We had a whole chocolate cheesecake for *dessert*.

The other one, *desert*, is used for all other meanings and has two pronunciations.

I promise that I won't *desert* you.

The snake slithered slowly across the *desert*.

do, due   *Do* is a verb, an action. You *do* something.

I always *do* my best work at night.

But a payment or an assignment is *due*; it is scheduled for a certain time.

Our first essay is *due* tomorrow.

Due can also be used before *to* in a phrase that means *because of.*

The outdoor concert was canceled *due to* rain.

feel, fill   *Feel* describes *feel*ings.

Whenever I stay up late, I *feel* sleepy in class.

Fill describes what you do to a cup or a gas tank.

Did they *fill* the pitcher to the top?

fourth, forth   The word *fourth* has *four* in it. (But note that *forty* does not. Remember the word *forty-fourth.*)

This is our *fourth* quiz in two weeks.

My grandparents celebrated their *forty-fourth* anniversary.

If you don't mean a number, use *forth.*

We wrote back and *forth* many times during my trip.

have, of   *Have* is a verb. Sometimes, in a contraction, it sounds like *of.* When you say *could've,* the *have* may sound like *of,* but it is not written that way. Always write *could have, would have, should have, might have.*

We should *have* planned our vacation sooner.

Then we could *have* used our coupon for a free one-way ticket.

Use *of* only in a prepositional phrase (see p. 65).

She sent me a box *of* chocolates for my birthday.

hear, here   The last three letters of *hear* spell "ear." You *hear* with your ear.

When I listen to a sea shell, I *hear* ocean sounds.

The other spelling *here* tells "where." Note that the three words indicating a place or pointing out something all have *here* in them: *here, there, where.*

I'll be *here* for three more weeks.

it's, its   *It's* is a contraction and means "it is" or "it has."

It's hot. (*It is* hot.)

It's been hot all week. (*It has* been hot all week.)

Its is a possessive. (Words such as *its, yours, hers, ours, theirs,* and *whose* are already possessive forms and never need an apostrophe. See p. 40.)

The jury had made *its* decision.

The dog pulled at *its* leash.

knew, new   *Knew* has to do with knowledge (both start with *k*).

New means "not old."

They *knew* that she wanted a *new* bike.

know, no   *Know* has to do with knowledge (both start with *k*).

By Friday, I must *know* all the state capitals.

No means "not any" or the opposite of "yes."

My boss has *no* patience. *No,* I need to work late.

E X E R C I S E S

Underline the correct word. Don't guess! If you aren't sure, turn back to the explanatory pages. When you've finished ten sentences, compare your answers with those at the back of the book. Correct each set of ten sentences before continuing so you'll catch your mistakes early.

Exercise 1

1. (It's, Its) not often that a company buys back (it's, its) own product (a, an) hundred years after selling it.

2. That's just what Levi Strauss & Co. (choose, chose) to (do, due) in May of 2001 after (a, an) anonymous person sold the company a pair of Levi's jeans dating back to the 1880s.

3. (Do, Due) to a rich 130-year history, the Levi Strauss company wanted to add the (knew, new) discovery to the archive of antique jeans the company (all ready, already) had.

4. The pair recently discovered was older than any found before and would therefore (fill, feel) a gap in the company's archive of historically accurate (clothes, cloths).

5. Adding to (it's, its) rarity, the 1880s pair was designed with (a, an) unique left-thigh pocket for tools, as well as other special features.

6. Before the auction, no one (knew, new) exactly how much the rare jeans would fetch, but their worth was estimated at approximately $30,000.

7. (Conscious, Conscience) of the jeans' incredible value, two different auction services participated in gathering the bids.

8. Collectors of vintage denim (clothes, cloths) from around the world bid for the privilege of owning this oldest surviving pair of Levi's, and they could (have, of) easily gone to someone other than the Levi Strauss company.

9. But the jeans' original maker really wanted them to (complement, compliment) the younger pairs in the archive, so the company made (it's, its) final bid and got the 120-year-old pants for $46,532.00.

10. While the company's high bid did not surprise anyone involved in the auction, it did (brake, break) the record for the highest amount ever paid for a pair of jeans.

Source: Levi Strauss & Co. Press Release (May 2001)

Exercise 2

1. I took my sister's (advice, advise) and (accepted, excepted) (are, our) mutual friends' invitation to have dinner with them last night.

2. Both Haroldine and Tom (are, our) studying to be professional chefs.

3. She plans to be (a, an) all-purpose cook, and he will specialize in (desserts, deserts).

4. As a final project for their latest cooking (coarse, course), they (choose, chose) a four-(coarse, course) menu with a spectacular (dessert, desert), and they invited me to help them judge the results.

5. I didn't have to (hear, here) more than that to make me (feel, fill) hungry.

6. I arrived with a guilty (conscious, conscience), however, because I (knew, new) I was more interested in the food than the company at first.

7. The (affect, effect) of the whole experience was a pleasant surprise: the tasty dishes (complemented, complimented) our lively conversations about movies, sports, and cooking techniques.

8. After the meal's (fourth, forth) (coarse, course), I was (all ready, already) for dessert, and the individual soufflés with soft chocolate centers ful-filled everyone's expectations.

9. Having dinner with Haroldine and Tom was a nice (brake, break) from my normal routine.

10. Looking back, I would (have, of) enjoyed the evening even if we had called out for pizza.

Exercise 3

1. I've been reading that (are, our) individual dreams say (a, an) awful lot about us but that some dreams (are, our) common to us all.

2. (It's, Its) strange, for example, that many people (feel, fill) as though they are falling or flying in a dream.

3. In another common dream experience, we realize suddenly that we are not wearing any (clothes, cloths), and we don't (know, no) how we got that way.

4. Or we dream that we have missed a deadline when a test or a paper was (do, due), but we have forgotten to (do, due) it.

5. Whether we are (conscious, conscience) of it or not, our dream lives can have (a, an) (affect, effect) on (are, our) real lives.

6. If in a dream we (brake, break) the heart of someone we love, we might wake up the next morning with a guilty (conscious, conscience).

7. Of (coarse, course), we may dream of eating (a, an) entire gallon of chocolate ice cream for (dessert, desert) and (feel, fill) another kind of guilt.

8. Dream experts give the following (advise, advice) to those who want to call (fourth, forth) the dreams that slip away from the (conscious, conscience) mind once we are awake.

9. They suggest that dreamers put paper and a pencil by the bed before going to sleep in order to write down a dream as soon as (it's, its) over.

10. We all (know, no) that (know, no) amount of coaxing will bring back a dream that our brain (all ready, already) (choose, chose) to forget.

Exercise 4

1. The T-shirt had (it's, its) modern beginnings when the U.S. Navy (choose, chose) it as (a, an) official undergarment in the early 1900s.

2. The first printed T-shirt was used during the 1948 presidential campaign as (a, an) ad for one of the candidates.

3. (It's, Its) message read "Dew it with Dewey," and (it's, its) now on display at the Smithsonian.

4. Whether he was (conscious, conscience) of it or not, Marlon Brando started a fashion trend by wearing (a, an) white T-shirt in the movie *A Streetcar Named Desire*.

5. James Dean's T-shirt and blue jeans also had an (affect, effect) on the look of the 1950s (do, due) to the popularity of his film *Rebel Without a Cause*.

6. After that, people began to (accept, except) T-shirts as regular (clothes, cloths).

7. Advertisers started to use the fronts and backs of T-shirts as spaces to (feel, fill) with slogans, brand names, and pictures of products.

8. In the 1960s, the (knew, new) look was colorful tie-dyed T-shirts used to (complement, compliment) bell-bottomed pants and sandals.

9. Of (coarse, course), an old T-shirt can be cut up into (clothes, cloths) that are the perfect texture to wax a car or to polish silver. The material is not too smooth and not too (coarse, course); (it's, its) just right.

10. Over the (coarse, course) of the last century, we have seen the T-shirt (feel, fill) many of (are, our) needs as comfortable and stylish (clothes, cloths) to wear and as useful (clothes, cloths) to clean with.

Exercise 5

1. You have probably (all ready, already) heard the expression "peeping Tom" used to describe a person who peers into neighbors' windows.

2. But you might not (know, no) (it's, its) origins.

3. (It's, Its) (a, an) old story that involves someone else you might (have, of) heard of—Lady Godiva—who lived in Coventry, England, in the eleventh century.

4. Lady Godiva's husband Leofric was (a, an) powerful man, the Earl of Coventry, but her (conscious, conscience) was bothered by his treatment of the townspeople.

5. Leofric forced the people to pay heavy taxes, but Lady Godiva couldn't (accept, except) his unfairness, so she asked him to reduce the tax.

6. Leofric made his wife (a, an) unusual offer: he would get rid of the tax if she would ride naked through the streets of Coventry on a horse with only her hair to cover her.

7. Lady Godiva (choose, chose) to (accept, except) her husband's challenge, for she believed that the townspeople would not (dessert, desert) her and would not look at her.

8. So Lady Godiva rode through Coventry without wearing any (clothes, cloths).

9. The townspeople promised to stay indoors with the shutters closed, and they did—(accept, except) one man, the tailor named Tom.

10. Tom magically was struck blind (do, due) to his decision to (brake, break) his promise to Lady Godiva, and (it's, its) from this story that we get (are, our) expression "peeping Tom."

Source: A Hog on Ice & Other Curious Expressions (Harper & Row, 1948)

PROOFREADING EXERCISE

Find and correct the ten errors contained in the following student paragraph. All of the errors involve Words Often Confused (Set 1).

My cat had six kittens last week, and they were all strong and active accept the littlest one born last—it was the runt. It's head and body were much smaller than those of it's brother and sisters. We named her first and called her Sweet Pea because we were all ready starting to fill that she was special. At first, the other kittens wouldn't let Sweet Pea eat, and we could here her cry for milk. It's almost as if the others were trying to get rid of her. We didn't know what to do, so we called the vet to get some advise. He told us that we could make sure Sweet Pea got enough milk by taking the others out of the box after they seemed full and that eventually Sweet Pea would be excepted by the others. The plan worked. By the second day, Sweet Pea was part of the family. We could of lost are favorite kitten if we hadn't received such good advice.

SENTENCE WRITING

The surest way to learn these Words Often Confused is to use them immediately in your own writing. Choose the five pairs or groups of words that you most often confuse from Set 1. Then use each of them correctly in a new sentence. No answers are provided at the back of the book, but you can see if you are using the words correctly by comparing your sentences to the examples in the explanations.

Words Often Confused (Set 2)

Study this second set of words carefully, with their examples, before attempting the exercises. Knowing all of the word groups in these two sets will take care of many of your spelling problems.

lead, led

Lead is the metal that rhymes with *head*.

Old paint is dangerous because it often contains *lead*.

The past form of the verb "to lead" is *led*.

What factors *led* to your decision?

I *led* our school's debating team to victory last year.

If you don't mean past time, use *lead*, which rhymes with *bead*.

I will *lead* the debating team again this year.

loose, lose

Loose means "not tight." Note how *l o o s e* that word is. It has plenty of room for two *o*'s.

My dog's tooth is *loose*.

Lose is the opposite of win.

If we *lose* this game, we will be out for the season.

passed, past

The past form of the verb "to pass" is *passed*.

She easily *passed* her math class.

The runner *passed* the baton to her teammate.

We *passed* your house twice before we saw the address.

Use *past* when it's not a verb.

> We drove *past* your house. (the same as "We drove *by* your house")

> I always use my *past* experiences to help me solve problems.

> In the *past*, he had to borrow his brother's car.

personal,
personnel

Pronounce these two correctly, and you won't confuse them—*pérsonal, personnél*.

> She shared her *personal* views as a parent.

Personnel means "a group of employees."

> I had an appointment in the *personnel* office.

piece, peace

Remember "piece of pie." The one meaning "a *piece* of something" always begins with *pie*.

> One child asked for an extra *piece* of candy.

The other one, *peace*, is the opposite of war.

> The two gangs discussed the possibility of a *peace* treaty.

principal,
principle

Principal means "main." Both words have *a* in them: princip*a*l, m*a*in.

> The *principal* concern is safety. (main concern)

> He lost both *principal* and interest. (main amount of money)

Also, think of a school's "princi*pal*" as your "*pal*."

> An elementary school *principal* must be kind. (main administrator)

A *principle* is a "rule." Both words end in *le*: princip*le*, ru*le*

> I am proud of my high *principles*. (rules of conduct)

> We value the *principle* of truth in advertising. (rule)

quiet, quite

Pronounce these two correctly, and you won't confuse them. *Quiet* means "free from noise" and rhymes with *diet*.

> Tennis players need *quiet* in order to concentrate.

Quite means "very" and rhymes with *bite*.

> It was *quite* hot in the auditorium.

right, write   *Right* means "correct" or "proper."

You will find your keys if you look in the *right* place.

It also means in the exact location, position, or moment.

Your keys are *right* where you left them.

Let's go *right* now.

Write means to compose sentences, poems, essays, and so forth.

I asked my teacher to *write* a letter of recommendation for me.

than, then   *Than* compares two things.

I am taller *than* my sister.

Then tells when (*then* and *when* rhyme, and both have *e* in them).

I always write a rough draft of a paper first; *then* I revise it.

their, there, they're   *Their* is a possessive, meaning belonging to them.

Their cars have always been red.

There points out something. (Remember that the three words indicating a place or pointing out something all have *here* in them: *here*, *there*, *where*.)

I know that I haven't been *there* before.

There was a rainbow in the sky.

They're is a contraction and means "they are."

They're living in Canada now. (*They are* living in Canada now.)

threw, through   *Threw* is the past form of "to throw."

We *threw* snowballs at each other.

I *threw* away my chance at a scholarship.

If you don't mean "to throw something," use *through*.

We could see our beautiful view *through* the new curtains.

They worked *through* their differences.

two, too, to   *Two* is a number.

>   We have written *two* papers so far in my English class.

Too means "extra" or "also," and so it has an extra *o*.

>   The movie was *too* long and *too* violent. (extra)

>   They are enrolled in that biology class *too*. (also)

Use *to* for all other meanings.

>   They like *to* ski. They're going *to* the mountains.

weather, whether   *Weather* refers to conditions of the atmosphere.

>   Snowy *weather* is too cold for me.

Whether means "if."

>   I don't know *whether* it is snowing there or not.

>   *Whether* I travel with you or not depends on the weather.

were, wear, where   These words are pronounced differently but are often confused in writing.

Were is the past form of the verb "to be."

>   We *were* interns at the time.

Wear means to have on, as in wearing clothes.

>   I always *wear* a scarf in winter.

Where refers to a place. (Remember that the three words indicating a place or pointing out something all have *here* in them: *here, there, where.*)

>   *Where* is the mailbox? There it is.

>   *Where* are the closing papers? Here they are.

who's, whose   *Who's* is a contraction and means "who is" or "who has."

>   *Who's* responsible for signing the checks? (*Who is* responsible?)

>   *Who's* been reading my journal? (*Who has* been reading my journal?)

Whose is a possessive. (Words such as *whose, its, yours, hers, ours,* and *theirs* are already possessive forms and never need an apostrophe. See p. 40.)

>   *Whose* keys are these?

woman, **women**	The difference here is one of number: wo*man* refers to one adult female; wo*men* refers to two or more adult females.

> I know a *woman* who won $8,000 on a single horse race.

> I bowl with a group of *women* from my work.

you're, your	*You're* is a contraction and means "you are."

> *You're* as smart as I am. (*You are* as smart as I am.)

Your is a possessive meaning belonging to you.

> I borrowed *your* lab book.

E X E R C I S E S

Underline the correct word. When you've finished ten sentences, compare your answers with those at the back of the book. Do only ten sentences at a time so that you will catch your mistakes early.

Exercise 1

1. Some people will go (threw, through) almost anything to look better.

2. Cosmetic surgeries for men and (woman, women) are more popular (than, then) ever.

3. A person (who's, whose) eyelids sag or someone (who's, whose) not happy with a "spare tire" can just get an eye-lift or a lunchtime lipo-suction job.

4. In the (passed, past), we could read people's ages on (their, there, they're) faces.

5. Now we can't tell (weather, whether) (their, there, they're) young or old except by a close look at (their, there, they're) elbows.

6. A man or a (woman, women) who chooses to (were, wear, where) makeup can even have it permanently applied by a tattoo artist.

7. One must be (quiet, quite) sure before getting makeup tattoos because (their, there, they're) irreversible.

8. Cosmetic surgery candidates should consider this (principal, principle): "If (you're, your) not absolutely certain, (than, then) don't do it."

9. Knowing (weather, whether) a surgical option is (right, write) or wrong is a (personal, personnel) decision.

10. (Their, There, They're) may be more to (loose, lose) (than, then) (their, there, they're) is to gain.

Exercise 2

1. (Their, There, They're) is a famous (piece, peace) of land that covers approximately 175 square miles of the Nazca Desert in Peru.

2. This part of the Peruvian desert is (were, wear, where) people of the (passed, past) carved intricate pictures in the rocky ground.

3. (Two, Too, To) surprising facts about these line drawings, called geoglyphs, are that (their, there, they're) 1,500 years old and are so large that (their, there, they're) whole shapes can be seen only from high up in the air.

4. In fact, these gigantic pictures were not discovered by the modern world until people (passed, past) over them in airplanes.

5. Someone (who's, whose) standing on the ground within or near the geoglyphs cannot see (their, there, they're) overall designs.

6. Most of the 12,000 Nazca line drawings are (quiet, quite) large—about the size of sports stadiums—and represent recognizable objects like birds, insects, sea creatures, and plants.

7. The most interesting of the Nazca geoglyphs are the ones (who's, whose) shapes are unrecognizable, for they most likely represent the (personal, personnel) artistic expressions of the ancient people who created them.

8. The age, size, and shapes of these drawings have all (lead, led) experts and others (two, too, to) wonder about how they (were, wear, where) made and how they (were, wear, where) seen by ancient people who did not have airplanes.

9. Of course, the mystery surrounding the Nazca geoglyphs has (lead, led) (two, too, to) speculation about UFOs, religious rituals, and ancient air travel.

10. Luckily for everyone, the dry (weather, whether) in the Nazca Desert has allowed the geoglyphs (two, too, to) survive without being washed away.

Source: Boys' Life, March 2001

Exercise 3

1. If you live (were, wear, where) there are pine trees, you can make (you're, your) own bird feeder very easily.

2. All you need is a pine cone or (two, too, to), a jar of peanut butter, some birdseed, and a long (piece, peace) of string.

3. The first step is (two, too, to) tie the string to the top of the pine cone securely.

4. Use a string that's long enough to allow the feeder to hang (were, wear, where) you will be able to see it later.

5. Try to use a pine cone that has a (loose, lose) rather (than, then) a tight shape.

6. Step (two, too, to) involves spreading the peanut butter in the spaces all around the outside of the pine cone.

7. This process can be (quiet, quite) messy, so you may want to (were, wear, where) rubber gloves and cover (you're, your) work surface with a (piece, peace) of newspaper.

8. Once (you're, your) finished with the second step, roll the peanut butter–covered pine cone in birdseed.

9. Hang the results from a tree branch, and sit back and watch the birds enjoy (their, there, they're) special treat in (piece, peace) and (quiet, quite).

10. And you can take (personal, personnel) pleasure in the fact that (you're, your) not adding more plastic to the environment since the pine cone bird feeder is made of all-natural ingredients.

Exercise 4

1. Test (you're, your) knowledge of animal history by answering the following question: which came first, sharks or dinosaurs?

2. (You're, Your) (right, write) if you answered sharks; they have been around for millions of years, and (their, there, they're) really (quiet, quite) amazing creatures.

3. Most sharks travel (through, threw) the water constantly without stopping, but some appear (two, too, to) sleep (right, write) on the bottom of the ocean.

4. (Their, There, They're) teeth never have a chance to (were, wear, where) down because each tooth is designed to come (loose, lose) easily, and (their, there, they're) is always another tooth waiting to take its place.

5. Sharks range in size from the six-inch cigar shark (two, too, to) the sixty-foot whale shark, and most of them are (quiet, quite) harmless (two, too, to) humans if they are left in (piece, peace).

6. More people die each year from being stung by bees (than, then) from being attacked by sharks, so (their, there, they're) reputation as killers is perhaps exaggerated.

7. Sharks can sense the movements of a fish in trouble or a swimmer (who's, whose) bleeding, and that's when (their, there, they're) likely to attack.

8. A shark doesn't chew its food, but bites off and swallows one big (piece, peace) at a time.

9. Baby sharks are called pups, and different species of sharks have different numbers of pups at a time—from (two, too, to) to close to a hundred.

10. A few sharks lay (their, there, they're) eggs in pouches with descriptive names like "mermaid's purses" and "devil's wheelbarrows"; these pouches are then laid on the ocean floor, and they stay (their, there, they're) until the shark pups hatch.

Source: 1996 Aqua Facts (Vancouver Aquarium)

Exercise 5

1. Last week, I went on a field trip with the children from the preschool (were, wear, where) I work; we took them to see a production of *The Wizard of Oz.*

2. The children (were, wear, where) told to (were, wear, where) their nicest clothes for our outing and to (right, write) their names on (their, there, they're) lunch bags.

3. On the bus (were, wear, where) twenty-five children and six (woman, women)—five teachers and one bus driver.

4. We weren't sure (weather, whether) the (principal, principle), Ms. Densmore, would be able to come with us.

5. As it turned out, she had to interview someone in the (personal, personnel) office at the same time, so she could not attend.

6. I (lead, led) my own small group of children (through, threw) the lobby of the theater, (passed, past) the ushers checking tickets, and down the row to our seats.

7. My children were on (their, there, they're) best behavior; they sat still and remained (quiet, quite) (through, threw) the whole performance.

8. At intermission, one of the children in the row ahead of ours (through, threw) a program out like a paper airplane and had to (loose, lose) the privilege of seeing the end of the show.

9. (Than, Then) as we boarded the bus back to school, we learned that another child's (loose, lose) tooth had come out in a (piece, peace) of chewing gum.

10. Once we figured out (who's, whose) tooth it was and once we (were, wear, where) all back on the bus, we headed for home.

PROOFREADING EXERCISE

See if you can correct the ten errors in this student paragraph. All errors involve Words Often Confused (Set 2).

When I was in high school, I past all my classes but didn't learn as much as I wanted too. All of my teachers did they're best, and the principle was an enthusiastic women who's love of education was contagious. Their was no shortage of school spirit; I just wasn't paying enough attention to make the hard information stick. Since I lead a carefree life at the time, I goofed off more then I should have. If I had those high school years to live over again, I would listen in class, do my homework carefully, and make sure that I knew all of the write answers on tests and that I didn't just forget the answers once the test was over.

SENTENCE WRITING

Write several sentences using any words you missed in doing the exercises for Words Often Confused (Set 2).

Sentence writing is a good idea not only because it will help you remember these words often confused but also because it will be a storehouse for ideas you can later use in writing papers. Here are some topics you might consider writing your sentences about:

— Your dream vacation spot

— Favorite singer/musical group

— A goal for the future

— A lesson you've learned

— How your values are changing

The Eight Parts of Speech

Choosing the right word is an important aspect of writing. Some words sound alike but are spelled differently and have different meanings (*past* and *passed*, for instance), and some words are spelled the same but sound different and mean different things (*lead*, for the action of "leading," and *lead*, for the stuff inside pencils).

One way to choose words more carefully is to understand the roles that words play in sentences. Just as one actor can play many different parts in movies (a hero, a villain, a humorous sidekick), single words can play different parts in sentences (a noun, a verb, an adjective). These are called the *eight parts of speech*, briefly defined with examples below.

1. **Nouns** name some*one*, *thing*, *place*, or *idea* and are used as subjects and objects in sentences.

   The **technician** fixed the **computers** in the **lab**.

2. **Pronouns** are special words that replace nouns to avoid repeating them.

   She (the technician) fixed **them** (the computers) in **it** (the lab).

3. **Adjectives** add description to nouns and pronouns—telling *which one, how many, what kind, color,* or *shape* they are.

> The **new** technician fixed **thirty old** computers in the **writing** lab.

4. **Verbs** show action or state of being.

> The new technician **fixed** the old computers in the writing lab; Terri **is** the technician's name.

5. **Adverbs** add information—such as *when, where, why,* or *how*—to verbs, adjectives and adverbs, or whole sentences.

> **Yesterday** the new technician **quickly** fixed the **very** old computers in the writing lab.

6. **Prepositions** show position in *space* and *time* and are followed by nouns to form prepositional phrases.

> The technician fixed the computers **in** the writing lab **at** noon.

7. **Conjunctions** are connecting words—such as *and, but,* and *or*—and words that begin dependent clauses—such as *because, since, when, while,* and *although.*

> Students still visited the lab **and** the media center **while** the computers were broken.

8. **Interjections** interrupt a sentence to show surprise or other emotions and are rarely used in Standard Written English.

> **Wow**, Terri is a valuable new employee.

To find out what parts of speech an individual word can play, look it up in a good dictionary (see p. 52). A list of definitions beginning with an abbreviated part of speech (n., adj., prep., and so on) will catalog its uses. However, seeing how a word is used in a particular sentence is the best way to identify its part of speech. Look at these examples:

> The **train** of a wedding gown flows elegantly behind it.
>
> (*Train* is a noun in this sentence, naming the part of a gown we call a "train.")

> Sammy and Helen **train** dolphins at Sea World.
>
> (*Train* is a verb in this example, expressing the action of teaching skills we call "training.")

> Doug's parents drove him to the **train** station.
>
> (*Train* is an adjective here, adding description to the noun "station," telling what *kind* of station it is.)

All of the words in a sentence work together to create meaning, but each one serves its own purpose by playing a part of speech. Think about how each of the words in the following sentence plays the particular part of speech labeled:

N.   PREP.   ADJ.   N.   ADV. V.   ADJ.   N. CONJ. PRO. V. PREP. N.
Students at community colleges often take morning classes, but they work at night.

Familiarizing yourself with the parts of speech will help you spell better now and understand phrases and clauses better later. Each of the eight parts of speech has characteristics that distinguish it from the other seven, but it takes practice to learn them.

E X E R C I S E S

Label the parts of speech above all of the words in the following sentences using the abbreviations N., PRO., ADJ., V., ADV., PREP., CONJ., and INTERJ. For clarity's sake, the sentences here are very brief, and you may ignore the words *a*, *an*, and *the*. These words are actually special forms of adjectives (called articles), but they are so numerous that there's no need to mark them. Refer back to the definitions and examples of the parts of speech whenever necessary. When in doubt, leave a word unmarked until you check the answers at the back of the book after each set of ten sentences. You'll find that many of the ones you found difficult to label will be *adverbs*, the most versatile of the parts of speech.

Exercise 1

1. Business owners hire employees.

2. Employees work hard and earn money.

3. At holidays, nice bosses offer bonuses to workers.

4. Business owners often show appreciation to customers.

5. A prosperous business is a wonderful accomplishment.

6. It reveals good planning and good luck.

7. Businesspeople speak a special language.

8. They know the difference between a dozen and a gross.

9. A dozen equals twelve.

10. A gross is twelve dozen.

Exercise 2

1. Plants need water and sunlight.
2. Sometimes house plants die unexpectedly.
3. Often people give them too much water or not enough water.
4. I saw an experiment on a television show once.
5. It involved two plants.
6. The same woman raised both plants with water and sunlight.
7. The plants grew in two different rooms.
8. She yelled at one plant but said sweet things to the other.
9. The verbally praised plant grew beautifully.
10. The verbally abused plant died.

Exercise 3

1. Wild Quaker parrots are interesting birds.
2. They originally came from Argentina.
3. They are noisy inhabitants of neighborhoods across the country.
4. These birds live in large nests at the top of tall trees.
5. Only Quaker parrots build nests.
6. These nests have three compartments.
7. The back part offers protection for the eggs.
8. The middle section houses the adults.
9. Parrots in the front compartment guard the entrance to the nest.
10. Some people raise Quaker parrots as pets.

Exercise 4

1. The *Titanic* collided with an iceberg and sank in 1912.
2. Robert Baboian is a corrosion expert.
3. He has a unique theory about the disaster.
4. Baboian believes in an additional cause for the sinking.

5. Rust weakened the rivets in the ship's hull because the builders made an error.
6. Builders used one kind of metal for the rivets.
7. They used another kind of metal for the hull.
8. Then they worked for one year on the interior of the ship.
9. The ship floated in the water for that year.
10. Before the fateful voyage, a photograph shows rust damage.

Source: Discover, August 2001

Exercise 5

1. I recently read some facts about movie kisses.
2. The first one occurs in a film by Thomas Edison in 1896.
3. The title of that short film is *The Kiss.*
4. A longer movie kiss holds the record for time.
5. In a 1941 film, Jane Wyman kisses Regis Toomey for three full minutes.
6. Mae West flirts with many men in her movies although she never kisses one of them.
7. *Don Juan* (1926) is a movie with many kisses in it.
8. John Barrymore delivers nearly two hundred of them.
9. In that movie, one kiss occurs for each minute of film.
10. Gee, I love trivial facts like these.

Source: I Was a Fugitive from a Hollywood Trivia Factory (Contemporary Books, 2000)

PARAGRAPH EXERCISE

Here is a brief excerpt from a book called *The Rat: An Owner's Guide to a Happy Healthy Pet,* by Ginger Cardinal. Label the parts of speech above as many of the words as you can before checking your answers at the back of the book.

Birds are not usually a good match with rats. In the wild, birds and rats are natural enemies. In survival of the biggest, rats eat small birds and bird eggs.

Large birds prey on rats as well. So, as a general rule, most birds are nervous and even frightened around rats.

SENTENCE WRITING

Write ten sentences imitating those in Exercise 1. Instead of beginning with "Business owners hire employees," you may begin with "College professors grade students" or "Good parents help children" then continue to imitate the rest of the sentences in Exercise 1. Label the parts of speech above the words in your imitation exercise.

The next two sections on contractions and possessives involve spelling words correctly through the use of apostrophes.

Contractions

When two words are shortened into one, the result is called a *contraction*:

is not   ·········➤   isn't   you have   ·········➤   you've

The letter or letters that are left out are replaced with an apostrophe. For example, if the two words *do not* are shortened into one, an apostrophe is put where the *o* is left out.

do not   don't

Note how the apostrophe goes in the exact place where the letter or letters are left out in these contractions:

I am	I'm
I have	I've
I shall, I will	I'll
I would	I'd
you are	you're
you have	you've
you will	you'll
she is, she has	she's
he is, he has	he's
it is, it has	it's
we are	we're
we have	we've
we will, we shall	we'll
they are	they're
they have	they've
are not	aren't
cannot	can't
do not	don't
does not	doesn't
have not	haven't
let us	let's
who is, who has	who's
where is	where's
were not	weren't
would not	wouldn't

could not	couldn't
should not	shouldn't
would have	would've
could have	could've
should have	should've
that is	that's
there is	there's
what is	what's

One contraction does not follow this rule: *will not* becomes *won't*.

In all other contractions that you're likely to use, the apostrophe goes exactly where the letter or letters are left out. Note especially *it's, they're, who's*, and *you're*. Use them when you mean two words. (See p. 40 for the possessive forms—*its, their, whose*, and *your*—which don't contain apostrophes.)

E X E R C I S E S

Put an apostrophe in each contraction. Then compare your answers with those at the back of the book. Be sure to correct each set of ten sentences before going on so you'll catch your mistakes early.

Exercise 1

1. Could a dog whos just playing around destroy his owner's house within the span of a few minutes?

2. Thats what happened in England recently.

3. A mischievous mutt named Sam wasnt doing anything unusual by chewing on various household objects.

4. While his owner, Wendy Rudge, wasnt looking, Sam started to gnaw on an aerosol can.

5. It didnt take long for Sam's teeth to puncture the metal and set the gas loose.

6. Unfortunately, this event didnt happen in the summer when the house's windows wouldve been open.

7. Instead the fireplace was roaring, and the heat and flames couldnt help but ignite the gas.

8. Its easy to imagine the hair spray canister shooting out flames as it rolled from the living room into the kitchen and set them both ablaze.

9. Now Sam isnt allowed anywhere near aerosol cans or any other potential source of fire.

10. After the shock he had, he probably wouldnt want to go near them anyway.

Source: Current Science, April 20, 2001

Exercise 2

1. Elephants arent considered ordinary animals in Thailand.

2. In fact, theyre the national animal of Thailand.

3. So its not uncommon for Thai elephants to be given special treatment.

4. And weve all heard of group weddings in which more than one couple is married at a time.

5. On Valentine's Day of 2001 in Thailand, two couples were wed in a grand ceremony in the city of Ayutthaya.

6. Its probably no surprise that these two couples were elephants.

7. One groom elephant named Sweetheart married his bride elephant, Blossoming Lotus.

8. The other wedding couple, Golden Tusk and Honey, tied the knot at the same time.

9. Hundreds of people attended the elephants' wedding to help raise awareness that these animals' numbers are shrinking, and theyre not as protected as they should be.

10. Lets hope that the four newlywed pachyderms live happily ever after.

Source: Current Science, April 20, 2001

Exercise 3

1. Africanized or "killer" bees arent coming to the United States—theyre already here.
2. They first arrived in Texas in 1990, and theyve continued to make their way into the country since then.
3. Theyre not any different in appearance than the bees youre used to seeing buzzing around flower gardens.
4. Yet weve probably all heard by now that theyre very different in their behavior.
5. Theyre more aggressive and more defensive than other bees.
6. People and animals are in the most danger when theyre near a hive.
7. Theres a good chance that the bees will warn someone whos too close to them, but theyve also been known to attack for no reason at all.
8. A person under attack shouldnt stand still or try to fight the bees off but should run as fast and as far away as possible.
9. The fact that the killer bees have arrived doesnt mean its time to panic.
10. After all, research shows that bee stings are one of the lowest ranked causes of death in the United States; thats the good news.

Source: Living with Killer Bees (Quick Trading Co., 1993)

Exercise 4

1. Im sure youve heard of Barbie and Ken, the famous toy couple.
2. These two may be boyfriend and girlfriend in their doll lives, but they werent that way to begin with.
3. In real life, shes his sister, hes her brother, and theyre both the children of Ruth Handler, whos the inventor of the Barbie doll.
4. Handler named the dolls after her own daughter and son, but thats where the similarity ends.

5. The Barbie doll was an idea that came when Handler noticed that her young daughter Barbie wanted to play with realistic, grown-up looking dolls instead of baby or little girl dolls.

6. Thats where the Barbie weve all seen got her start, and shes got lots of accessories and outfits that wouldnt fit any other doll.

7. When Barbie was first introduced at the 1959 New York Toy Show, the reaction wasnt positive at all.

8. Handler's idea didnt need any help in the stores, however; Barbie made $500 million by the late 1960s, and shes been extremely popular ever since.

9. Handler's husband Elliot cofounded the Mattel company before Barbie came along, and hes responsible for the success of its toy furniture and musical instruments.

10. Ruth Handler doesnt take anything for granted; shes used her life experiences in another positive way by helping design a more natural-looking artificial breast after her own bout with breast cancer.

Source: Mothers of Invention (Morrow, 1988)

Exercise 5

1. Ive just discovered that for most of the past century, Yellowstone National Park hasnt had any wolves in it.

2. With the help of an act of Congress in 1914, theyd been killed off in an effort to get rid of predators in Yellowstone and on other public lands.

3. Now its obvious that the policy was a mistake; people realized that Yellowstone wouldnt be complete without its wolves.

4. The Endangered Species Act in 1973 helped to start the plan of putting wolves back into Yellowstone, but its taken twenty years to get to the point where theyre actually being released.

5. The first wolves to be moved were from Alberta, Canada; thats where the land is similar to Yellowstone's and where theres no disease among the wolf population.

6. Once transplanted in Yellowstone, the Canadian wolves were kept in pens so that they wouldnt just try to go back home once released into the park.

7. But feeding the wolves in the acre-sized pens wasnt easy; its illegal to use motor vehicles in the wild part of Yellowstone, so the wolves' food had to be brought in on sleds pulled by mules.

8. Other animals dont like wolves, so as soon as a mule saw the hungry wolves circling for dinner, the mule wouldnt go any further; thats a problem which was eventually solved.

9. In March of 1995, the gate was opened on one of the pens to release the first group of wolves back into their natural habitat, but the wolves wouldnt use the gate.

10. Scientists realized that they shouldve known that the wolves wouldnt trust the opening that the humans used, so a hole was made in the fence near the spot where the wolves felt most comfortable, and thats where the wolves made their escape to freedom in Yellowstone.

Source: The Wolves of Yellowstone (Voyageur Press, 1996)

PROOFREADING EXERCISE

Can you correct the ten errors in this student paragraph? They could be from any of the areas studied so far.

Jokes can effect people differently. No too individuals have the same sense of humor. Thats why it may be risky to tell jokes at work or to people youv'e just met. I had a friend once who's timing and delivery were perfect. Jake could tell a joke to a person getting a root canal, and the person would of laughed. It was'nt the actual jokes that were so funny; it was the way Jake told them. I remember one of the short ones. Jake would ask, "What sits at the bottom of the ocean and shakes?" Hed tilt his head to the side a bit and look the person in the eye while waiting for an answer. Just as the person was about to respond with a stupid guess, Jake would blurt out, "A nervous wreck." The look on Jake's face was as funny as the punch line, and I think that must be the secret of a good comedian— he or shes funnier then the jokes themselves.

SENTENCE WRITING

Doing exercises will help you learn a rule, but even more helpful is using the rule in writing. Write ten sentences using contractions. You might write about your re- action to this week's big news story, or you can choose your own subject.

Possessives

Words that clarify ownership are called *possessives*. The trick in writing possessives is to ask the question "Who (or what) does the item belong to?" Modern usage has made *who* acceptable when it begins a question. More correctly, of course, the phrasing should be "*Whom* does the item belong to?" or even "*To whom* does the item belong?"

In any case, if the answer to this question does not end in *s* (e.g., *girl, person, people, children, month*), simply add an apostrophe and *s* to show the possessive. Look at the first five examples in the following chart.

However, if the answer to the question already ends in *s* (e.g., *girls, Brahms*), add only an apostrophe after the *s* to show the possessive. See the next two examples in the chart and say them aloud to hear that their sound does not change.

Finally, some *s*-ending words need another sound to make the possessive clear. If you need another *s* sound when you *say* the possessive (e.g., *boss* made possessive is *boss's*), add the apostrophe and another *s* to show the added sound.

a girl (uniform)	Whom does the uniform belong to?	a girl	Add *'s*	a girl's uniform
a person (clothes)	Whom do the clothes belong to?	a person	Add *'s*	a person's clothes
people (clothes)	Whom do the clothes belong to?	people	Add *'s*	people's clothes
children (games)	Whom do the games belong to?	children	Add *'s*	children's games
a month (pay)	What does the pay belong to?	a month	Add *'s*	a month's pay
girls (uniforms)	Whom do the uniforms belong to?	girls	Add *'*	girls' uniforms
Brahms (Lullaby)	Whom does the Lullaby belong to?	Brahms	Add *'*	Brahms' Lullaby
my boss (office)	Whom does the office belong to?	my boss	Add *'s*	my boss's office

The trick of asking "Whom does the item belong to?" will always work, but you must ask the question every time. Remember that the key word is *belong*. If you ask the question another way, you may get an answer that won't help you. Also, notice that the trick does not depend on whether the answer is *singular* or *plural*, but on whether it ends in *s* or not.

> ## To Make a Possessive
>
> **1.** Ask "Whom (or what) does the item belong to?"
>
> **2.** If the answer doesn't end in *s*, add an apostrophe and *s*.
>
> **3.** If the answer already ends in *s*, add just an apostrophe *or* an apostrophe and *s* if you need an extra sound to show the possessive (as in *boss's office*).

E X E R C I S E S

Follow the directions carefully for each of the following exercises. Because possessives can be tricky, we include explanations in some exercises to help you understand them better.

Exercise 1

Cover the right column and see if you can write the following possessives correctly. Ask the question "Whom (or what) does the item belong to?" each time. Don't look at the answer before you try!

1. a judge (sentence) _____ a judge's sentence

2. the men (locker room) _____ the men's locker room

3. Lee (sneeze) _____ Lee's sneeze

4. Tess (new job) _____ Tess's or Tess' new job

5. the Tomlins (cat) _____ the Tomlins' cat

6. a mouse (ears) _____ a mouse's ears

7. mice (ears) _____ mice's ears

8. Prof. Hibberts (tests) _____ Prof. Hibberts' tests

9. students (books) _____ students' books

10. a nation (resources) _____ a nation's resources

(Sometimes you may see a couple of choices when the word ends in *s*. *Tess's new job* may be written *Tess' new job*. That depends on whether you want your reader to say it with or without an extra *s* sound. Be consistent when given such choices.)

> **CAUTION** - Don't assume that every word that ends in *s* is a possessive. The *s* may indicate more than one of something, a plural noun. Make sure the word actually possesses something before you add an apostrophe.

A few commonly used words have their own possessive forms and don't need apostrophes added to them. Memorize this list:

our, ours	its
your, yours	their, theirs
his, her, hers	whose

Note particularly *its*, *their*, *whose*, and *your*. They are already possessive and don't take an apostrophe. (These words sound just like *it's*, *they're*, *who's*, and *you're*, which are *contractions* that use an apostrophe in place of their missing letters.)

Exercise 2

Cover the right column and see if you can write the required form. The answer might be a *contraction* or a *possessive*. If you miss any, go back and review the explanations.

1. Yes, (he) the one who called.	he's
2. (They) saving money for a vacation.	They're
3. Does (you) house face south?	your
4. (It) been snowing for two days.	It's
5. These are my keys; are those (her)?	hers
6. (They) muffler needs fixing.	Their
7. Do you know (who) seat that is?	whose
8. My backpack is useless; (it) strap is broken.	its

9. (You) welcome.   You're

10. (Who) going with you this summer?   Who's

Exercise 3

Here's another chance to check your progress with possessives. Cover the right column again as you did in Exercises 1 and 2, and add apostrophes correctly to any possessives. Each answer is followed by an explanation.

1. Our neighbors went to their grandparents house.

   grandparents' (You didn't add an apostrophe to *neighbors*, did you? The neighbors don't possess anything.)

2. The students bus broke down on their field trip.

   students' (Whom does the bus belong to?)

3. I invited Janet to my friends party.

   friend's (if it belongs to one friend), friends' (two or more friends)

4. Two of my sisters went to my dads alma mater.

   dad's (The sisters don't possess anything in the sentence.)

5. Karens apartment is similar to yours.

   Karen's (*Yours* is already possessive and doesn't take an apostrophe.)

6. Last weeks tips were the best yet.

   week's (The tips belong to last week.)

7. The Rogers farm house is just outside of town.

   The Rogers' (Whom does the farm belong to?)

8. The womens team played the mens team.

   women's, men's (Did you ask whom each team belongs to?)

9. The jurors handed the judge their verdict.

   No apostrophe. *Their* is already possessive, and the jurors don't possess anything in the sentence.

10. The sign by the gate said, "The Nelsons."

    Nelsons (meaning that the Nelsons live there) or Nelsons' (meaning that it's the Nelsons' house)

Exercises 4 and 5

Now you're ready to add apostrophes to the possessives that follow. But be careful. *First,* make sure the word really possesses something; not every word ending in *s* is a possessive. *Second,* remember that certain words already have possessive forms and don't use apostrophes. *Third,* even though a word ends in *s,* you can't tell where the apostrophe goes until you ask the question, "Whom (or what) does the item belong to?" The apostrophe or apostrophe and *s* should follow the answer to that question. Check your answers at the back of the book after the first set.

Exercise 4

1. David Mannings reputation as a movie reviewer was destroyed in the spring of 2001.

2. This critics words of praise had been printed on several of Columbia Pictures movie posters at the time and had helped to convince the public to see the films.

3. Mannings glowing quotations appeared on ads for *A Knights Tale, The Animal,* and *Hollow Man.*

4. However, there was a problem with this particular writers opinions.

5. David Mannings praise was empty because David Manning didn't exist.

6. One of the movie studios employees had invented Manning and made up the quotations printed on the posters.

7. A newswriter discovered that Mannings identity was a fake.

8. The publics reaction surprised both newspeople and entertainment industry executives.

9. Many moviegoers said that they expected movie poster quotations to be false and therefore weren't surprised when the studio admitted the truth.

10. The entertainment industry took the deception very seriously, however, and all of the films posters with phony quotes on them were reprinted.

Source: Newsweek, June 11, 2001

Exercise 5

1. The zippers history goes back more than a hundred years.

2. What began as an idea to help keep shoes fastened has evolved into the most popular method to secure clothes, suitcases, tents—just about anything we want to keep closed.

3. Until the zipper was perfected, peoples clothes and other items had to be held together with buttons, hooks, or some other form of fastener.

4. In 1893, a Chicago man named Whitcomb Judson patented a device similar to a modern zippers design but made of a series of hook-and-eye fasteners.

5. Judsons patented ancestor of the zipper doesn't compare with the modern zipper mechanisms two rows of interlocking teeth with a slider to join them.

6. Gideon Sundback is the person responsible for the 1917 patent of the zipper that we would all recognize, but the name "zipper" wasn't Sundbacks idea.

7. In 1923, the B. F. Goodrich company called the fasteners of its popular rain boots "Zippers," and the publics use of zippers took off from there.

8. Now an American purchases an average of 12 zippers a year; that adds up to around 1,000 in a persons lifetime.

9. Americas top-selling zippered clothing is blue jeans, and most jeans zippers are made of brass.

10. The overall demand for zippers is now so high that the worlds largest zipper company makes seven million zippers a day to keep up with it.

Source: Los Angeles Times, September 5, 1998

PROOFREADING EXERCISE

Find the five errors in this student paragraph. All of the errors involve possessives.

The Calderons are members of a family that has lived next door to me for twenty years. I have grown up with the Calderon's daughter, Kim. My family is bigger than her's. When I go to her house, Kims favorite pastime is putting together jigsaw puzzles. We always start off by separating a puzzles pieces into different categories. She makes piles of edge pieces, sky pieces, flower pieces, and so on. Then I start putting the edge piece's together to form the border. The Calderons' son, Simon, usually shows up just in time to put the last piece in the puzzle.

SENTENCE WRITING

Write ten sentences using the possessive forms of the names of your family members or the names of your friends. You could write about a memorable birthday or other occasion. Just tell the story of what happened that day.

REVIEW OF CONTRACTIONS AND POSSESSIVES

Here are two review exercises. First, add the necessary apostrophes to the following sentences. Try to get all the correct answers. Don't excuse an error by saying, "Oh, that was just a careless mistake." A mistake is a mistake. Be tough on yourself.

1. Ive never laughed as hard as I did when I saw Lucys chocolate factory episode.

2. The shows storyline is simple but very old-fashioned by todays standards.

3. Lucys husband, Ricky, and Ethels husband, Fred, switch places with their wives.

4. Ricky and Fred cant wait to see what its like to stay home and do all the housework.

5. They think itll be much easier than working to support the family.

6. Lucy and Ethels first step is to visit an employment agency and apply for a job that suits them; they take the employment agents suggestion and start work at a candy factory.

7. After Lucy watches one of the factorys best candy makers in action, Lucy tries to imitate the womans technique of pooling the chocolate, rolling the centers briefly around in it, and ending with a swirl of chocolate on the candies tops.

8. But Lucys candy centers get lost in her pool of chocolate, and she cant find any pieces big enough to deserve a swirl; Ethel hasnt done much better in her area.

9. Eventually, Ethel and Lucy are stationed at the candy wrapping conveyor belt; at first, they do fine, but as its speed increases, they dont know what to do and end up eating as many chocolates as they wrap.

10. Meanwhile, at home, Ricky and Freds experiences havent been any more successful than Lucy and Ethels, and they all decide that its best to switch back again.

Second, add the necessary apostrophes to the following short student essay.

Going to the Globe

I was very fortunate to attend a high school where theres an English teacher, Ms. Evans, who absolutely loves Shakespeare. Ever since shed heard that a new Globe Theater had been built in London, she said, "Im going to see it now that its finished, and Ill take a group of students with me."

Shakespeares original Globe Theater had been destroyed by a fire in 1613 during a performance of one of his plays, and it hadnt been rebuilt until recently. Im one of the lucky students who accompanied Ms. Evans on her first trip to the new Globe.

When we arrived in London, Ms. Evans excitement rubbed off on all of us. We found The Globes location across the Thames River from another of Londons most famous landmarks—Big Ben.

The theaters outside was just as beautiful as its inside, and it smelled like freshly cut lumber. In fact, thats what its almost entirely made of. Theres not a nail used in the whole outer frame structure. The huge wooden beams visible from the outside are held in place with more than 6,000 wooden pegs, just as Shakespeares craftsmen wouldve done.

We didnt get to see a performance at the Globe, but the tour guides description of one of them made it possible to imagine an audiences excitement, an actors challenges, and a playwrights satisfaction at the rebuilding of his Globe Theater.

Words That Can Be Broken into Parts

Breaking words into their parts will often help you spell them correctly. Each of the following words is made up of two shorter words. Note that the word then contains all the letters of the two shorter words.

chalk board	. . .	chalkboard	room mate	. . .	roommate
over due	. . .	overdue	home work	. . .	homework
super market	. . .	supermarket	under line	. . .	underline

Becoming aware of prefixes such as *dis*, *inter*, *mis*, and *un* is also helpful. When you add a prefix to a word, note that no letters are dropped, either from the prefix or from the word.

dis appear	disappear	mis represent	misrepresent
dis appoint	disappoint	mis spell	misspell
dis approve	disapprove	mis understood	misunderstood
dis satisfy	dissatisfy	un aware	unaware
inter act	interact	un involved	uninvolved
inter active	interactive	un necessary	unnecessary
inter related	interrelated	un sure	unsure

Have someone dictate the preceding list for you to write and then mark any words you miss. Memorize the correct spellings by noting how each word is made up of a prefix and a word.

Rule for Doubling a Final Letter

Most spelling rules have so many exceptions that they aren't much help. But here's one worth learning because it has almost no exceptions.

Double a final letter (consonants only) when adding an ending that begins with a vowel (such as *ing*, *ed*, *er*) if all three of the following are true:

1. The word ends in a single consonant,

2. which is preceded by a single vowel (the vowels are *a, e, i, o, u*),

3. and the accent is on the last syllable (or the word only has one syllable).

We'll try the rule on a few words to which we'll add *ing*, *ed*, or *er*.

begin   **1.** It ends in a single consonant—*n*,
           2. preceded by a single vowel—*i*,
           3. and the accent is on the last syllable—be gin′.
              Therefore, we double the final consonant and write *beginning, be-ginner.*

stop   **1.** It ends in a single consonant—*p*,
           2. preceded by a single vowel—*o*,
           3. and the accent is on the last syllable (there is only one).
              Therefore, we double the final consonant and write *stopping, stopped, stopper.*

filter   **1.** It ends in a single consonant—*r*,

2. preceded by a single vowel—*e*,

3. But the accent isn't on the last syllable. It's on the first—*fil'ter*. Therefore, we don't double the final consonant. We write *filtering, filtered*.

keep   **1.** It ends in a single consonant—*p*,

2. but it isn't preceded by a single vowel. There are two *e*'s. Therefore, we don't double the final consonant. We write *keeping, keeper*.

NOTE - Be aware that *qu* is treated as a consonant because *q* is almost never written without *u*. Think of it as *kw*. In words like *equip* and *quit*, the *qu* acts as a consonant. Therefore, *equip* and *quit* both end in a single consonant preceded by a single vowel, and the final consonant is doubled in *equipped* and *quitting*.

E X E R C I S E S

Add *ing* to these words. Correct each group of ten before continuing so you'll catch any errors early.

Exercise 1

1. steam		**6.** wed	
2. expel		**7.** stress	
3. sip		**8.** flop	
4. suffer		**9.** spin	
5. war		**10.** differ	

Exercise 2

1. shop		**4.** nail
2. offer		**5.** knit
3. wrap		**6.** omit

7. honor

8. brag

9. mark

10. hop

Exercise 3

1. get
2. trust
3. trip
4. plan
5. benefit

6. miss
7. read
8. occur
9. skim
10. scream

Exercise 4

1. creep
2. subtract
3. abandon
4. droop
5. happen

6. weed
7. fog
8. drop
9. refer
10. submit

Exercise 5

1. interpret
2. prefer
3. bet
4. stoop
5. flip

6. infer
7. guess
8. bug
9. jog
10. build

PROGRESS TEST

This test covers everything you've studied so far. One sentence in each pair is correct. The other is incorrect. Read both sentences carefully before you decide. Then write the letter of the incorrect sentence in the blank. Try to isolate and correct the error if you can.

1. _____ **A.** Last month, Trevon led the class with the highest test scores.

   B. He should of worked that hard all semester.

2. _____ **A.** Take your car in for a check-up when you've passed 60,000 miles on your odometer.

   B. That's the point when an engine might choose to brake down.

3. _____ **A.** The Greens' house is the one next to ours.

   B. Their childrens' voices are too soft to hear.

4. _____ **A.** I don't know weather I'll do the extra credit assignment or not.

   B. I'm sure it won't have any effect on our grade.

5. _____ **A.** Its important to be honest with your friends.

   B. After I lied, my conscience bothered me for days.

6. _____ **A.** My brother lost his voice but refused to stop talking.

   B. He should have listened to our advise.

7. _____ **A.** They worked on their scholarship applications together.

   B. His neat printing complimented her writing skills.

8. _____ **A.** Who's going to plan our vacation this year?

   B. Equiping ourselves for a camping trip can take weeks.

9. _____ **A.** My boss complemented me on a good day's work.

   B. I took an extra long coffee break in the employees' lounge.

10. _____ **A.** Their dog's ears hang down into it's dog food.

    B. They think it's cute, but I don't.

Using a Dictionary

Some dictionaries are more helpful than others. A tiny pocket-sized dictionary or one that fits on a single sheet in your notebook might help you find the spelling of very common words, but for all other uses, you will need a complete, recently published dictionary. Spend some time at a bookstore looking through the dictionaries to find one that you feel comfortable reading. Look up a word that you have had trouble with in the past, and see if you understand the definition. Try looking the same word up in another dictionary and compare.

Complete the following exercises using a good dictionary. Then you will understand what a valuable resource it is.

1. Pronunciation

Look up the word *sequester* and copy the pronunciation here.

_____

_____

For help with pronunciation of the syllables, you'll probably find key words at the bottom of one of the two dictionary pages open before you. Note especially that the upside-down *e* (ə) always has the sound of *uh* like the *a* in *ago* or *about*. Remember that sound because it's found in many words.

Slowly pronounce *sequester*, giving each syllable the same sound as its key word.

Note which syllable has the heavy accent mark. (In most dictionaries, the accent mark points to the stressed syllable, but other dictionaries place the accent mark in front of the stressed syllable.) The stressed syllable in *sequester* is *ques*. Now say the word, letting the full force of your voice fall on that syllable.

When more than one pronunciation is given, the first is preferred. If the complete pronunciation of a word isn't given, look at the word above it to find the pronunciation.

Find the pronunciation of these words, using the key words at the bottom of the dictionary page to help you pronounce each syllable. Then note which syllable has the heavy accent mark, and say the word aloud.

aubade   malign ·   longitude ·   piquant

2. Definitions

The dictionary may give more than one meaning for a word. Read all the meanings for each italicized word and then write a definition appropriate to the sentence.

1. Mark and Ruth have an M.A. and a Ph.D., *respectively.* _____

   _____

2. She was chosen to be the *penultimate* speaker at the conference. _____

   _____

3. They took their *biennial* trip to Yosemite. _____

   _____

4. As a lifeguard, he suffered from a *sporadic* fear of water. _____

   _____

3. Spelling

By making yourself look up each word you aren't sure how to spell, you'll soon become a better speller. When two spellings are given in the dictionary, the first one (or the one with the definition) is preferred.

Use a dictionary to find the preferred spelling for each of these words.

    cancelled, canceled   dialog, dialogue

    judgment, judgement   gray, grey

4. Parts of Speech

English has eight parts of speech: noun, pronoun, verb, adjective, adverb, preposition, conjunction, and interjection. At the beginning of each definition for a word, you'll find an abbreviation for the part of speech that the word is performing when so defined (N., PRON., V. [VI. OR VT.], ADJ., ADV., PREP., CONJ., INTERJ.). For more discussion of parts of speech, see page 25.

Identify the parts of speech listed in all the definitions for each of the following words.

    smile _____   well _____

    every _____   it   _____

5. Compound Words

If you want to find out whether two words are written separately, written with a hyphen between them, or written as one word, consult your dictionary. Look at these examples:

half brother	is written as two words
sister-in-law	is hyphenated
stepchild	is written as one word

Write each of the following as listed in the dictionary (as two words, as a hyphenated word, or as one word).

photo copy _____   sea gull   _____

one way   _____   week end   _____

6. Capitalization

If a word is capitalized in the dictionary, that means it should always be capitalized. If it is not capitalized in the dictionary, then it may or may not be capitalized, depending on how it is used (see p. 203). For example, *American* is always capitalized, but *college* is capitalized or not, according to how it is used.

Last year, I graduated from college.
Last year, I graduated from Monterey Peninsula College.

Write the following words as they're given in the dictionary (with or without a capital) to show whether they must always be capitalized or not. Take a guess before looking them up.

bakelite   _____   formica   _____

halloween   _____   autumn   _____

7. Usage

Just because a word is in the dictionary doesn't mean that it's in standard use. The following labels indicate whether a word is used today and, if so, where and by whom.

obsolete	no longer used
archaic	not now used in ordinary language but still found in some biblical, literary, and legal expressions
colloquial, informal	used in informal conversation but not in formal writing
dialectal, regional	used in some localities but not everywhere
slang	popular but nonstandard expression
nonstandard, substandard	not used in Standard Written English

Look up each italicized word and write any label indicating its usage. Dictionaries differ. One may list a word as *slang* whereas another will call it *colloquial*. Still another may give no designation, thus indicating that that particular dictionary considers the word in standard use.

1. The hula hoop was a *fad* that began in the 1950s. _____

2. You *guys* don't know how to have fun anymore. _____

3. That *tidbit* of gossip made my day. _____

4. That child has plenty of *spunk*. _____

5. I always say *hi* to my neighbors. _____

8. Derivations

The derivations or stories behind words will often help you remember the current meanings. For example, if you read that someone is *narcissistic* and you consult your dictionary, you'll find that *narcissism* is a condition named after Narcissus, who was a handsome young man in Greek mythology. One day Narcissus fell in love with his own reflection in a pool, but when he tried to get closer to it, he fell in the water and drowned. A flower that grew nearby is now named for Narcissus. And *narcissistic* has come to mean "in love with oneself."

Look up the derivation of each of these words. You'll find it in square brackets either just before or just after the definition.

procrustean _____

boycott _____

malapropism _____

Gordian _____

9. Synonyms

At the end of a definition, a group of synonyms is sometimes given. For example, at the end of the definition of *injure*, you'll find several synonyms, such as *damage* or *harm*. And if you look up *damage* or *harm*, you'll be referred to the same synonyms listed under *injure*.

List the synonyms given for the following words.

press _____

plan _____

summit _____

10. Abbreviations

Find the meaning of the following abbreviations.

R.S.V.P. _____   e.g.   _____

p.s.   _____   OPEC _____

11. Names of People

The names of famous people will be found either in the main part of your dictionary or in a separate biographical names section at the back.

Locate the following famous people (find out how to pronounce their names and what they're famous for).

Marcel Duchamp _____

Sappho _____

Miguel Covarubius _____

Martha Graham _____

12. Names of Places

The names of places will be found either in the main part of your dictionary or in a separate geographical names section at the back.

Locate the following places (find out how to pronounce them and where they're located).

Chiba _____

Big Sur _____

Tegucigalpa _____

Edinburgh _____

13. Foreign Words and Phrases

Find the language and the meaning of the italicized expressions.

1. The walls of the castle were lined with *objets d'art.* _____

_____

2. We were given *carte blanche* to gamble at the casino. _____

_____

3. I met my *doppelgänger* in a Chicago hotel. _____

_____

14. Miscellaneous Information

See if you can find these miscellaneous bits of information in a dictionary.

1. What part of the human body can suffer from *nystagmus?* _____

_____

2. How many zeroes does a *googol* have? _____

_____

3. How much time is a *fortnight?* _____

_____

4. In what year did *virtual reality* become an expression? _____

_____

5. What did ancient Greeks and Romans use a *strigil* for? _____

_____

PART 2

Sentence Structure

Sentence structure refers to the way sentences are built using words, phrases, and clauses. Words are single units, and words link up in sentences to form clauses and phrases. Clauses are word groups *with* subjects and verbs, and phrases are word groups *without* subjects and verbs. Clauses are the most important because they make statements—they tell who did what (or what something is) in a sentence. Look at the following sentence for example:

We bought oranges at the farmer's market on Main Street.

It contains ten words, each playing its own part in the meaning of the sentence. But which of the words together tell who did what? *We bought oranges* is correct. That word group is a clause. Notice that *at the farmer's market* and *on Main Street* also link up as word groups but don't have somebody (subject) doing something (verb). Instead, they are phrases to clarify *where* we bought the oranges.

Importantly, you could leave out one or both of the phrases and still have a sentence—*We bought oranges*. However, you cannot leave the clause out. Then you would just have *At the farmer's market on Main Street*. Remember, every sentence needs at least one clause that can stand by itself.

Learning about the structure of sentences helps you control your own. Once you know more about sentence structure, then you can understand writing errors and learn how to correct them.

Among the most common errors in writing are fragments, run-ons, and awkward phrasing.

Here are some fragments:

Wandering around the mall all afternoon.

Because I tried to do too many things at once.

By interviewing the applicants in groups.

They don't make complete statements—not one has a clause that can stand by itself. Who was *wandering*? What happened *because you tried to do too many things at once*? What was the result of *interviewing the applicants in groups*? These incomplete sentence structures fail to communicate a complete thought.

In contrast, here are some run-ons:

Computer prices are dropping they're still beyond my budget.

The forecast calls for rain I'll wait to wash my car.

A truck parked in front of my driveway I couldn't get to school.

Unlike fragments, run-ons make complete statements, but the trouble is they make *two* complete statements; the first *runs on* to the second without correct punctuation. The reader has to go back to see where there should have been a break.

So fragments don't include enough information, and run-ons include too much. Another problem occurs when the information in a sentence just doesn't make sense.

Here are a few sentences with awkward phrasing:

The problem from my grades started to end.

It was a time at the picnic.

She won me at chess.

Try to find the word groups that show who did what, that is, the clauses. Once you find them, then try to put the clauses and phrases together to form a precise meaning. It's difficult, isn't it? You'll see that many of the words themselves are misused or unclear, such as *from, it,* and *won.* These sentences don't communicate clearly because the clauses, phrases, and even words don't work together. They suffer from awkward phrasing.

Fragments, run-ons, awkward phrasing, and other sentence structure errors confuse the reader. Not until you get rid of them will your writing be clearer and easier to read. Unfortunately, there is no quick, effortless way to learn to avoid errors in sentence structure. First, you need to understand how clear sentences are built. Then you will be able to avoid common errors in your own writing.

This section will describe areas of sentence structure one at a time and then explain how to correct errors associated with the different areas. For instance, we start by helping you find subjects and verbs and understand dependent clauses; then we show you how to avoid fragments. You can go through the whole section yourself to learn all of the concepts and structures. Or your teacher may assign only parts based on errors the class is making.

Finding Subjects and Verbs

The most important words in sentences are those that make up its independent clause—the subject and the verb. When you write a sentence, you write about *something* or *someone*. That's the *subject*. Then you write what the subject *does* or *is*. That's the *verb*.

Lightning strikes.

The word *Lightning* is the thing you are writing about. It's the subject, and we'll underline all subjects once. *Strikes* tells what the subject does. It shows the action in the sentence. It's the verb, and we'll underline all of them twice. Most sentences do not include only two words (the subject and the verb). However, these two words still make up the core of the sentence even if other words and phrases are included with them.

Lightning strikes back and forth from the clouds to the ground very quickly.

Often lightning strikes people on golf courses or in boats.

When many words appear in sentences, the subject and verb can be harder to find. Because the verb often shows action, it's easier to spot than the subject. Therefore, always look for it first. For example, take this sentence:

The neighborhood cat folded its paws under its chest.

Which word shows the action? The action word is folded. It's the verb, so we'll underline it twice. Now ask yourself who or what folded? The answer is cat. That's the subject, so we'll underline it once.

Study the following sentences until you understand how to pick out subjects and verbs.

Tomorrow our school celebrates its fiftieth anniversary. (Which word shows the action? The action word is celebrates. It's the verb, so we'll underline it twice. Who or what celebrates? The school does. It's the subject. We'll underline it once.)

The team members ate several boxes of chocolates. (Which word shows the action? Ate shows the action. Who or what ate? Members ate.)

Internet users crowd the popular services. (Which word shows the action? The verb is crowd. Who or what crowd? Users crowd.)

Often the verb doesn't show action but merely tells what the subject *is* or *was*. Learn to spot such verbs—*is, am, are, was, were, seems, feels, appears, becomes, looks* . . . . (For more information on these special verbs, see the discussion of sentence patterns on p. 138).

Marshall is a neon artist. (First spot the verb <u>is</u>. Then ask who or what is? <u>Marshall</u> <u>is</u>.)

The bread appears moldy. (First spot the verb <u>appears</u>. Then ask who or what appears? <u>Bread</u> <u>appears</u>.)

Sometimes the subject comes after the verb, especially when a word like *there* or *here* begins the sentence without being a real subject. It's best not to start sentences with "There is . . . " or "There are . . . " for this reason.

In the audience were two reviewers from the *Times*. (Who or what were in the audience? Two <u>reviewers</u> from the *Times* <u>were</u> in the audience.)

There was a fortune-teller at the carnival. (Who or what was there? A <u>fortune-teller</u> <u>was</u> there at the carnival.)

There were name tags for all the participants. (Who or what were there? <u>Name tags</u> <u>were</u> there for all the participants.)

Here are the contracts. (Who or what are here? The <u>contracts</u> <u>are</u> here.)

NOTE - Remember that *there* and *here* (as used in the last three sentences) are not subjects. They simply point to something.

In commands, often the subject is not expressed. An unwritten *you* is understood by the reader.

Sit down. (<u>You</u> <u>sit</u> down.)

Place flap A into slot B. (<u>You</u> <u>place</u> flap A into slot B.)

Meet me at 7:00. (<u>You</u> <u>meet</u> me at 7:00.)

Commonly, a sentence may have more than one subject.

<u>Toys</u> and <u>memorabilia</u> from the 1950s <u>are</u> high-priced collectibles.

Celebrity <u>dolls</u>, board <u>games</u>, and even cereal <u>boxes</u> from that decade <u>line</u> the shelves of antique stores.

A sentence may also have more than one verb.

Water boils at a consistent temperature and freezes at another.

The ice tray fell out of my hand, skidded across the floor, and landed under the table.

E X E R C I S E S

Underline the subjects once and the verbs twice in the following sentences. When you've finished the first set, compare your answers carefully with those at the back of the book.

Exercise 1

1. Human beings are creatures of habit.
2. They visit predictable places and do predictable things.
3. In their work, scientists study such behavior.
4. George Karev is a member of the Bulgarian Academy of Sciences.
5. Karev studied the habits of people in movie theaters.
6. Karev's results about moviegoers make a lot of sense.
7. Most people prefer seats on the right side of the theater and always sit there.
8. Therefore, their left eye sees most of the movie.
9. The left eye generally reports to the right hemisphere of the brain.
10. The right hemisphere connects people with their own feelings and with the emotions of others.

Source: Current Science, May 11, 2001

Exercise 2

1. Traffic reports on the radio and TV affect people's lives.
2. But such reports are not always available.

3. On the road, drivers without radios miss important warnings.

4. There are many possible results.

5. Sometimes a bad accident or a construction site slows traffic to a halt.

6. At such times, drivers and their passengers sit in traffic jams for hours.

7. Police and transportation officials often provide detours in these cases.

8. Informed drivers avoid wasted hours through the use of such detours.

9. Traffic reports on the radio are invaluable.

10. They help drivers out of many difficult situations.

Exercise 3

1. There is a long-standing tradition in school lunch rooms.

2. Children get peanut butter-and-jelly sandwiches in their lunchboxes.

3. The PB&J sandwich seems an almost fool-proof choice for a kid's lunch.

4. Most kids love the sight, smell, and taste of this combination of salty peanut butter, sweet jelly, and soft bread.

5. But peanuts are dangerous to children with peanut allergies.

6. Most youngsters eat peanuts and feel fine.

7. A mildly allergic child reacts with watery eyes and hives.

8. In extreme cases, children with peanut allergies die.

9. So there are peanut-free zones in some schools.

10. With each new academic year, schools increase their awareness of risks such as peanut allergies.

Exercise 4

1. I never knew much about curses and magic spells.

2. According to *Smithsonian* magazine, the Greeks and Romans used them all the time.

3. There were magicians for hire back then.

4. These magicians made money through their knowledge of the art of cursing.

5. Some ancient citizens took revenge on their enemies with special curses for failure.

6. Others wanted only love and placed spells on the objects of their desire.

7. The magicians wrote the commissioned curses or love spells on lead tablets.

8. Then they positioned these curse tablets near their intended victims.

9. Archeologists found one 1,700-year-old curse tablet over the starting gate of an ancient race course.

10. It named the horses and drivers of specific chariots and itemized the specifics of the curse.

Source: Smithsonian, April 1996

Exercise 5

1. Plastic snow domes are popular souvenir items.

2. They are clear domes usually on white oval bases.

3. People display these water-filled objects or use them as paperweights.

4. Inside are tiny replicas of famous tourist attractions like the Eiffel Tower or Big Ben.

5. Snow or glitter mixes with the water for a snowstorm effect.

6. These souvenirs often hold startling combinations.

7. In a snow dome, even the Bahamas has blizzards.

8. There is also a Los Angeles dome with smog instead of snow.

9. Snow dome collectors regard them as valuable objects.

10. Others treat them as mere trinkets.

PARAGRAPH EXERCISE

Underline the subjects once and the verbs twice in the following student paragraph.

Al Levis invented the popular snack Slim Jims. Slim Jims are stick-shaped meat snacks. Levis was a high-school dropout but eventually made a fortune from his snack product. Slim Jims originally came in jars full of vinegar. In the 1940s and 50s, bar customers ate Slim Jims with their cocktails. Then Levis's company offered Slim Jims in individual packages. People ate them on camping trips and at sporting events. Levis sold his invention in the late 1960s but continued his good work. Before his death in March of 2001, Levis donated millions of dollars to worthy causes.

SENTENCE WRITING

Write ten sentences about any subject—your favorite color, for instance. Keeping your subject matter simple in these sentence writing exercises will make it easier to find your sentence structures later. After you have written your sentences, go back and underline your subjects once and your verbs twice.

Locating Prepositional Phrases

Prepositional phrases are among the easiest structures in English to learn. Remember that a phrase is just a group of related words (at least two) without a subject and a verb. And don't let a term like *prepositional* scare you. If you look in the middle of that long word, you'll find a familiar one—*position*. In English, we tell the *positions* of people and things in sentences using prepositional phrases.

Look at the following sentence with its prepositional phrases in parentheses:

Our field trip (to the desert) begins (at 6:00) (in the morning) (on Friday).

One phrase tells where the field trip is going (*to the desert*), and three phrases tell when the trip begins (*at 6:00, in the morning,* and *on Friday*). As you can see, prepositional phrases show the position of someone or something in space or in time.

Here is a list of some prepositions that can show positions in space:

under	across	outside	against
around	by	inside	at
through	beyond	over	beneath
above	among	on	in
below	near	behind	past
between	without	from	to

Here are some prepositions that can show positions in time:

before	throughout	past	within
after	by	until	in
since	at	during	for

These lists include only individual words, *not phrases.* Remember, a preposition must be followed by an object—someone or something—to create a prepositional phrase. Notice that in the added prepositional phrases that follow, the position of the balloon in relation to the object, *the clouds,* changes completely.

The hot-air balloon floated *above the clouds.*
below the clouds.
within the clouds.
between the clouds.
past the clouds.
around the clouds.

Now notice the different positions in time:

The balloon landed *at 3:30.*
by 3:30.
past 3:30.
before the thunderstorm.
during the thunderstorm.
after the thunderstorm.

NOTE - A few words—such as *of, as,* and *like*—are prepositions that do not fit neatly into either the space or time category, yet they are very common prepositions (box *of candy,* note *of apology,* type *of bicycle*—act *as a substitute,* use *as an example,* testified *as an expert*—vitamins *like A, C, and E,* acts *like a child,* moves *like a snake*).

By locating prepositional phrases, you will be able to find subjects and verbs more easily. For example, you might have difficulty finding the subject and verb in a long sentence like this:

After the rainy season, one of the windows in the attic leaked at the corners of its molding.

But if you put parentheses around all the prepositional phrases like this

(After the rainy season), <u>one</u> (of the windows) (in the attic) <u>leaked</u> (at the corners) (of its molding).

then you have only two words left—the subject and the verb. Even in short sentences like the following, you might pick the wrong word as the subject if you don't put parentheses around the prepositional phrases first.

<u>Two</u> (of the characters) <u>lied</u> (to each other) (throughout the play).

The <u>waves</u> (around the ship) <u>looked</u> real.

> **NOTE** - Don't mistake *to* plus a verb for a prepositional phrase. Special forms of verbals always start with *to*, but they are not prepositional phrases (see p. 127). For example, in the sentence "I like to run to the beach," *to run* is a verbal, not a prepositional phrase. However, *to the beach* is a prepositional phrase because it begins with a preposition (to), ends with a noun (beach), and shows position in space.

EXERCISES

Put parentheses around the prepositional phrases in the following sentences. Be sure to start with the preposition itself (*in, on, to, at, of* . . .) and include the word or words that go with it (*in the morning, on our sidewalk, to Hawaii* . . .). Then underline the sentences' subjects once and verbs twice. Remember that subjects and verbs are not found inside prepositional phrases, so if you locate the prepositional phrases *first,* the subjects and verbs will be much easier to find. Review the answers given at the back for each set of ten sentences before continuing.

Exercise 1

1. In February of 2001, a powerful earthquake struck Seattle, Washington, and its surrounding communities.
2. One of those communities was Port Townsend.
3. At Mind Over Matter, a Port Townsend specialty store, the shaking of the earth caused more than just damage.
4. A favorite display at the store was a pendulum with sand beneath it.
5. With its powerful shaking, the earthquake moved the pendulum and drew a picture in the shape of a rose.
6. Jason Ward, the store's owner, noticed the unique drawing in the sand right after the quake.
7. During some earthquakes, the ground moves back and forth in one direction.
8. In the Seattle quake, the ground shook in many directions.

9. Ward and others marveled at the beauty of the quake's design and planned a casting of it.

10. But Ward's son knocked the sand tray by mistake and erased nature's handiwork.

Source: Current Science, May 11, 2001

Exercise 2

1. The many cases of food poisoning in America each year alarm people.
2. Some food scientists point to food irradiation as one possible solution.
3. The irradiation of food kills bacteria through exposure to gamma rays.
4. With irradiation, farmers spray fewer pesticides on their crops.
5. And irradiated food lasts longer on the shelf or in the refrigerator.
6. However, many scientists and consumers worry about the risks of food irradiation.
7. Irradiation reduces vitamins and changes nutrients in the food.
8. The radioactive materials at the irradiation plants are also potentially dangerous.
9. Critics predict accidents in the transportation and use of these radioactive substances.
10. In the United States, the controversy about food irradiation continues.

Exercise 3

1. *Romeo and Juliet* is many people's favorite play by William Shakespeare.
2. The Bard's love story remains one of the most famous in the world.
3. Many movies use aspects of this story as part of their plots.
4. One thing about the story surprises people.
5. Both Romeo and Juliet have other love interests at some point in the play.
6. Romeo has his eyes on Rosaline before Juliet.

7. And Juliet accepts Paris's marriage proposal against her will.

8. But before her unwanted wedding day, Juliet elopes with Romeo in secret.

9. Friar Lawrence helps the newlyweds with a plan for their escape without anyone's notice.

10. However, the complicated timing of the plan has tragic results on the lives of Romeo and Juliet.

Exercise 4

1. For a change of pace, I shopped for my Mother's Day gift at an antique mall.

2. I found old Bakelite jewelry in every shade of yellow, red, blue, and green.

3. There were even linens from all the way back to the pioneer days.

4. One booth sold only drinking glasses with advertising slogans and cartoon characters on them.

5. Another stocked old metal banks with elaborate mechanisms for children's pennies.

6. In the back corner of the mall, I found a light blue pitcher with a dark blue design.

7. My mother had one like it in the early years of my childhood.

8. My sisters and I liked to drink punch from it on hot days in the summer.

9. I checked the price on the tag underneath the pitcher's handle.

10. But at a moment like that, my mind was not on money.

Exercise 5

1. Over the weekend, I watched a hilarious old movie, *Genevieve*, on late-night television.

2. The whole story takes place in the countryside of England.

3. It is a black-and-white movie from the 1930s or 1940s.

4. The clothes and manners of the characters in *Genevieve* are very proper and old-fashioned.

5. Two young couples enter their cars in a road rally for fun.

6. They participate in the race strictly for adventure.

7. Genevieve is the name of the main couple's car.

8. During the road rally, the two couples' polite manners disappear in the rush for the finish line.

9. Predictably, they begin to fight with each other and to sabotage each other's cars.

10. But like all good comedies, *Genevieve* and its ending hold a surprise for everyone.

PARAGRAPH EXERCISE

Put parentheses around the prepositional phrases, then underline the subjects once and the verbs twice in this excerpt from the book *Weather: A Golden Guide,* by Paul E. Lehr, R. Will Burnett, and Herbert S. Zim:

Meteors are visitors from outer space. They hit our atmosphere at tremendous speeds—perhaps 90,000 miles per hour. Friction with the air of the upper atmosphere heats them to incandescence, and most of them vaporize into gases or disintegrate into harmless dust . . . within 30 miles of the earth's surface. Thus our atmosphere protects us. Millions of meteors, most of them smaller than grains of sand, hit our atmosphere every day. Very few ever reach the ground.

SENTENCE WRITING

Write ten simple sentences on the topic of your favorite food—or choose any topic you like. When you go back over your sentences, put parentheses around your prepositional phrases and underline your subjects once and your verbs twice.

Understanding Dependent Clauses

All clauses contain a subject and a verb, yet there are two kinds of clauses: *independent* and *dependent*. Independent clauses have a subject and a verb and make complete statements by themselves. Dependent clauses have a subject and a verb but don't make complete statements because of the words they begin with. Here are some of the words (conjunctions) that begin dependent clauses:

after	since	whereas
although	so that	wherever
as	than	whether
as if	that	which
because	though	whichever
before	unless	while
even if	until	who
even though	what	whom
ever since	whatever	whose
how	when	why
if	whenever	where

Whenever a clause starts with one of these dependent words, it is a dependent clause. To show you the difference between an independent and a dependent clause, look at this example of an independent clause:

> We ate dinner together.

It has a subject (We) and a verb (ate), and it makes a complete statement. But as soon as we put one of the dependent words in front of it, the clause becomes dependent because it no longer makes a complete statement:

> *After* we ate dinner together . . .
>
> *Although* we ate dinner together . . .
>
> *As* we ate dinner together . . .
>
> *Before* we ate dinner together . . .
>
> *Since* we ate dinner together . . .
>
> *That* we ate dinner together . . .
>
> *When* we ate dinner together . . .
>
> *While* we ate dinner together . . .

Each of these dependent clauses leaves the reader expecting something more. Each would depend on another clause—an independent clause—to make a sentence. For the rest of this discussion, we'll place a broken line beneath dependent clauses.

> *After* we ate dinner together, we went to the evening seminar.
>
> We went to the evening seminar *after* we ate dinner together.
>
> The speaker didn't know *that* we ate dinner together.
>
> *While* we ate dinner together, the restaurant became crowded.

As you can see in these examples, *when a dependent clause comes before an independent clause, it is followed by a comma.* Often the comma prevents misreading, as in the following sentence:

> *When* he returned, the DVD was on the floor.

Without a comma after *returned*, the reader would read *When he returned the DVD* before realizing that this was not what the author meant. The comma prevents misreading. Sometimes if the dependent clause is short and there is no danger of misreading, the comma can be left off, but it's safer simply to follow the rule that a dependent clause coming before an independent clause is followed by a comma. You'll learn more about the punctuation of dependent clauses on page 183, but right now just remember the previous rule.

Note that a few of the dependent words (*that, who, which, what*) can do "double duty" as both the dependent word and the subject of the dependent clause:

Thelma wrote a book *that* sold a thousand copies.

The manager saw *what* happened.

Sometimes the dependent clause is in the middle of the independent clause:

The book *that* sold a thousand copies was Thelma's.

The events *that* followed the parade delighted everyone.

The dependent clause can even be the subject of the entire sentence:

What you do also affects me.

How your project looks counts for ten percent of the grade.

Also note that sometimes the *that* of a dependent clause is omitted:

I know *that* you feel strongly about this issue.

I know you feel strongly about this issue.

Everyone received the classes *that* they wanted.

Everyone received the classes they wanted.

Of course, the word *that* doesn't always introduce a dependent clause. It may be a pronoun and serve as the subject or object of the sentence:

That <u>was</u> a long movie.

<u>We</u> <u>knew</u> that already.

That can also be an adjective, a descriptive word telling *which one:*

That <u>movie</u> always <u>makes</u> me cry.

<u>We</u> <u>took</u> them to *that* park last week.

E X E R C I S E S

Draw a broken line beneath any dependent clauses in the following sentences. Some sentences have no dependent clauses, and others have more than one. The best way to begin is to look for the dependent words (*when, since, that, because, after . . .*) and be sure they are followed by subjects and verbs. Finally, underline the subjects once and the verbs twice in both the independent and dependent clauses. Compare your underlines with those at the back of the book carefully after each set.

Exercise 1

1. People who need glasses often wear contact lenses.
2. Clear contact lenses maintain a person's appearance because they fit over the eye and have no frames.
3. But there are contact lenses that change a person's eye color.
4. Someone who has green eyes makes them blue or brown with colored contact lenses.
5. Now even people who don't need glasses change their eye color with contact lenses.
6. Colored lenses are fashion statements that are especially popular with young people.
7. Unless a doctor fits them, contact lenses that people buy or trade with friends invite injuries.
8. Ill-fitting lenses squeeze or scratch the eyes as they move around under the eyelids.

9. After a scratch occurs, germs easily infect the eyes' surface.

10. Such infections sometimes lead to damage that is permanent.

Source: Current Science, May 11, 2001

Exercise 2

1. I am not very talkative in school.

2. Whenever my teacher asks a question in class, I get nervous.

3. If I know the answer, I usually look straight ahead.

4. When I forget the answer, I check my shoes or a note in my notebook.

5. Usually, the teacher chooses someone else before I finish my fidgeting.

6. Obviously, when I take a speech class, I talk sometimes.

7. In my last speech class, we all demonstrated some sort of process.

8. The speech that I gave explained how I make crepes.

9. Since I work at a French restaurant, I borrowed a crepe pan for my demonstration.

10. The crepes cooked so quickly that the teacher and students passed the plates around before I said anything at all.

Exercise 3

1. Many people remember when microwave ovens first arrived in stores.

2. People worried about whether they were safe or not.

3. Before they had the microwave oven, people cooked all food with direct heat.

4. At first, microwave ovens were strange because they heated only the food.

5. And microwave ovens cooked food so much faster than ordinary ovens did.

6. Eventually, people welcomed the convenience that microwave ovens offered.

7. Since they are fast and cool, microwave ovens work well almost anywhere.

8. People who are on a budget bring lunch from home and heat it up at work or school.

9. Now that microwave ovens are here, people even make popcorn without a pan.

10. As each new technology arrives, people wonder how they ever lived without it.

Exercise 4

1. Since we all want perfect documents, nearly everyone uses correction fluid or tape sometimes.

2. Bette Nesmith invented Liquid Paper or, as she first called it, "Mistake Out."

3. After the young bank secretary noticed that sign painters always painted over their errors instead of erasing them, she had an idea.

4. Nesmith started filling up small bottles with white paint, which she used for her typing mistakes.

5. As soon as her friends saw how well Nesmith's paint worked, they all wanted their own bottles.

6. Once she realized that the idea was a success, she developed a liquid that was more than just paint.

7. She patented her formula and called it Liquid Paper.

8. She took the product to a big corporation.

9. After IBM rejected Nesmith's invention, she formed The Liquid Paper Company herself and earned a large fortune.

10. Michael Nesmith, who is Bette Nesmith's son, helped his mother in her business even after he became a member of the famous group The Monkees.

Source: Mothers of Invention (Morrow, 1988)

Exercise 5

1. When I first heard the expression "white elephant," I didn't know what it meant.
2. Yesterday I finally learned what "white elephant" means.
3. A white elephant is an unwanted object that is difficult to get rid of.
4. Most white elephants are gifts that friends or relatives give us.
5. As I read the story behind the expression, I understood it better.
6. The ruler of an ancient land received any white elephants born in his country; it was a custom that sometimes came in handy.
7. The ruler then gave the white elephants as presents to people who angered him.
8. The elephants ate so much and were so costly that they ruined the lives of the people who received them as "gifts."
9. That is why we now use the term for objects that cause us to feel responsible and burdened.
10. Whenever I give a present, I choose it carefully so that it is not a white elephant.

Source: A Hog on Ice & Other Curious Expressions (Harper & Row, 1948)

PARAGRAPH EXERCISE

Draw a broken line beneath the dependent clauses in these paragraphs from *The Story of My Life*, by Helen Keller (1880–1968), the famous American woman who, after a severe childhood illness, lost her sight, her hearing, and her ability to speak. Against all odds, Keller graduated from Radcliffe College and became an accomplished writer and political and social activist. When looking for dependent clauses, remember to find the dependent words (*when, since, that, because, after . . .*) and be sure they are followed by subjects and verbs. Underline the subjects once and the verbs twice in both the independent and dependent clauses.

I do not remember when I first realized that I was different from other people; but I knew it before my teacher came to me. I had noticed that my mother and my friends did not use signs as I did when they wanted anything done, but talked with their mouths. Sometimes I stood between two persons who were conversing and touched their lips. I could not understand, and was vexed. I moved my lips and gesticulated frantically without result. This made me so angry at times that I kicked and screamed until I was exhausted.

I think I knew when I was naughty, for I knew that it hurt Ella, my nurse, to kick her, and when my fit of temper was over I had a feeling akin to regret. But I cannot remember any instance in which this feeling prevented me from repeating the naughtiness when I failed to get what I wanted.

SENTENCE WRITING

Write ten sentences about one of your weekend routines (sleeping late, eating a big breakfast, doing house or yard work, etc.). Try to write sentences that contain both independent and dependent clauses. Then find the dependent words and draw a broken line beneath your dependent clauses.

Correcting Fragments

Sometimes a group of words looks like a sentence—with a capital letter at the beginning and a period at the end—but it may be missing a subject or a verb or both. Such incomplete sentence structures are called *fragments*. Here are a few examples:

> Just ran around with his arms in the air. (*Who* did? There is no subject.)
>
> Paul and his sister with the twins. (*Did* what? There is no verb.)
>
> Nothing to do at night. (This fragment is missing a subject and a real verb. *To do* is a verbal, see p. 127.)

To change these fragments into sentences, we must make sure each has a subject and a real verb:

> The lottery winner just ran around with his arms in the air. (We added a subject.)
>
> Paul and his sister with the twins reconciled. (We added a verb.)
>
> The jurors had nothing to do at night. (We added a subject and a real verb.)

Sometimes we can simply attach such a fragment to the previous sentence.

> I want a fulfilling job. A teaching career, for example.
>
> I want a fulfilling job—a teaching career, for example.

Or we can add a subject or a verb to the fragment and make it a complete sentence.

> I want a fulfilling job. A teaching career is one example.

Phrases

By definition, phrases are word groups without subjects and verbs, so whenever a phrase is punctuated as a sentence, it is a fragment. Look at this example of a sentence followed by a phrase fragment beginning with *hoping* (see p. 127 for more about verbal phrases):

> Actors waited outside the director's office. Hoping for a chance at an audition.

We can correct this fragment by attaching it to the previous sentence.

Actors <u>waited</u> outside the director's office, hoping for a chance at an audition.

Or we can change it to include a subject and a real verb.

Actors <u>waited</u> outside the director's office. They <u>hoped</u> for a chance at an audition.

Here's another example of a sentence followed by a phrase fragment:

Philosophy <u>classes</u> <u>are</u> challenging. When taught by great thinkers.

Here the two have been combined into one complete sentence:

Philosophy <u>classes</u> taught by great thinkers <u>are</u> challenging.

Or a better revision might be

Philosophy <u>classes</u> <u>are</u> challenging when taught by great thinkers.

Sometimes, prepositional phrases are also incorrectly punctuated as sentences. Here a prepositional phrase follows a sentence, but the word group is a fragment—it has no subject and verb of its own. Therefore, it needs to be corrected.

<u>I</u> <u>live</u> a simple life. With my family on our farm in central California.

Here is one possible correction:

<u>I</u> <u>live</u> a simple life with my family on our farm in central California.

Or it could be corrected this way:

My <u>family</u> and <u>I</u> <u>live</u> a simple life on our farm in central California.

Dependent Clauses

Dependent clauses punctuated as sentences are still another kind of fragment. A sentence needs a subject, a verb, *and* a complete thought. As discussed in the previous section, a dependent clause has a subject and a verb, but it begins with a word that makes its meaning incomplete, such as *after, while, because, since, although, when, if, where, who, which,* and *that.* (See p. 71 for a longer list of these conjunctions.) To correct such fragments, we need to eliminate the word that makes the clause dependent *or* add an independent clause.

Fragment

> *While* some of us wrote in our journals.

Corrected

> Some of us wrote in our journals.

or

> *While* some of us wrote in our journals, the fire alarm rang.

Fragment

> *Which* kept me from finishing my journal entry.

Corrected

> The fire alarm kept me from finishing my journal entry.

or

> We responded to the fire alarm, *which* kept me from finishing my journal entry.

Are fragments ever permissible? Professional writers sometimes use fragments in advertising and other kinds of writing. But professional writers use these fragments intentionally, not in error. Until you're an experienced writer, it's best to write in complete sentences. Especially in college writing, you should avoid using fragments.

EXERCISES

Some—but not all—of the following word groups are sentences. The sentences include subjects and verbs and make complete statements. Write the word "sentence" next to each of the sentences. Any word groups that do *not* include subjects and verbs and make complete statements are fragments. Write the word "fragment" next to each of these incomplete sentence structures. Then change the fragments into sentences by ensuring that each has a subject and a real verb and makes a complete statement.

Exercise 1

1. Duct tape has many uses.
2. Holds objects together firmly.
3. Patches holes in backpacks and tents.
4. People are very creative with duct tape.
5. Books written about the unique uses for it.
6. A yearly contest by the makers of Duck Brand duct tape.
7. High school prom couples make their outfits entirely from duct tape.
8. Strips of duct tape forming tuxedos, cummerbunds, gowns, hats, and corsages.
9. A $2,500 prize to the couple with the best use of duct tape and another $2,500 to their high school.
10. Hundreds of couples from across the country participate in this contest every year.

Source: http://www.ducktapeclub.com/prom

Exercise 2

1. The largest of the dinosaurs were probably vegetarians.
2. Tyrannosaurus rex a meat-eater or carnivore.
3. Supposedly the biggest of the carnivorous dinosaurs.
4. In 1995, scientists discovered the remains of a bigger carnivore than T. Rex.
5. In Africa, living ninety million years ago.
6. Scientists named it Carcharodontosaurus saharicus.
7. Meaning having shark-like teeth and living in the Sahara Desert.
8. It was almost fifty feet long and weighed eight tons.

9. A skull five and a half feet in length.

10. T. Rex may have been smaller but will always have an easier name to re-member.

Source: Newsweek, May 27, 1996

Exercise 3

Correct each phrase fragment by changing or adding words or by attaching the phrase to the complete sentence nearby.

1. We shopped all day at the mall. Looking for the perfect suitcases for our cruise this summer.

2. We knew of a specialty store. With hard and soft luggage, large and small sizes, and lots of accessories to choose from.

3. Walking from store to store and getting tired. We gave up after a while and sat down.

4. Resting on a bench for a few minutes. We enjoyed ourselves by "people-watching."

5. We could not believe the crowds at the mall on a weekday. In every shop and at the food court, too.

6. Crowding the walkways and window shopping. Human beings circulated in every direction.

7. Teenagers gathered in groups. Laughing at each other and ignoring the shoppers.

8. Using the mall as an exercise facility. Pairs of older people walked briskly around the balconies.

9. We finally resumed our search and found the perfect luggage at a little store. Near the elevators at the end of the mall.

10. Because of all the interesting people and the final outcome. Our shopping trip was a complete success.

Exercise 4

Correct each dependent clause fragment by eliminating its dependent word or by attaching the dependent clause to the independent clause before or after it.

1. Thrift stores, yard sales, and flea markets are popular places to shop. Because they sell items that aren't available anywhere else as cheaply.

2. Also, most thrift stores benefit charities. Which use the profits to help people in need.

3. Although the styles of clothing and furniture found in thrift stores are often five to thirty years old. Many people prefer these vintage designs.

4. For instance, thrift stores sell old shelving units made of solid wood or thick metal. Which are much more substantial than modern ones made of cheap wood or plastic.

5. There are also famous stories of people becoming rich. Because they shopped at yard sales and flea markets.

6. One man bought a framed picture for a few dollars at a flea market. Since he liked the frame itself but not the picture.

7. When he removed the picture from the frame at home. He found one of the original copies of the "Declaration of Independence."

8. At a yard sale, a woman bought a small table. Which she later discovered was worth half a million dollars.

9. Of course, collectors always shop at these places. Where they hope to find treasures like rare cookie jars, pens, paintings, records, toys, and other objects of value.

10. In a way, shopping at thrift stores, yard sales, and flea markets is a kind of recycling. Which is something that benefits everyone.

Exercise 5

All of the following word groups contain subjects and verbs and are therefore clauses. If the clause *does not* begin with a dependent word (a conjunction such as *when, while, after, because, since, as, where, if, who, which,* or *that*), put a period after it. If the clause *does* begin with a dependent word (making it a dependent clause fragment), add an independent clause or revise the dependent clause to make it a sentence. These ten clauses are not about the same topic.

1. As the players walked off the field

2. She was a tough comedienne with a painful past

3. Luckily, a relative saw the amnesia victim's story on the news

4. If cars could fly

5. Tragically, Mozart died at an early age

6. That we had no fire insurance at the time

7. Since that car costs too much

8. Finally, I asked someone for directions to the museum

9. Because the government protects endangered species

10. Where the technology of cloning will be in ten years

PROOFREADING EXERCISE

Find and correct the five fragments in the following paragraph.

Shark attacks have been on the rise. We've all heard the heartbreaking news stories. Of people on their honeymoons or children playing in only a few feet of water being attacked by sharks. Movies like *Jaws* make us wary and scared. When we watch them. But their effects fade over time, and we forget about the risks. Of entering the habitats of dangerous animals. Experts try to convince us. That sharks and other powerful species are not targeting human beings on purpose. To a shark, a person is no different from a seal or a sea turtle. Facts such as these prompt many of us to think twice. Before we take a dip in the ocean.

SENTENCE WRITING

Write ten fragments and then revise them so that they are complete sentences. Or exchange papers with another student and turn your classmate's ten fragments into sentences.

Correcting Run-on Sentences

Any word group having a subject and a verb is a clause. As we have seen, the clause may be independent (making a complete statement and able to stand alone as a sentence), or it may be dependent (beginning with a dependent word and unable to stand alone as a sentence). When two *independent* clauses are written together without proper punctuation between them, the result is called a *run-on sentence*. Here are some examples.

> Classical music is soothing I listen to it in the evenings.
>
> I love the sound of piano therefore, Chopin is one of my favorites.

Run-on sentences can be corrected in one of four ways:

1. Make the two independent clauses into two sentences.

> Classical music is soothing. I listen to it in the evenings.
>
> I love the sound of piano. Therefore, Chopin is one of my favorites.

2. Connect the two independent clauses with a semicolon.

> Classical music is soothing; I listen to it in the evenings.
>
> I love the sound of piano; therefore, Chopin is one of my favorites.

When a connecting word (transition) such as

also	however	otherwise
consequently	likewise	then
finally	moreover	therefore
furthermore	nevertheless	thus

is used to join two independent clauses, the semicolon comes before the connecting word, and a comma usually comes after it.

> Mobile phones are convenient; however, they are very expensive.
>
> Earthquakes scare me; therefore, I don't live in Los Angeles.
>
> Yasmin traveled to London; then she took the "Chunnel" to Paris.
>
> The college recently built a large new library; thus we have more quiet study areas.

NOTE - The use of the comma after the connecting word depends on how long the connecting word is. If it is only a short word, like *then* or *thus*, the comma is not necessary.

---

3. Connect the two independent clauses with a comma and one of the following seven words (the first letters of which create the word *fanboys*): *for*, *and*, *nor*, *but*, *or*, *yet*, *so*.

> Classical music is soothing, *so* I listen to it in the evenings.
>
> Chopin is one of my favorites, *for* I love the sound of piano.

Each of the *fanboys* has its own meaning (for example, *so* means "as a result," and *for* means "because").

Swans are beautiful birds, *and* they mate for life.

Students may register for classes by phone, *or* they may do so in person.

I applied for financial aid, *but* I was still working at the time.

Brian doesn't know how to use a computer, *nor* does he plan to learn.

Before you put a comma before a *fanboys*, be sure there are two independent clauses. Note that the first sentence that follows has two independent clauses. However, the second sentence contains one independent clause with two verbs and therefore needs no comma.

The snow began falling at dusk, and it continued to fall through the night.

The snow began falling at dusk and continued to fall through the night.

4. Make one of the clauses dependent by adding a dependent word (such as *since*, *when*, *as*, *after*, *while*, or *because*—see p. 71 for a longer list of these conjunctions).

Since classical music is soothing, I listen to it in the evenings.

Chopin is one of my favorites *because* I love the sound of piano.

Learn these ways to join two clauses, and you'll avoid run-on sentences.

Ways to Correct Run-on Sentences

They were learning a new song. They needed to practice. (two sentences)

They were learning a new song; they needed to practice. (semicolon)

They were learning a new song; therefore, they needed to practice. (semicolon + transition)

They were learning a new song, so they needed to practice. (comma + *fanboys*)

Because they were learning a new song, they needed to practice. (dependent clause first)

They needed to practice because they were learning a new song. (dependent clause last)

E X E R C I S E S

Exercises 1 and 2
CORRECTING RUN-ONS WITH PUNCTUATION

Most—but not all—of the following sentences are run-ons. If the sentence has two independent clauses, separate them with correct punctuation. For the first two exercises, *don't create any dependent clauses*; use only a period, a semicolon, or a comma to separate the two independent clauses. Remember to insert a comma only when the words *for, and, nor, but, or, yet,* or *so* are used to join two independent clauses.

Exercise 1

1. Nearly everyone yawns but few understand the dynamics of yawning.
2. One person's yawn often triggers another person's yawn.
3. Yawning clearly seems to be a contagious activity.
4. Scientific studies of yawning verify this phenomenon and also explain the reasons for it.
5. Groups of people do similar things for they are acting somewhat like herds of animals.
6. During times of transition, such as getting up from or going to bed, members of a family or a dorm full of roommates synchronize their activities through yawning.
7. The yawning helps the group act as one so it minimizes conflict.
8. There are a few misconceptions about yawns one of them has to do with oxygen levels.
9. Some people explain yawning as the body's way to increase oxygen intake.
10. Surprisingly, studies show no changes in yawning patterns due to levels of oxygen in fact, research subjects inhaling pure oxygen yawned the same number of times as those breathing normally.

Source: Discover, June 2001

Exercise 2

1. I am writing a research paper on Margaret Fuller she is a famous American writer and philosopher from the early 1800s.

2. She lived at the same time and in the same area as Ralph Waldo Emerson, Henry David Thoreau, Nathaniel Hawthorne, Herman Melville, and others.

3. Historians sometimes call this famous group of people the "Concord Circle" for they lived in and around Concord, Massachusetts.

4. Fuller's father chose to educate her himself therefore, they had a very close and intense relationship.

5. She read Latin at the age of six and became extremely well-educated but her famous neighbors found the mixture of her intellect and her lively personality puzzling.

6. Fuller wrote a book called *Woman in the Nineteenth Century* after that, she moved to Italy.

7. She married an Italian named Giovanni Ossoli they had a son and planned to return to America.

8. Some of her acquaintances back in America frowned on her marriage to a younger and less intelligent man so they dreaded her return.

9. Fuller had nightmares of drowning in a shipwreck she wrote of these fears in letters to her mother and others.

10. In 1850 Margaret Fuller, her husband, and their son died their ship sank in a storm just a few hundred yards off the coast of America.

Exercises 3 and 4
CORRECTING RUN-ONS WITH DEPENDENT CLAUSES

Most—but not all—of the following sentences are run-ons. Correct any run-on sentences by making one or more of the clauses *dependent*. You may rephrase the clauses but be sure to use dependent words (such as *since, when, as, after, while, because* or the other conjunctions listed on p. 71) to begin dependent clauses. In some sentences, you will want to put the dependent clauses first; in others, you may want to put them last (or in the middle of the sentence). Since various words can be used to start dependent clauses, your answers may differ from those suggested at the back of the book.

Exercise 3

1. On summer evenings, people around the world enjoy the sight of little lights they are flying around in the air.
2. Most people know the glowing insects as fireflies they are also called lightning bugs and glowworms.
3. Glowworms are unique they don't fly.
4. The term *fireflies* is a little misleading they are not technically flies.
5. Lightning bugs are beetles they have special substances in their bodies.
6. These substances make them glow these substances are luciferin and luciferase.
7. The luciferin and luciferase combine with oxygen they produce a greenish light.
8. The light can be very intense people in some countries use caged fireflies as lamps.
9. In addition to their ability to light up, fireflies blink on and off.
10. Incredibly, groups of fireflies blink out of order at first they seem to coordinate their blinking within a few minutes.

Source: Current Science, May 11, 2001

Exercise 4

1. My family and I get a lot of annoying phone calls in the early evenings.
2. The calls are made by companies their salespeople try to interest us in the newest calling plan or credit card offer.
3. They don't call during the day then nobody is home.
4. I feel sorry for some of the salespeople they're just doing their job.

5. My father tells them to call during business hours they hang up right away.

6. I pick up the receiver sometimes and hear a computerized voice trying to sell me a subscription to a magazine.

7. My mother answers she is too polite, so they just keep talking.

8. We try to ignore the ringing it drives us all crazy.

9. One time my brother pretended to be my father and almost ordered a new roof for the house.

10. We never buy anything over the phone maybe these companies will all get the message and leave us alone.

Exercise 5

Correct the following run-on sentences using any of the methods studied in this section: adding a period, a semicolon, a semicolon + a transition word, a comma + a *fanboys*, or using dependent words to create dependent clauses.

1. In 2001, American businessman Dennis Tito did something and no one had done it before.

2. Tito became the world's first tourist in space he paid twenty million dollars for a ride to the International Space Station.

3. Tito wanted the United States to take him into space NASA said no.

4. NASA declined Tito's offer Russian space officials accepted it gladly.

5. In early May 2001, Tito boarded a Russian Soyuz rocket he blasted off into outer space.

6. Tito could talk to the cosmonauts on board he studied Russian for six months before his trip.

7. Dennis Tito's first-of-its-kind vacation was just the beginning of civilian travel into outer space more and more individuals will want to follow Tito's example.

8. There will be travel agents they will specialize in space travel.

9. Other countries besides Russia will welcome the income from such trips China may soon have the ability to take people into space.

10. In 2001, NASA chose not to let Tito on one of its space shuttles in the future space programs may be funded through space tourism NASA may not have a choice.

Source: USA Today, May 4, 2001

REVIEW OF FRAGMENTS AND RUN-ON SENTENCES

If you remember that all clauses include a subject and a verb, but only independent clauses can be punctuated as sentences (since only they can stand alone), then you will avoid fragments in your writing. And if you memorize these six rules for the punctuation of clauses, you will be able to avoid most punctuation errors.

Punctuating Clauses

I am a student. I am still learning.	(two sentences)
I am a student; I am still learning.	(two independent clauses)
I am a student; therefore, I am still learning.	(two independent clauses connected by a word such as *also, consequently, finally, furthermore, however, likewise, moreover, nevertheless, otherwise, then, therefore, thus*)
I am a student, so I am still learning.	(two independent clauses connected by *for, and, nor, but, or, yet, so*)
Because I am a student, I am still learning.	(dependent clause at beginning of sentence)
I am still learning because I am a student.	(dependent clause at end of sentence) The dependent words are *after, although, as, as if, because, before, even if, even though, ever since, how, if, in order that, since, so that, than, that, though, unless, until, what, whatever, when, whenever, where, whereas, wherever, whether, which, whichever, while, who, whom, whose, why.*

It is essential that you learn the italicized words in the previous table—which ones come between independent clauses and which ones introduce dependent clauses.

PROOFREADING EXERCISE

Rewrite the following paragraph, making the necessary changes so there will be no fragments or run-on sentences.

In April of 2001, a writer named Terry Ryan published a book about her mother. The title of the book *The Prize Winner of Defiance: How My Mother Raised 10 Kids on 25 Words or Less*. Ryan had already written two poetry books and was busy writing a comic strip for a San Francisco newspaper. When she decided to tell her mom's story. Terry's mother, Evelyn Ryan, was a remarkable woman she entered contest after contest in the 1950s and won most of them. In those days, companies sponsored competitions and they gave prizes to the writers of the best slogan, poem, or jingle about their product. Evelyn Ryan being such a naturally good writer that she won countless prizes, ranging from small appliances to large cash awards. All of them earned through skill and perseverance. Terry Ryan especially remembers her mother's organizational skills and generosity. Evelyn Ryan, her daughter explains, was also motivated by her circumstances as the wife of an alcoholic. She did it all for her family winning such contests was her way of staying at home, supporting ten children, and keeping the family together.

Source: The San Diego Union-Tribune, April 29, 2001

SENTENCE WRITING

Write a sample sentence of your own to demonstrate each of the six ways a writer can use to punctuate two clauses. You may model your sentences on the examples used in the preceding review chart.

Identifying Verb Phrases

Sometimes a verb is one word, but often the whole verb includes more than one word. These are called verb phrases. Look at several of the many forms of the verb *speak*, for example. Most of them are verb phrases, made up of the main verb (*speak*) and one or more helping verbs.

speak	is speaking	had been speaking
speaks	am speaking	will have been speaking
spoke	are speaking	is spoken
will speak	was speaking	was spoken
has spoken	were speaking	will be spoken
have spoken	will be speaking	can speak
had spoken	has been speaking	must speak
will have spoken	have been speaking	should have spoken

Note that words like the following are never verbs even though they may be near a verb or in the middle of a verb phrase:

already	ever	not	really
also	finally	now	sometimes
always	just	often	usually
probably	never	only	possibly

Jason has *never* spoken to his instructor before. She *always* talks with other students.

Two verb forms—*speaking* and *to speak*—look like verbs, but neither form can ever be the only verb in a sentence. No *ing* word by itself can be the verb of a sentence; it must be helped by another verb in a verb phrase. (See the discussion of verbal phrases on p. 127.)

Jeanine speaking French. (not a sentence because there is no complete verb phrase)

Jeanine is speaking French. (a sentence with a verb phrase)

And no verb with *to* in front of it can ever be the verb of a sentence.

Ted to speak in front of groups. (not a sentence because there is no real verb)

Ted <u>hates</u> to speak in front of groups. (a sentence with *hates* as the verb)

These two forms, *speaking* and *to speak*, may be used as subjects or other parts of a sentence.

<u>Speaking</u> on stage <u>is</u> scary. <u>To speak</u> on stage <u>is</u> scary. <u>Ted</u> <u>had</u> a *speaking* part in that play.

E X E R C I S E S

Underline the subjects once and the verbs or verb phrases twice in the following sentences. It's a good idea to put parentheses around prepositional phrases first. (See p. 65 if you need help in locating prepositional phrases.) The sentences may contain independent *and* dependent clauses, so there could be several verbs and verb phrases. (Remember that *ing* verbs alone and the *to* ____ forms of verbs are never real verbs in sentences. We will learn more about them on p. 127.)

Exercise 1

1. Shopping for holiday items has taken a turn for the worse in recent years.
2. Before one holiday has arrived, another holiday's decorations line the shelves of stores.
3. In early July, for instance, shoppers will not find banners to celebrate Independence Day.
4. Instead, they will see Halloween items already for sale.
5. And by October, store owners will have placed turkeys and pilgrims in full view.
6. Of course, Kwanza, Hanukah, and Christmas sales begin in September on their own special aisle.
7. What can people do about this trend?
8. Shoppers could protest and boycott early displays.
9. They could tell store managers about their concerns.

10. But they might just miss the chance to buy that cute little bunny at the spring sale in January.

Exercise 2

1. On December 16, 2000, the London stage production of Agatha Christie's play *The Mousetrap* marked a milestone.

2. On that night, actors were performing Christie's play for the twenty-thousandth time.

3. In fact, *The Mousetrap* broke the record as the world's longest running play.

4. The play opened in London on November 25, 1952, and had been running continually ever since.

5. More than ten million people had attended the London performances.

6. There are other interesting facts about this production.

7. Two pieces of the original set—the clock and the armchair—had survived on stage for half a century.

8. The cast, however, had changed more often.

9. Some actors had remained in the show for years while others had played parts for only a short time.

10. One actress understudied for over six thousand performances, but she was needed on stage only seventy-two times.

Exercise 3

1. Felix Hoffmann, a chemist, was trying to ease his own father's pain when he discovered aspirin in 1897.

2. Although aspirin can cause side effects, each year people around the world give themselves fifty billion doses of the popular pain killer.

3. But different countries take this medicine in different ways.

4. The British like to dissolve aspirin powder in water.

5. The French have insisted that slow-release methods work best.
6. Italians prefer aspirin drinks with a little fizz.
7. And Americans have always chosen to take their aspirin in pill form.
8. However it is taken, aspirin continues to surprise researchers with benefits to human health.
9. It has been found to benefit people susceptible to heart attack, colon cancer, and Alzheimer's disease.
10. Where would we be without aspirin?

Source: Newsweek, August 18, 1997

Exercise 4

1. I have just read about the life of Philo T. Farnsworth.
2. Thirteen-year-old Philo T. Farnsworth was plowing a field in 1922 when he visualized the concept that led to television as we know it.
3. Others were working on the idea of sending images through the air, but Farnsworth actually solved the problem in that open field.
4. He looked at the rows that the plow had made in the earth.
5. And he reasoned that images could be broken down into rows and sent line by line through the air and onto a screen.
6. Farnsworth's idea made television a reality, but historically he has not been fully recognized for this and his other accomplishments.
7. In 1957, he was featured as a guest on *I've Got a Secret,* a television show that presented mystery contestants.
8. The panelists on the show were supposed to guess the guest's secret, which the audience was shown so that everyone knew the answer except the people asking the questions.
9. They asked if he had invented something painful, and he replied that he had; the panelists never guessed that he was the inventor of television.

10. Farnsworth did receive a box of cigarettes and eighty dollars for being on the show.

Exercise 5

1. I like to walk around the park with my two little dogs in the early evenings.
2. The three of us have enjoyed this ritual for several years now.
3. On Friday evening, we were just passing the duck pond, and a big dog with no owner ran over to us.
4. It was obviously looking for other dogs to play with.
5. Yip and Yap have never barked so loudly before.
6. I had originally named them for their distinct barking noises.
7. But lately I had not heard these short, ear-splitting sounds very often.
8. The big dog was shocked by the fierceness of my little dogs' reply and quickly ran to find other friends.
9. Even I could not believe it.
10. I will never worry about their safety around big dogs again.

REVIEW EXERCISE

To practice finding all of the sentence structures we have studied so far, mark the following excerpt from Nancy Cartwright's book *My Life as a 10-Year-Old Boy.* Cartwright is the actress who plays the part of Bart Simpson. First, put parentheses around prepositional phrases, then underline subjects once and verbs or verb phrases twice. Finally, put a broken line beneath dependent clauses. Begin by marking the first paragraph, then check your answers at the back of the book before marking the rest. (Remember that *ing* verbs alone and the *to* _____ forms of verbs are never real verbs in sentences. We will learn more about them on p. 127.)

While computer and digital technology are slowly taking over most of the animation industry, *The Simpsons* remains 100 percent hand-painted. Did you get that—100 percent *hand-painted*! If you consider that it takes anywhere from fifteen to twenty-four pieces of art for every second that you see on the screen and that the show is anywhere from twenty-two to twenty-three minutes long—we are talking somewhere between 18,900 and 33,220 hand-painted cels per episode! This attention to detail and the continual use of actual artists instead of computers makes *The Simpsons* the leader in this rapidly emerging industry.

The painting is done in Korea or, quite frankly, it would never happen. It would be too expensive. . . .

When the shipment first arrives in Korea, the exposure sheets [are] translated into Korean. Then the work is divided up and distributed to the staff. They have exactly the same character and background model sheets as we do and all the tools they need to do the job. There, a team of unsung heroes draws all the in-between poses and copies them to cels, and then another team flips them over and, using the paint by number instructions of the color department, paints what we see on some future Sunday evening.

Using Standard English Verbs

The next two discussions are for those who need to practice using Standard English verbs. Many of us grew up doing more speaking than writing. But in college and in the business and professional world, the use of Standard Written English is essential.

The following charts show the forms of four verbs as they are used in Standard Written English. These forms might differ from the way you use these verbs when you speak. Memorize the Standard English forms of these important verbs. The first verb (*talk*) is one of the regular verbs (verbs that all end the same way according to a pattern); most verbs in English are regular. The other three verbs charted here (*have*, *be*, and *do*) are irregular and are important because they are used not only as main verbs but also as helping verbs in verb phrases.

Don't go on to the exercises until you have memorized the forms of these Standard English verbs.

Sometimes you may have difficulty with the correct endings of verbs because you don't hear the words correctly. Note carefully the *s* sound and the *ed* sound at the end of words. Occasionally, the *ed* is not clearly pronounced, as in *They tried to help*, but most of the time you can hear it if you listen.

Regular Verb: Talk

Present Time

Past Time

I
you
we
they } talk

I
you
we
they
he, she, it } talked

he, she, it   talks

Irregular Verb: Have

Present Time

Past Time

I
you
we
they } have

I
you
we
they
he, she, it } had

he, she, it   has

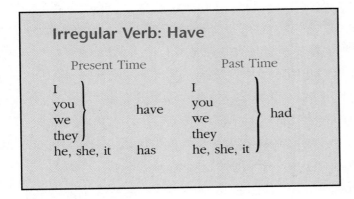

Irregular Verb: Be

Present Time

Past Time

I   am
you
we } are
they
he, she, it   is

I   was
you
we } were
they
he, she, it   was

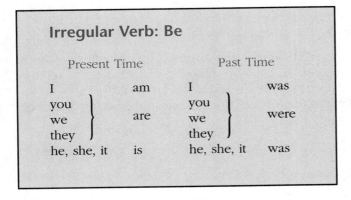

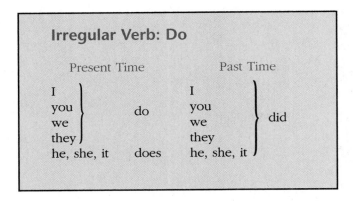

Irregular Verb: Do

Present Time		Past Time	
I		I	
you	do	you	did
we		we	
they		they	
he, she, it	does	he, she, it	

Read the following sentences aloud, making sure that you say every sound.

1. He seems satisfied with his new job.

2. She likes saving money for the future.

3. It takes strength of character to control spending.

4. Todd makes salad for every potluck he attends.

5. I used to know all their names.

6. They supposed that they were right.

7. He recognized the suspect and excused himself from the jury.

8. Shao Ming sponsored Dorothy in the school's charity event.

Now read some other sentences aloud from this text, making sure that you say all the *s*'s and *ed*'s. Reading aloud and listening to others will help you use the correct verb endings automatically.

E X E R C I S E S

In these pairs of sentences, use the *present* form of the verb in the first sentence and the *past* form in the second. All the verbs follow the pattern of the regular verb *talk* except the irregular verbs *have*, *be*, and *do*. Keep referring to the tables if you're not sure which form to use. Check your answers in the back of the book after each set.

Exercise 1

1. (walk)   I often _____ around the block for exercise. I _____ around it twice yesterday.

2. (be)   Max _____ glad to be graduating. He _____ unsure about his future just two years ago.

3. (have)   The Clarks _____ an SUV now. They _____ a small car before.

4. (do)   I _____ my studying in the afternoons. I _____ my studying in the evenings in high school.

5. (need)   She _____ to wear bifocals now. She _____ only single lenses before.

6. (be)   Now I _____ a fully paid employee. I _____ a work-study student last year.

7. (have)   My class ring _____ a large green stone in its setting. It _____ other stones around it, but they fell out.

8. (be)   They _____ my first choice as roommates. They _____ not my parents' first choice.

9. (do)   My sister usually _____ my taxes. She _____ my taxes last year.

10. (work)   He _____ for two companies right now. He _____ for only one company before.

Exercise 2

1. (be)   She _____ a lawyer now. She _____ a law student last year.

2. (do)   They _____ their best work on the weekends. They _____ a great job last weekend.

3. (have)   I _____ a new ed-plan. I originally _____ a plan that would have taken too long to complete.

4. (ask)   She _____ for help when she needs it. She _____ her tutor for help with her latest essay.

5. (have)   I always _____ the flu at this time of year. I _____ the flu last year right on schedule.

6. (learn)   We _____ something about writing each week. Yesterday we _____ how to write a thesis.

7. (be)   Most of us _____ right handed. Therefore, we _____ not comfortable drawing with our left hands.

8. (do)   She _____ well on all of her assignments. She _____ very well on the term project.

9. (play)   He _____ the piano now. He _____ the guitar as his first instrument.

10. (be)   I _____ a natural comedian. However, last month I _____ too depressed to be funny.

Underline the Standard English verb forms. All the verbs follow the pattern of the regular verb *talk* except the three irregular verbs *have*, *be*, and *do*. Keep referring to the tables if you are not sure which form to use.

Exercise 3

1. I (start, started) a new volunteer job last month, and so far I really (like, likes) it.

2. The organization (offer, offers) relief boxes to victims of crime or natural disasters around the world.

3. The other volunteers (is, are) all really nice, so we (has, have) a good work environment.

4. Yesterday, we (finish, finished) a project that (need, needed) lots of boxes.

5. The supervisors who (run, runs) the organization always (do, does) their best to explain the victims' situations to us.

6. And they (advise, advises) us to make sure that the boxes (comfort, comforts) the victims as much as possible.

7. I can tell that the supervisors (enjoy, enjoys) their work; they (is, are) always happy to see the relief on the victims' faces.

8. My fellow volunteers and I (complete, completed) our latest project in just one week even though the supervisor (expect, expected) it to take us two weeks.

9. We (has, have) our supervisors to thank for a smooth-running organization.

10. And I (thank, thanks) my coworkers for being my friends.

Exercise 4

1. My brother and I (do, does) our homework together every night so that we (don't, doesn't) fall behind.

2. I (is, am) better at math, and my brother Dan (is, am) better in English.

3. When I (need, needs) help with grammar, Dan (explain, explains) the rule to me.

4. And if he gets stuck on a math problem, I (help, helps) him understand it; then he (do, does) it himself.

5. This system (work, works) very well for us, and I (hope, hopes) we will always use it.

6. Before we (do, did) it this way, I (drop, dropped) an English class.

7. It (was, were) too hard for me, but now I (do, does) as well as the other students.

8. Dan and I both (work, works) hard, and we (check, checks) each other's progress.

9. When I (learn, learns) more English skills and Dan (learn, learns) more math skills, we will be equal.

10. Our parents (expect, expects) a lot from both of us, and we (don't, doesn't) want to let them down.

Exercise 5

Correct any of following sentences that do not use Standard English verb forms.

1. Last year our high school theater class performed Meredith Wilson's *The Music Man.*

2. Fifty of us and one teacher rehearse the musical for three months.

3. We was all very excited about opening night.

4. Before the curtain went up, we join hands and wished each other luck.

5. We discover that audiences love musicals.

6. Once we was performing, their reactions settle all our nerves.

7. I saw smiling faces stretching from the front row to the back.

8. My mom was smiling so hard that she said her face hurt afterward.

9. After the first performance, all of us in the show celebrate at our teacher's house.

10. She order a cake that was shaped like the "Wells Fargo Wagon," and we all loved it.

PROOFREADING EXERCISE

In the following paragraph, correct any sentences that do not use Standard English verb forms.

Everyday as we drive though our neighborhoods on the way to school or to work, we see things that needs to be fixed. Many of them cause us only a little bit of trouble, so we forget them until we face them again. Every morning, drivers in my neighborhood has to deal with a truck that someone park right at the corner of our street. It block our view as we try to turn onto the main avenue. We need to move out past the truck into the oncoming lane of traffic just to make a left turn. One day last week, I turn too soon, and a car almost hit me. This truck don't need to be parked in such a dangerous place.

SENTENCE WRITING

Write ten sentences about a different problem in your own neighborhood. Check your sentences to be sure that they use Standard English verb forms. Try exchanging papers with another student if possible.

Using Regular and Irregular Verbs

All regular verbs end the same way in the past form and when used with helping verbs. Here is a table showing all the forms of some *regular* verbs and the various helping verbs with which they are used.

Regular Verbs				
BASE FORM	**PRESENT**	**PAST**	**PAST PARTICIPLE**	***ING* FORM**
(Use after can, may, shall, will, could, might, should, would, must, do, does, did.)			*(Use after have, has, had. Some can be used after forms of be.)*	*(Use after forms of be.)*
ask	ask *(s)*	asked	asked	asking
bake	bake *(s)*	baked	baked	baking
count	count *(s)*	counted	counted	counting
dance	dance *(s)*	danced	danced	dancing
decide	decide *(s)*	decided	decided	deciding
enjoy	enjoy *(s)*	enjoyed	enjoyed	enjoying
finish	finish *(es)*	finished	finished	finishing
happen	happen *(s)*	happened	happened	happening
learn	learn *(s)*	learned	learned	learning
like	like *(s)*	liked	liked	liking
look	look *(s)*	looked	looked	looking
mend	mend *(s)*	mended	mended	mending
need	need *(s)*	needed	needed	needing
open	open *(s)*	opened	opened	opening
start	start *(s)*	started	started	starting
suppose	suppose *(s)*	supposed	supposed	supposing
tap	tap *(s)*	tapped	tapped	tapping
walk	walk *(s)*	walked	walked	walking
want	want *(s)*	wanted	wanted	wanting

NOTE - When there are several helping verbs, the last one determines which form of the main verb should be used: they *should* finish soon; they should *have* finished an hour ago.

When do you write *ask, finish, suppose, use*? And when do you write *asked, finished, supposed, used*? Here are some rules that will help you decide.

Write *ask*, *finish*, *suppose*, *use* (or their *s* forms) when writing about the present time, repeated actions, or facts:

He *ask*s questions whenever he is confused.

They always *finish* their projects on time.

I *suppose* you want me to help you move.

Birds *use* leaves, twigs, and feathers to build their nests.

Write *asked*, *finished*, *supposed*, *used*

1. **When writing about the past:**

   He *asked* the teacher for another explanation.

   She *finished* her internship last year.

   They *supposed* that there were others bidding on that house.

   I *used* to study piano.

2. **When some form of *be* (other than the word *be* itself) comes before the word:**

   He was *asked* the most difficult questions.

   She is *finished* with her training now.

   They were *supposed* to sign at the bottom of the form.

   My essay was *used* as a sample of clear narration.

3. **When some form of *have* comes before the word:**

   The teacher has *asked* us that question before.

   She will have *finished* all of her exams by the end of May.

   I had *supposed* too much without any proof.

   We have *used* many models in my drawing class this semester.

All the verbs in the chart on page 108 are *regular*. That is, they're all formed in the same way—with an *ed* ending on the past form and on the past participle. But many verbs are irregular. Their past and past participle forms change spelling instead of just adding an *ed*. Here's a chart of some *irregular* verbs. Notice that the base, present, and *ing* forms end the same as regular verbs. Refer to this list when you aren't sure which verb form to use. Memorize all the forms you don't know.

Irregular Verbs

BASE FORM	PRESENT	PAST	PAST PARTICIPLE	*ING* FORM
(Use after can, may, shall, will, could, might, should, would, must, do, does, did.)			*(Use after have, has, had. Some can be used after forms of be.)*	*(Use after forms of be.)*
be	is, am, are	was, were	been	being
become	become *(s)*	became	become	becoming
begin	begin *(s)*	began	begun	beginning
break	break *(s)*	broke	broken	breaking
bring	bring *(s)*	brought	brought	bringing
buy	buy *(s)*	bought	bought	buying
build	build *(s)*	built	built	building
catch	catch *(es)*	caught	caught	catching
choose	choose *(s)*	chose	chosen	choosing
come	come *(s)*	came	come	coming
do	do *(es)*	did	done	doing
draw	draw *(s)*	drew	drawn	drawing
drink	drink *(s)*	drank	drunk	drinking
drive	drive *(s)*	drove	driven	driving
eat	eat *(s)*	ate	eaten	eating
fall	fall *(s)*	fell	fallen	falling
feel	feel *(s)*	felt	felt	feeling
fight	fight *(s)*	fought	fought	fighting
find	find *(s)*	found	found	finding
forget	forget *(s)*	forgot	forgotten	forgetting
forgive	forgive *(s)*	forgave	forgiven	forgiving
freeze	freeze *(s)*	froze	frozen	freezing
get	get *(s)*	got	got *or* gotten	getting
give	give *(s)*	gave	given	giving
go	go *(es)*	went	gone	going
grow	grow *(s)*	grew	grown	growing
have	have *or* has	had	had	having
hear	hear *(s)*	heard	heard	hearing
hold	hold *(s)*	held	held	holding
keep	keep *(s)*	kept	kept	keeping
know	know *(s)*	knew	known	knowing

BASE FORM	PRESENT	PAST	PAST PARTICIPLE	*ING* FORM
lay (to put)	lay *(s)*	laid	laid	laying
lead (like "bead")	lead *(s)*	led	led	leading
leave	leave *(s)*	left	left	leaving
lie (to rest)	lie *(s)*	lay	lain	lying
lose	lose *(s)*	lost	lost	losing
make	make *(s)*	made	made	making
meet	meet *(s)*	met	met	meeting
pay	pay *(s)*	paid	paid	paying
read	read *(s)*	read	read	reading
(pron. "reed")		(pron. "red")	(pron. "red")	
ride	ride *(s)*	rode	ridden	riding
ring	ring *(s)*	rang	rung	ringing
rise	rise *(s)*	rose	risen	rising
run	run *(s)*	ran	run	running
say	say *(s)*	said	said	saying
see	see *(s)*	saw	seen	seeing
sell	sell *(s)*	sold	sold	selling
shake	shake *(s)*	shook	shaken	shaking
shine (give light)	shine *(s)*	shone	shone	shining
shine (polish)	shine *(s)*	shined	shined	shining
sing	sing *(s)*	sang	sung	singing
sleep	sleep *(s)*	slept	slept	sleeping
speak	speak *(s)*	spoke	spoken	speaking
spend	spend *(s)*	spent	spent	spending
stand	stand *(s)*	stood	stood	standing
steal	steal *(s)*	stole	stolen	stealing
strike	strike *(s)*	struck	struck	striking
swim	swim *(s)*	swam	swum	swimming
swing	swing *(s)*	swung	swung	swinging
take	take *(s)*	took	taken	taking
teach	teach *(es)*	taught	taught	teaching
tear	tear *(s)*	tore	torn	tearing
tell	tell *(s)*	told	told	telling
think	think *(s)*	thought	thought	thinking
throw	throw *(s)*	threw	thrown	throwing
wear	wear *(s)*	wore	worn	wearing
win	win *(s)*	won	won	winning
write	write *(s)*	wrote	written	writing

Sometimes verbs from the past participle column are used after some form of the verb *be* (or verbs that take the place of *be* like *appear, seem, look, feel, get, act, become*) to describe the subject or to say something in a passive, rather than an active, way.

She is contented.
You appear pleased. (You *are* pleased.)
He seems delighted. (He *is* delighted.)
She looked surprised. (She *was* surprised.)
I feel shaken. (I *am* shaken.)
They get bored easily. (They *are* bored easily.)
You acted concerned. (You *were* concerned.)
They were thrown out of the game. (Active: *The referee threw them out of the game.*)
We were disappointed by the news. (Active: *The news disappointed us.*)

Often these verb forms become words that describe the subject; at other times they still act as part of the verb in the sentence. What you call them doesn't matter. The only important thing is to be sure you use the correct form from the past participle column.

E X E R C I S E S

Write the correct form of the verbs in the blanks. Refer to the tables and explanations on the preceding pages if you aren't sure which form to use after a certain helping verb. Check your answers after each exercise.

Exercise 1

1. (look) Once again, I have _____ everywhere for my keys.

2. (look) I could _____ in a few more places, but I'm late.

3. (look) I feel so foolish while I am _____ for them.

4. (look) I know that if I _____ too hard I won't find them.

5. (look) Once I _____ for them for over two hours.

6. (look) I can _____ right past them if I am too frantic.

7. (look) I have _____ in places where they would never be.

8. (look)   My daughter once caught me while I was _____ for them in the refrigerator.

9. (look)   In fact, my family now _____ at me with scorn whenever I ask, "Has anybody seen my keys?"

10. (look)   From now on I will _____ in the obvious places first and keep my problem to myself.

Exercise 2

1. (drive)   I always _____ my sister to school; in fact, I have _____ her to school for a whole year now.

2. (think)   The other day, I was _____ of new ways to get her there in the morning, but she _____ that they were all bad ideas.

3. (take)   She could _____ a school bus that stops nearby; instead she _____ me for granted.

4. (tell)   It all started when she _____ our mother that some of the other children were _____ her to stay out of their seats.

5. (write)   I _____ a note to the bus driver to see if she could help ease my sister's mind, but so far she hasn't _____ back.

6. (know)   When I was my sister's age, I _____ some tough kids at school, so I _____ how she must feel.

7. (teach)   But experiences like that _____ us how to get along with everyone; they sure _____ me.

8. (tear)   Now I am _____ between wanting to help her avoid the tough kids and _____ my hair out from having to take her to school every day.

9. (ride)   We have _____ together for so long that I might miss her if I _____ alone.

10. (make)   I have _____ up my mind. I will _____ the best of it while she still needs me. What else are big sisters for?

Exercise 3

1. (be, hear)

We _____ surprised when we _____ from our Aunt Shelby yesterday.

2. (see, begin)

We hadn't _____ her in over a year, and we had _____ to wonder if she would ever visit us again.

3. (fly, eat)

She had _____ in from France earlier in the day but hadn't _____ dinner yet.

4. (get, do)

We _____ back to her at her hotel and _____ our best to convince her to join us for dinner.

5. (take, eat)

It did not _____ much to convince her, and soon we were _____ dinner together.

6. (write, come, lose)

She said that she had _____ to tell us that she was _____, and she asked if we had _____ the letter.

7. (swear, feel)

We _____ that we never received it, and she _____ better.

8. (buy, pay)

Just to make sure there were no hard feelings, we _____ her dinner, and she _____ the tip.

9. (get, think)

It was _____ late, so she _____ that she should go back to her hotel to get some sleep.

10. (see, tell, lie)

When we _____ Shelby the next day, she _____ us that she was so tired the night before that as soon as she _____ down on the hotel pillow, she fell asleep.

Exercise 4

1. (use, suppose)

My brothers and I _____ to stay up all night in our room when we were _____ to be sleeping.

2. (catch, come, hear) Our parents would _____ us sometimes when they _____ upstairs and _____ us talking.

3. (be, leave) We _____ not very smart about it; sometimes we even _____ the light on.

4. (read, draw, build) That way we could _____ or _____ or _____ our secret inventions.

5. (feel, draw) Those nights _____ really special, and I _____ some of my best pictures then.

6. (do, sleep) We _____ suffer from fatigue during the day as we _____ through our classes at school.

7. (know, spend) We _____ that we had to fix the problem, so we _____ several nights withdrawing from our late-night schedule.

8. (go, be) Gradually we _____ to bed earlier and earlier until we _____ back to a normal sleeping pattern.

9. (wake, stay) We _____ up on time and _____ awake in our classes.

10. (forget, spend, be) I will never _____ the quiet, creative, and carefree nights I _____ with my brothers when we _____ just kids.

Exercise 5

1. (lay, lie, feel) I _____ my blanket down on the cool grass under a big tree and was _____ face-down on the blanket when I _____ a wasp land on the back of my ankle.

2. (know, be) I _____ that special sensation of a wasp's legs on my skin because I have _____ stung by one before.

3. (break, have)   Last time, I _____ out in hives and _____ to
go to the hospital to get an injection of antihista-
mine.

4. (become, think)   My eyes _____ swollen, and I _____ that I was
going to die.

5. (be)   I _____ not going to let that happen again.

6. (read, frighten) I had _____ that insects like wasps only sting
when they're _____.

7. (keep, shake)   So this time I _____ calm and gently _____
my ankle to shoo away the wasp without angering
it.

8. (work, rise, sneak) My plan _____, and as soon as the wasp
_____ in the air to find a new spot to land, I
_____ away.

9. (leave, go)   I _____ my blanket under the tree, and I didn't
even _____ back to the park for it later.

10. (lose, sting)   Of course, I would rather _____ a blanket than
be _____ by a wasp again.

PROGRESS TEST

This test covers everything you've learned in the Sentence Structure section so far. One sentence in each pair is correct. The other is incorrect. Read both sentences carefully before you decide. Then write the letter of the incorrect sentence in the blank. Try to name the error and correct it if you can.

1. _____ A. I haven't ever ridden my bike to school.

            B. There are secure parking areas for bikes but they are always too crowded.

2. _____ A. Several important officials attended the meeting.

            B. Concerned about the condition of the city's schools.

3. _____ A. Everyday, she write sentences on the chalkboard.

            B. I can't see them because I need glasses.

4. _____ A. Whenever I hand in late assignments.

            B. My teachers reduce the grades.

5. _____ A. Coach Sutter must have forgotten about us.

            B. She was suppose to meet us on the field at noon.

6. _____ A. He has saved his money, and is finally taking his trip to Yosemite.

            B. He has reserved his campsite and has packed his bags.

7. _____ A. The whole audience recognized her when she arrived.

            B. When she left everyone remained quiet for a few seconds.

8. _____ A. We had already gone to dinner by the time you arrived.

            B. We ate sushi it was delicious.

9. _____ A. Those two employees deserves a raise.

            B. They work hard at their jobs, and people are starting to notice.

10. _____ A. I plan to transfer to a university at the end of the next school year.

            B. Just as soon as I pass my last math class.

Maintaining Subject/Verb Agreement

As we have seen, the subject and verb in a sentence work together, so they must always agree. Different subjects need different forms of verbs. When the correct verb follows a subject, we call it subject/verb agreement.

The following sentences illustrate the rule that *s* verbs follow most singular subjects but not plural subjects.

One <u>turtle</u> <u>walks</u>.

The <u>baby</u> <u>cries</u>.

A <u>democracy</u> <u>listens</u> to the people.

One <u>child</u> <u>plays</u>.

Three <u>turtles</u> <u>walk</u>.

The <u>babies</u> <u>cry</u>.

<u>Democracies</u> <u>listen</u> to the people.

Many <u>children</u> <u>play</u>.

The following sentences show how forms of the verb *be* (*is, am, are, was, were*) and helping verbs (*be, have,* and *do*) are made to agree with their subjects.

This <u>puzzle</u> <u>is</u> difficult.

I <u>am</u> amazed.

He <u>was</u> sleeping.

That <u>class</u> <u>has</u> been canceled.

<u>She</u> <u>does</u> not want to participate.

These <u>puzzles</u> <u>are</u> difficult.

<u>You</u> <u>are</u> amazed.

<u>They</u> <u>were</u> sleeping.

Those <u>classes</u> <u>have</u> been canceled.

<u>They</u> <u>do</u> not want to participate.

The following words are always singular and take an *s* verb or the irregular equivalent (*is, was, has, does*):

one	anybody	each
anyone	everybody	
everyone	nobody	
no one	somebody	
someone		

<u>Someone</u> <u>feeds</u> my dog in the morning.

<u>Everybody</u> <u>was</u> at the party.

<u>Each</u> <u>does</u> her own homework.

Remember that prepositional phrases often come between subjects and verbs. You should ignore these interrupting phrases, or you may mistake the wrong word for the subject and use a verb form that doesn't agree.

<u>Someone</u> from the apartments <u>feeds</u> my dog in the morning. (*Someone* is the subject, not *apartments*.)

<u>Everybody</u> on the list of celebrities <u>was</u> at the party. (*Everybody* is the subject, not *celebrities*.)

<u>Each</u> of the twins <u>does</u> her own homework. (*Each* is the subject, not *twins*.)

However, the words *some, any, all, none,* and *most* are exceptions to this rule of ignoring prepositional phrases. These words can be singular or plural, depending on the words that follow them in prepositional phrases.

<u>Some</u> of the *pie* <u>is</u> gone.

<u>Some</u> of the *cookies* <u>are</u> gone.

<u>Is</u> <u>any</u> of the *paper* still in the supply cabinet?

<u>Are</u> <u>any</u> of the *pencils* still in the supply cabinet?

<u>All</u> of her *work* <u>has</u> been published.

<u>All</u> of her *poems* <u>have</u> been published.

<u>None</u> of the *jewelry* <u>is</u> missing.

<u>None</u> of the *clothes* <u>are</u> missing.

On July 4th, <u>most</u> of the *country* <u>celebrates</u>.

On July 4th, <u>most</u> of the *citizens* <u>celebrate</u>.

When a sentence has more than one subject joined by *and,* the subject is plural:

The <u>teacher</u> and the <u>tutors</u> <u>eat</u> lunch at noon.

A glazed <u>doughnut</u> and an onion <u>bagel</u> <u>were</u> sitting on the plate.

However, when two subjects are joined by *or*, then the subject *closest* to the verb determines the verb form:

Either the <u>teacher</u> *or* the <u>tutors</u> <u>eat</u> lunch at noon.

Either the <u>tutors</u> *or* the <u>teacher</u> <u>eats</u> lunch at noon.

A glazed <u>donut</u> *or* an onion <u>bagel</u> <u>was</u> sitting on the plate.

In most sentences, the subject comes before the verb. However, in some cases, the subject follows the verb, and subject/verb agreement needs special attention. Study the following examples:

Over the building <u>flies</u> a solitary <u>flag</u>. (flag flies)

Over the building <u>fly</u> several <u>flags</u>. (flags fly)

There <u>is</u> a good <u>reason</u> for my actions. (reason is)

There <u>are</u> good <u>reasons</u> for my actions. (reasons are)

E X E R C I S E S

Underline the correct verbs in parentheses to maintain subject/verb agreement in the following sentences. Remember to ignore prepositional phrases, unless the subjects are *some, any, all, none,* or *most.* Check your answers ten at a time.

Exercise 1

1. There (is, are) good news about Luna, the old-growth redwood tree that activist Julia Butterfly Hill lived in for over two years.

2. After Hill succeeded in getting Luna and other ancient redwoods nearby protected from logging efforts, Luna's trunk (was, were) cut deeply all around her base by someone with a chainsaw.

3. No one (know, knows) for certain how many of Luna's life functions (has, have) been affected by the wound.

4. But a team of tree experts (has, have) come together to save her life again.

5. Probably there (has, have) been significant damage; however, arborists and biologists (expect, expects) Luna to survive with help in the form of braces and cables.

6. All of the experts (is, are) interested in learning more about coast red-wood trees from Luna's progress.

7. Even some of the loggers who (was, were) against Hill's tree-sitting protest (has, have) helped design the huge steel braces that now (hold, holds) Luna's trunk together.

8. There (is, are) also a system of cables connected to other trees around Luna.

9. All of the trees (work, works) together to keep Luna steady in storms or earthquakes.

10. For now Luna's future (look, looks) secure, but the question of why someone would harm her in the first place (remain, remains).

Source: Earth Island Journal, Autumn 2001

Exercise 2

1. One of the world's most popular places (is, are) Disneyland in Buena Park, California.

2. Some of Disneyland's little-known facts (surprise, surprises) people.

3. For instance, the buildings on Main Street itself (isn't, aren't) really as tall as they appear.

4. Each of the upper floors (is, are) built in smaller scale than the floor below to create the illusion of height.

5. In one of Main Street's Fire House windows (shine, shines) a light in honor of Walt Disney, the park's creator.

6. None of the characters roaming the park in full-body costumes ever (speak, speaks).

7. Only the "human" characters, such as Snow White, Cinderella, and Aladdin (talk, talks).

8. There (is, are) also a "kid switch" policy to help parents with small children go on the adult rides.

9. One parent stands in line and (enjoy, enjoys) the ride.

10. At the exit gate (waits, wait) the other parent to switch places once the ride has finished so that both of the adults have a good time without waiting in line twice.

Source: Avenues, March–April 1997

Exercise 3

1. No one in my film class (has, have) ever seen *2001: A Space Odyssey* before, except me.

2. All of them (has, have) heard of it, but none of them (has, have) actually watched it.

3. Most of my friends outside of school (love, loves) old movies, especially science fiction ones like *Slaughterhouse Five* and *Fahrenheit 451*.

4. Each of these sci-fi movies (make, makes) its own point about the human situation.

5. But everybody I know (say, says) *2001: A Space Odyssey* makes the biggest point of all.

6. One of my roommates (think, thinks) that it is the greatest movie ever made.

7. I believe that either it or *Fahrenheit 451* (is, are) the best, but I (hasn't, haven't) decided which one yet.

8. Now George Orwell's famous year 1984 (has, have) passed.

9. And each of us (look, looks) back at the shocking events of the real year 2001.

10. No one really (know, knows) what surprises await us in the future.

Exercise 4

1. Some of the world's gems (has, have) been designated as birthstones.
2. Each of these stones (is, are) unique.
3. Either a zodiac sign or a month of the year (is, are) represented by a particular gem.
4. The stone for January (is, are) garnet, and February's (is, are) amethyst.
5. Aquamarine and diamond (is, are) March and April's birthstones.
6. Someone who is born in May (has, have) emerald as a birthstone.
7. The pearl, the ruby, and peridot (represent, represents) those with birthdays in June, July, and August, respectively.
8. And the remaining months—September, October, November, and December—(is, are) associated with sapphire, opal, topaz, and turquoise—in that order.
9. The custom of assigning birthstones to signs of the zodiac (come, comes) from the connection between gems and the stars.
10. Both gemstones and stars (shine, shines).

Source: Gem Stones (Dorling Kindersley, 1994)

Exercise 5

1. Everyone in my circle of friends (has, have) plans for the summer vacation.
2. Each of us (is, are) going to pass the time differently.
3. One of my best friends (is, are) driving all the way to New Orleans.
4. Another of them always (visit, visits) relatives in Palm Springs.
5. Most of the students at my school (travel, travels) somewhere to get away.
6. Because of my family's limited funds, normally either my sister or I (get, gets) to go on a trip during the summer.

7. In the past, my backup plans (has, have) involved driving to the beach nearby and staying with my cousin's family.

8. But this year my parents (has, have) surprised us with news of a special family trip.

9. My sister and I (get, gets) to go with them to Hawaii.

10. Both of us (is, are) really looking forward to it.

PROOFREADING EXERCISE

Find and correct the ten subject/verb agreement errors in the following paragraph.

My teachers for this school year are really interesting. Each of their personalities are different. Some of them requires us to be on time every day and follow directions to the letter. Others treats students almost as casual friends. The expectations of my geography teacher is higher than I expected. Students in that class has to do just what the teacher says, or they risk failing. Most of my other professors takes a more lenient approach. But two of them has an odd grading technique, at least it seems odd to me. These two teachers wants us to turn in all of our papers over the Internet. We can't turn in any handwritten work. I guess there is good reasons behind their demands. My friends says that turning in work over the Internet makes the teachers' jobs easier because it eliminate the possibility of plagiarizing.

SENTENCE WRITING

Write ten sentences in which you describe the clothes you are wearing. Use verbs in the present time. Then go back over your sentences—underline your subjects once, underline your verbs twice, and be sure they agree. Exchange papers with another sftudent and check each other's subject/verb agreement.

Avoiding Shifts in Time

People often worry about using different time frames in writing. Let common sense guide you. If you begin writing a paper in past time, don't shift back and forth to the present unnecessarily; and if you begin in the present, don't shift to the past without good reason. In the following paragraph, the writer starts in the present and then shifts to the past, then shifts again to the present:

> In the novel *To Kill a Mockingbird*, Jean Louise Finch is a little girl who lives in the South with her father, Atticus, and her brother, Jem. Everybody in town calls Jean Louise "Scout" as a nickname. When Atticus, a lawyer, chose to defend a black man against the charges of a white woman, some of their neighbors turned against him. Scout protected her father by appealing to the humanity of one member of the angry mob. In this chapter, five-year-old Scout turns out to be stronger than a group of adult men.

All the verbs should be in the present:

> In the novel *To Kill a Mockingbird*, Jean Louise Finch is a little girl who lives in the South with her father, Atticus, and her brother, Jem. Everybody in town calls Jean Louise "Scout" as a nickname. When Atticus, a lawyer, chooses to defend a black man against the charges of a white woman, some of their neighbors turn against him. Scout protects her father by appealing to

the humanity of one member of the angry mob. In this chapter, five-year-old Scout turns out to be stronger than a group of adult men.

This sample paragraph discusses only the events that happen within the novel's plot, so it needs to maintain one time frame—the present, which we use to write about literature and repeated actions.

However, sometimes you will write about the present, the past, and even the future together. Then it may be necessary to use these different time frames within the same paragraph, each for its own reason. For example, if you were to give biographical information about Harper Lee, author of *To Kill a Mockingbird*, within a discussion of the novel and its influence, you might need to use all three time frames:

> Harper Lee grew up in Alabama, and she based elements in the book on experiences from her childhood. Like the character Atticus, Lee's father was a lawyer. She wrote the novel in his law offices. *To Kill a Mockingbird* is Harper Lee's most famous work, and it received the Pulitzer Prize for fiction in 1960. Lee's book turned forty years old in the year 2000. It will always remain one of the most moving and compassionate novels in American literature.

This paragraph uses past (*grew, based, was, wrote, received, turned*), present (*is*), and future (*will remain*) in the same paragraph without committing the error of shifting. Shifting occurs when the writer changes time frames *inconsistently* or *for no reason*, confusing the reader (as in the first example given).

PROOFREADING EXERCISES

Which of the following student paragraphs shift *unnecessarily* back and forth between time frames? In those that do, change the verbs to maintain one time frame, thus making the entire paragraph read smoothly. (First, read the paragraphs to determine whether unnecessary shifting takes place. One of the paragraphs is correct.)

1. I am taking an art history class right now. Everyday, we watched slide shows of great pieces of art throughout history. We memorized each piece of art, its time period, and the artist who created it. I enjoy these slide shows, but I had trouble remembering the facts about them. I always get swept away by the beautiful paintings, drawings, and sculptures and forgot to take notes that I could study from at home.

2. My Shakespeare teacher recently told us that in Shakespeare's day, all of the characters' parts were played by male actors. That information surprised me. The Elizabethans, of course, probably accepted all-male actors without question. Now that we are so used to realistic action and special effects on stage, I have a hard time imagining a man playing Juliet convincingly. Yet as a theater major, I know how much costume and voice really help to create a believable character. And I was glad to read that, more recently, there have been all-female casts of *Hamlet* and other plays. These productions seem to balance the scales somehow.

3. I loved traveling by train. The rocking motion makes me so calm, and the clackety-clack of the railroad ties as we ride over them sounds like a heartbeat to me. I also enjoy walking down the aisles of all the cars and looking at the different passengers. Whole families sat together, with children facing their parents. I noticed the kids liked to ride backward more than the adults. The food that we ate in the dining car was expensive, but it is always fancy and delicious. My favorite part of the train is the observation car. It is made of glass from the seats up so that we could see everything that we passed along the way.

Recognizing Verbal Phrases

We know (from the discussion on p. 95) that a verb phrase is made up of a main verb and at least one helping verb. But sometimes certain forms of verbs are used not as real verbs but as some other part of a sentence. Verbs put to other uses are called *verbals*.

A verbal can be a subject:

Skiing is my favorite Olympic sport. (*Skiing* is the subject, not the verb. The verb is *is*.)

A verbal can be a descriptive word:

His *bruised* ankle healed very quickly. (*Bruised* describes the subject, ankle. *Healed* is the verb.)

A verbal can be an object:

I like *to read* during the summer. (*To read* is the object. *Like* is the verb.)

Verbals link up with other words to form *verbal phrases*. To see the difference between a real verb phrase and a verbal phrase, look at these two sentences:

I <u>was bowling</u> with my best friends. (*Bowling* is the main verb in a verb phrase. Along with the helping verb *was*, it shows the action of the sentence.)

I <u>enjoyed</u> *bowling* with my best friends. (Here the real verb is *enjoyed*. *Bowling* is not the verb; it is part of a verbal phrase—*bowling with my best friends*—which is what I enjoyed.)

Three Kinds of Verbals

1. *ing* verbs used without helping verbs (*running, thinking, baking . . .*)

2. verb forms that often end in *ed, en,* or *t* (*tossed, spoken, burnt . . .*)

3. verbs that follow *to* _____ (*to walk, to eat, to cause . . .*)

Look at the following sentences using the previous examples in verbal phrases:

Running two miles a day <u>is</u> great exercise. (real verb = is)

<u>She</u> <u>spent</u> two hours *thinking of a title for her essay.* (real verb = spent)

<u>We</u> <u>had</u> such fun *baking those cherry vanilla cupcakes.* (real verb = had)

Tossed in a salad, artichoke <u>hearts</u> <u>add</u> zesty flavor. (real verb = add)

Spoken in Spanish, the <u>dialogue</u> <u>sounds</u> even more beautiful. (real verb = sounds)

The gourmet <u>pizza</u>, *burnt by a careless chef,* <u>shrunk</u> to half its normal size. (real verb = shrunk)

<u>I</u> <u>like</u> *to walk around the zoo by myself.* (real verb = like)

To eat exotic foods <u>takes</u> courage. (real verb = takes)

<u>They</u> actually <u>wanted</u> *to cause an argument.* (real verb = wanted)

E X E R C I S E S

Each of the following sentences contains at least one verbal or verbal phrase. Double underline the real verbs or verb phrases and put brackets around the verbals and verbal phrases. Remember to locate the verbals first (*running, wounded, to sleep* . . .) and include any word(s) that go with them (*running a race, wounded in the fight, to sleep all night*). Real verbs will never be inside verbal phrases. Check your answers after the first set before going on to the next.

Exercise 1

1. Many people dislike speaking in front of strangers.
2. That is why there is an almost universal fear of giving speeches.
3. Feeling insecure and exposed, people get dry mouths and sweaty hands.
4. Note cards become useless, rearranging themselves in the worst possible order.
5. To combat this problem, people try to memorize a speech, only to forget the whole thing as the audience stares back at them expectantly.
6. And when they do remember parts of it, the microphone decides to quit at the punch line of their best joke.
7. Embarrassed and humiliated, they struggle to regain their composure.
8. Then the audience usually begins to sympathize with and encourage the speaker.
9. Finally used to the spotlight, the speaker relaxes and finds the courage to finish.
10. No one expects giving a speech to get any easier.

Exercise 2

1. I have learned how to manage my time when I am not working.
2. I like to go to the movies on Friday nights.
3. Watching a good film takes me away from the stress of my job.

4. I especially enjoy eating buttery popcorn and drinking a cold soda.

5. It is the perfect way for me to begin the weekend.

6. I get to escape from deadlines and the pressure to succeed.

7. I indulge myself and try to give myself a break—nobody's perfect, and everybody has setbacks.

8. All day Saturday I enjoy lounging around the house in my weekend clothes.

9. I do a little gardening and try to relax my mind.

10. By Sunday evening, after resting for two days, I am ready to start my busy week all over again.

Exercise 3

1. Choosing a major is one of the most important decisions for students.

2. Many students take a long time to decide about their majors.

3. But they fear wasting time on the wrong major more than indecision.

4. They spend several semesters as undecided majors taking general education classes.

5. Distracted by class work, students can forget to pay attention to their interests.

6. Finally, a particular subject area will attract them to study it further.

7. One student might find happiness in doing a psychology experiment.

8. Writing a poem in an English class may be the assignment to make another decide.

9. Attracted by telescopes, a student might choose to major in astronomy.

10. Finding a major takes time and patience.

Exercise 4

1. Astronaut Shannon Lucid blasted off in March of 1996 to join the cosmonauts on Mir space station.

2. Lucid, a woman in her fifties, thrived in her weightless environment, setting a record for the longest trip in space by an American.

3. One of the dangers of living without gravity is that bones and muscles deteriorate rapidly without exercise.

4. During her time aboard Mir, Lucid kept in shape by exercising on a specially designed treadmill and bicycle.

5. Part of her mission required her to conduct various experiments.

6. NASA designed these experiments to study the effects of weightlessness; they included burning candles, growing crystals, and incubating quail eggs in zero gravity.

7. Lucid took along books to keep her busy between experiments and exercising.

8. When she ran out of reading material, Lucid's daughter helped by sending a new book up on a cargo ship carrying other supplies to Mir from Earth.

9. Chocolate turned out to be in short supply aboard the space station while Lucid was there.

10. Waiting for her when she landed after being in space for 188 days was a gift from President Clinton—it was a gigantic box of M&M's wrapped in gold paper.

Source: Newsweek, October 7, 1996

Exercise 5

1. We have all seen stage shows where magicians try to hypnotize people beginning with the suggestion, "You are getting very sleepy . . . ."

2. Then they order their hypnotized subjects to cluck like chickens or to cry like babies.

3. Hypnotists can even convince subjects to feel very cold even if the room is actually warm.

4. More important, hallucinating on command and the ability to control pain have been achieved through hypnosis.

5. Now researchers are studying the brains of supposedly hypnotized people to see if there is such a thing as a real hypnotic state.

6. Measuring the altered blood flow to different locations in the brain allows scientists to visualize the effects of hypnosis.

7. And studies show that these effects can indeed be measured by changes in the brains of hypnotized subjects.

8. To identify people only pretending to be hypnotized, scientists secretly filmed all participants while only an audiotape made suggestions to the subjects.

9. Subjects genuinely able to be hypnotized responded to either the audio-tape or the hypnotist himself.

10. Those who did not respond unless a hypnotist was in the room were judged to be faking the effects of hypnosis, and their brain measurements revealed less change than the others.

Source: New Scientist, July 4, 1998

PARAGRAPH EXERCISE

Double underline the real verbs or verb phrases and put brackets around the verbals and verbal phrases in the following excerpt from the book *First Ladies of the White House*, by Nancy J. Skarmeas.

Born in May of 1860 in Savannah, Georgia, Ellen Axson was a sensitive and refined woman with a talent for painting and an interest in music and literature. She married Woodrow Wilson on June 24, 1885.

Mrs. Wilson spent much of her brief time in the White House painting and drawing in an attic studio. She had worked previously as a professional painter, but as first lady she donated her work to be auctioned for charity. As an outgrowth of her own interest in art, Mrs. Wilson devoted a room of the White House to the display of craftworks by the women of the Blue Ridge Mountains. One of Mrs. Wilson's more public projects was her work to improve the condition of the poor neighborhoods of Washington, D.C. The first lady took congressmen on tours of the city's bleakest areas and initiated legislation aimed at eliminating the slums.

SENTENCE WRITING

Write ten sentences that contain verbal phrases. Use the ten verbals listed here to begin your verbal phrases: *speaking, typing, driving, reading, to eat, to go, to chat, to cook, impressed, taken.* The last two are particularly difficult to use as verbals. There are sample sentences listed in the Answers section at the back of the book. But first, try to write your own so that you can compare the two.

Correcting Misplaced or Dangling Modifiers

When we modify something, we change whatever it is by adding something to it. We might modify a car, for example, by adding special tires. In English, we call words, phrases, and clauses *modifiers* when they add information to part of a sentence. To do its job properly, a modifier should be in the right spot—as close to the word it describes as possible. If we put new tires on the roof of the car instead of where they belong, they would be misplaced. In the following sentence, the modifier is too far away from the word it modifies to make sense. It is a misplaced modifier:

> Swinging from tree to tree, we watched the monkeys at the zoo.

Was it *we* who were swinging from tree to tree? That's what the sentence says because the modifying phrase *Swinging from tree to tree* is next to *we*. It should be next to *monkeys*.

> At the zoo, we watched the monkeys swinging from tree to tree.

The next example has no word at all for the modifier to modify:

> At the age of eight, my family finally bought a dog.

Obviously, the family was not eight when it bought a dog. Nor was the dog eight. The modifier *At the age of eight* is dangling there with no word to attach itself to, no word for it to modify. We can get rid of the dangling modifier by turning it into a dependent clause. (See p. 71 for a discussion of dependent clauses.)

> When I was eight, my family finally bought a dog.

Here the clause has its own subject and verb—*I was*—and there's no chance of misunderstanding the sentence. Here's another dangling modifier:

> After a two-hour nap, the train pulled into the station.

Did the train take a two-hour nap? Who did?

> After a two-hour nap, I awoke just as the train pulled into the station.

EXERCISES

Carefully rephrase any of the following sentences that contain misplaced or dangling modifiers. Some sentences are correct.

Exercise 1

1. After watching TV for half an hour, the pasta was ready.
2. I found a dollar jogging around the block.
3. The children ate the cupcakes sitting in their chairs.
4. One year after becoming manager, the company closed the store.
5. That tutor works well with all of the instructors.
6. My mom's smiling face appeared with a bouquet of flowers for my birthday.
7. The usher slipped and fell on someone's program.
8. They gave directions to the driver through the window.
9. Trying to fix my clock, I broke it instead.
10. I bought a new shirt with silver buttons.

Exercise 2

1. Five people stood behind the bench and waited for the bus.
2. The applicants listened to each of the employers taking careful notes.
3. I saw that movie with my sister three times.
4. Giving my order in a low voice, the waiter asked me to speak louder.
5. I went to a play with my theater class last week.
6. We received an invitation to their party in a pink envelope.
7. Filled with gas, we were able to drive our car all the way to San Francisco.
8. After setting the table, our guests started eating.
9. Taped to the door, I wrote a note that I would return shortly.
10. The student workers built a nice wall with gloves and safety goggles.

Exercise 3

1. Clamped down on my windshield, I saw a parking ticket.
2. Team leaders will have many responsibilities at the new camp.

3. Using red ink, mistakes can be marked more clearly.

4. They noticed a loophole reading their policy very carefully.

5. She kicked her friend in the arena by accident.

6. The teacher handed the tests back to the students with a frown.

7. Talking with the other students, class finally started.

8. We bought a cat for our friend with a fluffy tail.

9. The pre-schoolers planted seedlings dressed in farmer outfits.

10. At the age of sixteen, driving permits are easy to obtain.

Exercise 4

1. After calling roll, the students placed their homework on the teacher's desk.

2. Sharon asked her boss for a raise and got one.

3. The actors accepted the flowers with open arms.

4. A "Ramp Closed" sign caused a backup on the freeway.

5. Celebrating too soon, the coach warned the players to wait until the end of the game.

6. I sent her a picture of us in a big envelope.

7. She found an old handkerchief going through her coat pockets.

8. Promising to return, our guide left us alone in the museum.

9. The Girl Scouts went camping with their troop leaders.

10. After shouting "Happy birthday!" the room went completely quiet.

Exercise 5

1. One day after turning forty, my new car broke down on the freeway.

2. Liking the rush of fresh air on his face, my brother lets his dog hang out the window of the car.

3. I ran through the park to try out my new shoes.

4. Studying in the writing lab, my comma problems disappeared.

5. Helping other people gives me great pleasure.

6. Chasing each other up and down a tree, we saw a pair of squirrels.

7. I like to watch television at night.

8. We are proud of our sister for graduating with honors.

9. Lifting the heavy television, her face turned red.

10. I enjoy collecting things from days gone by.

PROOFREADING EXERCISE

Find and correct any misplaced or dangling modifiers in the following paragraphs.

I love parades, so last year my family and I traveled to Pasadena, California, to see one of the biggest parades of all—the Tournament of Roses Parade on New Year's Day. It turned out to be even more wonderful than I expected.

Arriving one day early, the city was already crowded with people. Lots of families were setting up campsites on Colorado Boulevard. We didn't want to miss one float in the parade, so we found our own spot and made ourselves at home. When the parade began, I had as much fun watching the spectators as the parade itself. I saw children pointing at the breathtaking horses and floats sitting on their fathers' shoulders. Decorated completely with flowers or plant material, I couldn't believe how beautiful the floats were and how good they smelled.

The crowd was overwhelmed by the sights and sounds of the parade. Marching and playing their instruments with perfect precision, everyone especially enjoyed hearing the school bands. They must have practiced for the whole year to be that good.

My experience didn't end with the parade, however. After the last float had passed by, I found a twenty dollar bill walking down Colorado Boulevard. Now hanging on my wall at home, I framed it as a souvenir of my trip to the Rose Parade.

SENTENCE WRITING

Write five sentences that contain misplaced or dangling modifiers; then revise those sentences to put the modifiers where they belong. Use the examples in the explanations as models.

Following Sentence Patterns

Sentences are built according to a few basic patterns. For proof, rearrange each of the following sets of words to form a complete statement (not a question):

apples a ate raccoon the

the crashing beach were waves the on

your in am partner I life

been she school has to walking

you wonderful in look green

There are only one or two possible combinations for each due to English sentence patterns. Either *A raccoon ate the apples,* or *The apples ate a raccoon,* and so on. But in each case, the verb or verb phrase makes its way to the middle of the statement.

To understand sentence patterns, you need to know that verbs can do three things.

1. Verbs can show actions:

The raccoon ate the apples.

The waves were crashing on the beach.

She has been walking to school.

2. Verbs can link subjects with descriptive words:

I am your partner in life.

You look wonderful in green.

3. Verbs can help other verbs form verb phrases:

The waves were crashing on the beach.

She has been walking to school.

Look at these sentences for more examples:

Mel grabbed a slice of pizza. (The verb *grabbed* shows Mel's action.)

His slice was the largest one in the box. (The verb *was* links *slice* with its description as *the largest one.*)

Mel had been craving pizza for a week. (The verbs *had* and *been* help the main verb *craving* in a verb phrase.)

Knowing what a verb does in a clause helps you gain an understanding of the three basic sentence patterns:

Subject + Action Verb + Object Pattern

Some action verbs must be followed by a person or an object that receives the action.

S   AV   OBJ
Sylvia completed the difficult math test. (*Sylvia completed* makes no sense without being followed by the object that she completed—*test.*)

Subject + Action Verb (+ No Object) Pattern

At other times, the action verb itself completes the meaning and needs no object after it.

> S   AV
> She celebrated at home with her family. (*She celebrated* makes sense alone. The two prepositional phrases—*at home* and *with her family*—are not needed to understand the meaning of the clause.)

Subject + Linking Verb + Description Pattern

A special kind of verb that does not show an action but links a subject with a description is called a *linking verb*. It acts like an equal sign in a clause. Learn to recognize the most common linking verbs: *is, am, are, was, were, seem, feel, appear, become, look.*

> S   LV   DESC
> Sylvia is an excellent student. (*Sylvia* equals *an excellent student.*)

> S   LV   DESC
> Sylvia has become very intelligent. (*Very intelligent* describes *Sylvia.*)

NOTE - We learned on page 95 that a verb phrase includes a main verb and its helping verbs. Helping verbs can be used in any of the sentence patterns.

> S   AV
> Sylvia is going to Seattle for a vacation. (Here the verb *is* helps the main verb *going*, which is an action verb with no object followed by two prepositional phrases—*to Seattle* and *for a vacation.*)

The following chart outlines the patterns using short sentences that you could memorize:

Three Basic Sentence Patterns

S + AV + OBJ

<u>Kids</u> <u><u>like</u></u> candy.

S + AV

<u>They</u> <u><u>play</u></u> (with their friends) (on the playground).
                    not objects

S + LV + DESC

<u>They</u> <u><u>are</u></u> fourth-graders.

<u>They</u> <u><u>look</u></u> happy.

These are the basic patterns for most of the clauses used in English sentences. Knowing them can help writers control their sentences and improve their use of words.

E X E R C I S E S

First, put parentheses around any prepositional phrases. Next, underline the subjects once and the verbs or verb phrases twice. Then mark the sentence patterns above the words. Remember that the patterns never mix together. For example, unlike an action verb, a linking verb will almost never be used alone (for example, "He seems."), nor will an action verb be followed by a description of the subject (for example, "She took tall."). And if there are two clauses, each one may have a different pattern. Check your answers after the first set of ten.

Exercise 1

1. I am a fan of televised golf.

2. The game of golf eases my mind.

3. During a weekend tournament, I work in my office at home and watch the action on a portable TV.

4. With the soft sound of the announcers' voices, I can relax and participate at the same time.

5. I use the ongoing competition as a distraction.

6. By the middle of the tournament, I have finished the bills and have started next month's budget.

7. Then I pay closer attention to the leaders.

8. Occasionally, the competition becomes really intense.

9. I especially love tied scores and extra rounds.

10. I will always be a golf fan.

Exercise 2

1. People often travel with their dogs, cats, or other pets.

2. Veterinarians offer some suggestions about traveling with pets.

3. First, a pet should be old enough to travel.

4. All pets should travel in special carriers with food and water dishes.

5. Ordinary water in a pet's dish spills easily.

6. But ice cubes in the water dish will melt slowly.

7. During long car rides, pets should have enough shade and fresh air.

8. Small pets can ride with passengers.

9. However, a loose pet could cause an accident.

10. Sedatives for pets are risky but sometimes necessary.

Exercise 3

1. We live in a world with photocopiers, scanners, and fax machines.

2. If we need copies of documents, these machines make them for us.

3. Up until the late 1800s, people copied all documents by hand.

4. As a solution to this problem, Thomas Edison invented an electric pen.

5. Unlike ordinary pens, Edison's electric pen made stencils; the pen itself was inkless.

6. Its sharp tip poked holes in the paper, and later a roller spread ink over the holes.

7. The ink went though the holes onto another sheet of paper underneath.

8. And an exact copy was the result; in fact, one stencil produced many copies.

9. The first documents Edison reproduced with his electric pen were a speech from *Richard III* and the outline of a photograph of Edison's wife, Mary.

10. Although Edison sold many thousands of his electric pens at the time, only six of them have survived.

Source: Smithsonian, July 1998

Exercise 4

1. On November 4, 1922, archaeologist Howard Carter discovered the tomb of King Tutankhamen.

2. Carter had been excavating in Egypt for years without success.

3. Then he made his famous discovery.

4. With the help of his workers, Carter found the top step of a stone stairway.

5. They followed the staircase down a total of sixteen steps.

6. At the bottom, Carter and his team encountered a sealed door.

7. They had found a tomb undisturbed for thousands of years.

8. It held the personal belongings of a young Egyptian king.

9. Some of the objects were precious; others were just ordinary household effects.

10. The job of cataloging and removing the items took ten years.

Exercise 5

1. In 1993, Sears discontinued its famous catalog.
2. For 97 years, a person could buy almost anything through the Sears catalog.
3. People called it "The Big Book."
4. The final issue contained 1,500 pages of merchandise for sale.
5. In 1897, before the government regulated such things, even medicines with opium were available through the catalog.
6. In 1910, Sears manufactured its own motor car; the Sears catalog advertised the automobile for sale at a cost of just under four hundred dollars.
7. From the 1918 version of the catalog, people could purchase a kit that included building instructions and the materials for an entire house; the price was fifteen hundred dollars.
8. Sears sold more than 100,000 houses through its catalog.
9. Before 1992, all customers used mail order forms, not phone calls, to place their orders.
10. When the merchandise arrived at the catalog center, customers went and picked it up; for most of its history, the catalog offered no delivery service.

Source: Time, February 8, 1993

PARAGRAPH EXERCISE

Label the sentence patterns in the following paragraphs. They are from a book by Nancy J. Skarmeas titled *Our Presidents: Their Lives and Stories.* It helps to put parentheses around prepositional phrases first to isolate them from the words that make up the sentence patterns—the subjects, the verbs, and any objects after action verbs or any descriptive words after linking verbs (*is, was, were, seem, appear . . .*).

Franklin Delano Roosevelt
1882–1945
Thirty-Second President 1933–1945

Four times Americans went to the polls and elected Franklin Delano Roosevelt as their president. An inspirational and controversial leader, Roosevelt steered Americans through the dark, troubled days of the Great Depression and World War II.

Franklin Roosevelt grew up in the luxurious family home in Hyde Park, New York, and spent summers on beautiful Campobello Island. . . . In his twelve years as president, Roosevelt oversaw an unprecedented expansion of the federal government. . . .

Roosevelt's wife, Eleanor, a niece of former president Theodore Roosevelt and a distant cousin to Franklin, was, like her husband, a popular and controversial figure. She was an outspoken advocate of civil and human rights and as first lady took an active role in American public life.

SENTENCE WRITING

Write ten sentences describing the weather today and your feelings about it. Keep your sentences short and clear. Then go back and label the sentence patterns you have used.

Avoiding Clichés, Awkward Phrasing, and Wordiness

Clichés

A cliché is an expression that has been used so often it has lost its originality and effectiveness. Whoever first said "light as a feather" had thought of an original way to express lightness, but today that expression is worn out. Most of us use an occasional cliché in speaking, but clichés have no place in writing. The good writer thinks up fresh new ways to express ideas.

Here are a few clichés. Add some more to the list.

the bottom line
older but wiser
last but not least
in this day and age
different as night and day
out of this world
white as a ghost
sick as a dog
tried and true
at the top of their lungs
the thrill of victory
one in a million
busy as a bee
easier said than done
better late than never

Clichés lack freshness because the reader always knows what's coming next. Can you complete these expressions?

the agony of . . .
breathe a sigh of . . .
lend a helping . . .
odds and . . .
raining cats and . . .
as American as . . .
been there . . .
worth its weight . . .

Clichés are expressions too many people use. Try to avoid them in your writing.

Awkward Phrasing

Another problem—awkward phrasing—comes from writing sentence structures that *no one* else would use because they break basic sentence patterns, omit necessary words, or use words incorrectly. Like clichés, awkward sentences might *sound* acceptable when spoken, but as polished writing, they are usually unacceptable.

Awkward

> There should be great efforts in terms of the communication between teachers and their students.

Corrected

> Teachers and their students must communicate.

Awkward

> During the experiment, the use of key principles was essential to ensure the success of it.

Corrected

> The experiment was a success. *or* We did the experiment carefully.

Awkward

> My favorite was when the guy with the ball ran the wrong way all the way across the field.

Corrected

> In my favorite part, the receiver ran across the field in the wrong direction.

Wordiness

Good writing is concise writing. Don't use ten words if you can say it better in five. "In today's society" isn't as effective as "today," and it's a cliché. "At this point in time" could be "presently" or "now."

Another kind of wordiness comes from saying something twice. There's no need to write "in the month of August" or "9 a.m. in the morning" or "my personal opinion." August *is* a month, 9 a.m. *is* morning, and anyone's opinion *is* personal. All you need to write is "in August," "9 a.m.," and "my opinion."

Still another kind of wordiness comes from using expressions that add nothing to the meaning of the sentence. "The point is that we can't afford it" says no more than "We can't afford it."

Here is a sample wordy sentence:

The construction company actually worked on that particular building for a period of six months.

And here it is after eliminating wordiness:

The construction company worked on that building for six months.

Wordy Writing	Concise Writing
advance planning	planning
an unexpected surprise	a surprise
ask a question	ask
at a later date	later
basic fundamentals	fundamentals
green in color	green
but nevertheless	but (or nevertheless)
combine together	combine
completely empty	empty
down below	below
each and every	each (or every)
end result	result
fewer in number	fewer
free gift	gift
in order to	to
in spite of the fact that	although
just exactly	exactly

large in size	large
new innovation	innovation
on a regular basis	regularly
past history	history
rectangular in shape	rectangular
refer back	refer
repeat again	repeat
serious crisis	crisis
sufficient enough	sufficient (or enough)
there in person	there
two different kinds	two kinds
very unique	unique

E X E R C I S E S

Exercise 1

Rewrite the following sentences to eliminate *clichés* and *awkward phrasing*. If a whole sentence is a cliché, eliminate it.

1. I like to shop around before I buy something.
2. Three or four different stores is not unusual for me to go to.
3. I always keep my eye on the bottom line.
4. I can save a hundred dollars on one item with this foolproof method.
5. Stranger things have happened.
6. Prices may vary significantly on the exact same merchandise.
7. But buying at the right time is easier said than done.
8. Once I waited so long for a sale on a computer that I was left empty handed.

9. There is a real feeling of satisfaction I get when I do find a bargain though.

10. Looking for good prices is as American as apple pie.

Exercise 2

Rewrite the following sentences to eliminate *wordiness*. See how few words you can use without changing the meaning of the sentence.

1. I received an unexpected surprise in class today.

2. It came in the form of a grade I'm not used to getting on my papers.

3. I discovered as I looked at the piece of lined paper that I turned in that I had received an A on a quiz.

4. I had a hard time believing that I could get such a good grade as an A on any kind of a test.

5. After I thought about it for a long period of time, I kind of remembered that it seemed sort of easy when I took it.

6. Due to the fact that I had read the homework and saw the tutor before class, I really knew the material that was on the quiz.

7. Sure enough, as soon as I saw the grade, I also saw that Mr. Talbot could tell that I was surprised by such a perfect score since I got them all right.

8. He must have wondered why I did so well on this test when I hadn't done too well on other tests before this one.

9. I told him that on this particular occasion I studied and did all the work really carefully, and that's why I did so well on the test.

10. There were not many other students who did as well as I did, and Mr. Talbot asked me to tell them how I got such a good grade, so I told them all how it happened.

Exercise 3

Revise the sentences in the remaining exercises to eliminate any clichés, awkward phrasing, or wordiness.

1. The most beautiful thing I have ever seen in my life has got to be the blossoms in Fresno County, California.
2. Each spring, like clockwork, the orchards of trees and fields of flowers burst into bloom.
3. Cars, vans, and buses of all shapes and sizes drive along a preplanned route called the Blossom Trail.
4. There are flowers for as far as the eye can see—for over 60 miles, in fact.
5. The apple trees' blossoms have petals that are as white as snow.
6. And the bright orange poppies completely covering the hillsides are a feast for the eyes.
7. As an added bonus, the apricot, peach, and nectarine trees have blooms on them that are pink and even red.
8. Add the purples and blues of lupines, clover, and other wildflowers, and they complete the rainbow of colors.
9. The absolute best time to see the blooms is the end of February or the beginning of March.
10. That's when the beauty of the Blossom Trail is at its peak.

Source: Fresno County Blossom Trail (Fresno Convention and Visitors Bureau, 1998)

Exercise 4

1. In this day and age, it's hard to find a place that is really and truly old-fashioned.
2. Knott's Berry Farm is that kind of place; it's near Disneyland, but in my personal opinion, these two amusement parks are as different as night and day.
3. First of all, Knott's was a real berry farm way back in 1920 when Walter and Cordelia Knott started selling dinners in a Western-style ghost-town hotel that Walter brought from Arizona.

4. There is also a real old passenger train that people can ride on and get robbed by Knott's Berry Farm bandits.

5. The Knott's merry-go-round is something special too; its animals were carved by hand by a really famous carousel maker named Gustav Dentzel; its history goes all the way back to 1902 when it was made.

6. There is even an old schoolhouse, just like the ones in old Western movies; Walter and Cordelia's grandchildren actually went to school there before it became just one part of the ghost-town area of the park.

7. Talk about old-fashioned, Knott's hires real live blacksmiths to make things like horseshoes for the horses in the park and to show the way they do their magic to the visitors.

8. And many Native American craftspeople make pots and jewelry and canoes so that people can see how they make them.

9. Last but not least, the park has its share of roller coasters with people screaming at the top of their lungs.

10. Now Knott's Berry Farm is one in a million because it's the only big amusement park in the whole United States that is still owned and operated by the family that started it almost 80 years ago.

Source: Avenues, March–April 1997

Exercise 5

1. The other day I had to stay home from school because I was as sick as a dog with the flu.

2. I called my teacher and told her that one day of complete and utter rest would make me feel much better, but that was easier said than done.

3. I had forgotten that on Mondays nearly every house on the block has its gardeners come to take care of the plants and trees in the yards.

4. Each and every one of them always uses a power leaf blower and a tree-trimming saw to get the work done.

5. The noise around the neighborhood made my head spin, and I couldn't get to sleep for the life of me.

6. I tried watching television in order to drown out the noise and put me to sleep.

7. That was like jumping out of the frying pan into the fire; the shows on daytime TV were really hard to take.

8. Once the gardeners finished, I finally got to go to sleep at about 3 p.m. in the afternoon.

9. It was better late than never.

10. I got just about sixteen hours of sleep, felt better, and was as happy as a clam to be back at school the next day.

PROOFREADING EXERCISE

Revise the sentences in the following paragraphs to eliminate any clichés, awkward phrasing, or wordiness.

Without a doubt, one of the most important reference works in the entire history of the universe has got to be The *Oxford English Dictionary*, a book which is better known as the *OED*. At the present time, I'm reading a biography about the original editor of the *OED*; his name was Dr. James Murray. The book is about Dr. Murray and one particular man who contributed thousands and thousands of definitions and examples to the *OED* dictionary through the mail before the editor realized that the man was in an insane asylum and guilty of murdering another man several years earlier. The book that I'm reading is called *The Professor and the Madman*, and it's written by Simon Winchester.

The part of the story about these two men that interests me the most and makes chills run up and down my spine is the part that tells about the possible reasons why the insane man went crazy in the first place. The man had been a doctor during the civil war, and as a doctor, he was used to helping people, not hurting people. But Dr. William Minor, that was his name, was given a command as part of his military duties to place a scar on the face of a soldier who was caught as a deserter from the army. Dr. Minor had to use a hot metal instrument to brand the deserter's face with a big letter "D." To make a long story short, doing this terrible thing could have contributed to the doctor going crazy, which later made him become paranoid and kill an innocent man. The book explains that one way that Dr. Minor tried to pay his debt to society was to use his incredible intellect and academic ability to write definitions for the *Oxford English Dictionary.*

Personally, I'll never look up another word in the *OED* without wondering if it was defined by the "madman" in the book I'm reading. Just when I think I've seen it all and heard it all, stories like this one make me truly believe that truth is stranger than fiction after all.

SENTENCE WRITING

Go back to the sentences you wrote for the Sentence Writing exercise on page 25 or page 78 and revise them to eliminate any clichés, awkward phrasing, or wordiness.

Correcting for Parallel Structure

Your writing will be clearer and more memorable if you use parallel structure. That is, when you write two pieces of information or any kind of list, put the items in similar form. Look at this sentence, for example:

My favorite movies are comic, romantic, or the ones about outer space.

The sentence lacks parallel structure. The third item in the list doesn't match the other two. Now look at this sentence:

My favorite movie categories are comedies, love stories, and sci-fi fantasies.

Here the items are parallel; they are all plural nouns. Or you could write the following:

I like movies that make me laugh, that make me cry, and that make me think.

Again the sentence has parallel structure because all three items in the list are dependent clauses. Here are some more examples. Note how much easier it is to read the sentences with parallel structure.

Without Parallel Structure	With Parallel Structure
I like to hike, to ski, and going sailing.	I like to hike, to ski, and to sail. (all "to _____" verbs)
The office has run out of pens, paper, ink cartridges, and we need more toner, too.	The office needs more pens, paper, ink cartridges, and toner. (all nouns)
They decided that they needed a change, that they could afford a new house, and wanted to move to Arizona.	They decided that they needed a change, that they could afford a new house, and that they wanted to move to Arizona. (all dependent clauses)

The parts of an outline should always be parallel. Following are two brief outlines about food irradiation. The parts of the outline on the *left* are not parallel. The first subtopic (I.) is a question; the other (II.) is just a noun. And the supporting points (A., B., C.) are written as nouns, verbs, and even clauses. The parts of the outline on the *right* are parallel. Both subtopics (I. and II.) are plural nouns, and all details (A., B., C.) are action verbs followed by objects.

Not Parallel	Parallel
Food Irradiation	Food Irradiation
I. How is it good?	I. Benefits
A. Longer shelf life	A. Extends shelf life
B. Using fewer pesticides	B. Requires fewer pesticides
C. Kills bacteria	C. Kills bacteria
II. Concerns	II. Concerns
A. Nutritional value	A. Lowers nutritional value
B. Consumers are worried	B. Alarms consumers
C. Workers' safety	C. Endangers workers

Using parallel structure will make your writing more effective. Note the parallelism in these well-known quotations:

A place for everything and everything in its place.

Isabella Mary Beeton

Ask not what your country can do for you; ask what you can do for your country.

John F. Kennedy

We hold these truths to be self-evident, that all men are created equal, that they are endowed by their creator with certain unalienable rights, that among these are Life, Liberty, and the pursuit of Happiness.

Thomas Jefferson

E X E R C I S E S

Rephrase the following sentences so that any pairs or lists contain parallel structure.

Exercise 1

1. Do you know who invented the hot dog and the origin of its name?
2. Some people mistakenly believe that hot dogs originally had dog meat in them.
3. Actually, Harry M. Stevens, the person in charge of feeding New York Giants fans one hundred years ago, helped to invent the hot dog.
4. Tasty hot German sausages were becoming very popular as fast food, but it was hard for people to eat them.

5. Stevens had the idea of serving the sausages in a roll of bread, and people could put hot mustard on them.

6. At the Giants' stadium, these treats were called "red hots"; wandering vendors sold them during the games.

7. Sports cartoonist T. A. Dorgan was the one who gave the "hot dog" its current name.

8. Soon after Stevens' innovation, Dorgan drew a cartoon portraying a "red hot" as a Dachshund.

9. Dorgan was spoofing the fact that both "red hots" and Dachshunds were cylindrical in shape, red in color, and they both came from Germany.

10. Now you know more about the man who helped invent the hot dog, also how the name got started.

Source: Dogwatching (Three Rivers Press, 1986)

Exercise 2

1. There are many interesting facts about the lives of the men who have held the office of President of the United States.

2. Three presidents died on the Fourth of July, and one president had his birthday on Independence Day.

3. The ones who died on July 4th were John Adams, Thomas Jefferson, and James Monroe; and Calvin Coolidge was the one whose birthday was on that day.

4. James Buchanan was the only unmarried president.

5. The person who was the youngest to be elected president was John F. Kennedy, at 43 years old, but Theodore Roosevelt became president at 42 because of McKinley's assassination.

6. Gerald Ford was never elected as vice president or for the position of president; he came to both positions through the resignations of Spiro Agnew and Richard Nixon, respectively.

7. The various careers of these men prior to becoming president included farming, editing, teaching, lawyers, military positions, businessmen, acting, and a tailor.

8. John Tyler, U.S. President from 1841 to 1845, had fifteen children.

9. Franklin D. Roosevelt's family tree linked him to eleven other presidents either directly or through marriage.

10. FDR holds two other distinctions in presidential history: he was the first to be on TV, and twelve years in office made his term as president the longest.

Sources: The Presidents of the United States of America (White House Historical Assn., 1995) and *Some Facts about the Presidents* (Bright of America, 1997)

Exercise 3

1. Researchers have designed a new kind of robot.

2. It doesn't look like other robots, and what it does is different too.

3. Its "head" contains a microphone for ears, a small screen for a face, and a video camera to act as its eyes.

4. It does not have a body, just a pole to hold up its "head."

5. The pole connects to a box-shaped base with rollers to give it motion.

6. The difference between this and other kinds of robots is that the PRoP, as it's called, becomes an extension of anyone who controls it through the Internet.

7. A person in one city will be able to log on to the PRoP in another city and wander around—seeing what it sees, speaking to people it meets, and the person is able to hear what it hears.

8. The face of the person controlling the PRoP will be displayed on the small screen on its "head," so it will assume the user's identity.

9. The inventors of the PRoP believe that research labs and those in the business world will be most interested in the PRoPs at first.

10. But in the future, PRoPs could make it possible to take a vacation or maybe you could play a game of chess with a faraway friend without ever leaving your desk.

Source: New Scientist, September 26, 1998

Exercise 4

1. People don't seem to agree about how they're going to spell the word *millennium.*

2. The word *millennium* is a combination of *mille* and *annus.*

3. These are the Latin root words meaning "thousand" and the other one means "year."

4. Now that we have entered a new millennium, we should try to resolve the question of this word's spelling.

5. Some companies with *millennium* in their names have chosen to take out letters or are making it plural.

6. There is the Millenium Hotel, and a car model is named Millenia.

7. Some companies spell it with all its letters only to have phone books or business card printers misspell it.

8. We worry not only about how to spell *millennium* but also we worry about whether people will get tired of it.

9. A company relies on two things above all: customer loyalty and the ability to recognize its name.

10. How will customers recognize the name of a company that uses the word *millennium* but then the company chooses to spell it differently?

Exercise 5

Make the following discussion of handy hints parallel. The information is from the book *691 of the Best Household Tips*.

1. I've been learning to cook lately, but making the same mistake is something I always do.
2. I always put too much salt in, or I sweeten a dish too much.
3. I've just read about a few ways to correct these cooking mistakes.
4. To correct the use of too much salt, I could add a little sugar.
5. For soups or in the case of stews, a slice of raw potato can absorb the excess salt.
6. If the salt is still too overpowering, double the dish's ingredients and don't add any new salt to the new batch.
7. Then, if there's too much food, put half in the freezer for later.
8. For sweetening with too much sugar when baking, one remedy is to add some salt.
9. For overly sweet vegetables or entrees, some vinegar could be added.
10. By following these cooking tips, I hope to make better dishes in the future.

PROOFREADING EXERCISE

Proofread the following paragraph about Carry Nation and revise it to correct any errors in parallel structure.

Carry A. Nation was an American woman who lived from 1846 to the year 1911. She is most famous for two things: her name, which helped inspire her to be an activist, and the habit that she had of wrecking any saloon in sight. Carry Nation hated alcohol as well as any place that sold it. She was a powerful woman who was almost six feet tall. During her adult life, she went on a mission to destroy saloons across the country one at a time. Her crusade began in Wichita. She used a hatchet to smash saloon windows, chop up saloon furniture, she cracked saloon mirrors, and made especially sure to break as many of a saloon's liquor bottles as possible. Carry A. Nation repeated this offense from the east coast to California's coast. Whenever she landed in jail, this enterprising American sold toy replicas of her hatchet and speeches were given by her to raise money for her bail. Carry Nation took action based on her beliefs. She caused a lot of trouble for some people, but people were also helped by her. She donated funds to the poor, and drunkard's wives were given shelter in a home that she founded.

Source: *Guess Who? A Cavalcade of Famous Americans* (Platt and Munk, 1969)

SENTENCE WRITING

Write ten sentences that use parallel structure in a list or a pair of objects, actions, locations, or ideas. You may choose your own subject or describe a process that you carry out at your job.

Using Pronouns

Nouns name people, places, things, and ideas—such as *students, school, computers*, and *cyberspace*. Pronouns take the place of nouns to avoid repetition and to clarify meaning. Look at the following two sentences:

> Naomi's father worried that the children at the party were too loud, so Naomi's father told the children that the party would have to end if the children didn't calm down.

Naomi's father worried that the children at the party were too loud, so *he* told *them* that *it* would have to end if *they* didn't calm down.

Nouns are needlessly repeated in the first sentence. The second sentence uses pronouns in their place. *He* replaces *father*, *they* and *them* replace *children*, and *it* takes the place of *party*.

Of the many kinds of pronouns, the following cause the most difficulty because they include two ways of identifying the same person (or people), but only one form is correct in a given situation:

Subject Group	Object Group
I	me
he	him
she	her
we	us
they	them

Use a pronoun from the Subject Group in two instances:

1. Before a verb as a subject:

He is my cousin. (*He* is the subject of the verb *is*.)

He is taller than *I*. (The sentence is not written out in full. It means "*He* is taller than *I* am." *I* is the subject of the verb *am*.)

Whenever you see *than* in a sentence, ask yourself whether a verb has been left off the end of the sentence. Add the verb, and then you'll automatically use the correct pronoun. In both speaking and writing, always add the verb. Instead of saying, "She's smarter than (I, me)," say, "She's smarter than I *am*." Then you will use the correct pronoun.

2. After a linking verb (is, am, are, was, were) as a pronoun that renames the subject:

The one who should apologize is *he*. (*He* is *the one who should apologize.* Therefore, the pronoun from the Subject Group is used.)

The winner of the lottery was *she*. (*She* was *the winner of the lottery.* Therefore, the pronoun from the Subject Group is used.)

Modern usage allows some exceptions to this rule, however. For example, *It's me* or *It is her* (instead of the grammatically correct *It is I* and *It is she*) may be common in spoken English.

Use pronouns from the Object Group for all other purposes. In the following sentence, *me* is not the subject, nor does it rename the subject. It follows a preposition; therefore, it comes from the Object Group.

My boss went to lunch with Jenny and *me.*

A good way to tell whether to use a pronoun from the Subject Group or the Object Group is to leave out any extra name (and the word *and*). By leaving out *Jenny and,* you will say, *My boss went to lunch with me.* You would never say, *My boss went to lunch with I.*

My father and *I* play chess on Sundays. (*I* play chess on Sundays.)

She and her friends rented a video. (*She* rented a video.)

We saw Kevin and *them* last night. (We saw *them* last night.)

The teacher gave *us* students certificates. (Teacher gave *us* certificates.)

The coach asked Craig and *me* to wash the benches. (Coach asked *me* to wash the benches.)

Pronoun Agreement

Just as subjects and verbs must agree, pronouns should agree with the words they refer to. If the word referred to is singular, the pronoun should be singular. If the noun referred to is plural, the pronoun should be plural.

Each classroom has its own chalkboard.

The pronoun *its* refers to the singular noun *classroom* and therefore is singular.

Both classrooms have their own chalkboards.

The pronoun *their* refers to the plural noun *classrooms* and therefore is plural.

The same rules that we use to maintain the agreement of subjects and verbs also apply to pronoun agreement. For instance, ignore any prepositional phrases that come between the word and the pronoun that takes its place.

The *box* of chocolates has lost *its* label.

Boxes of chocolates often lose *their* labels.

A *player* with the best concentration usually beats *her or his* opponent.

Players with the best concentration usually beat *their* opponents.

When a pronoun refers to more than one word joined by *and*, the pronoun is plural:

> The *teacher* <u>and</u> the *tutors* eat *their* lunches at noon.
>
> The *salt* <u>and</u> *pepper* were in *their* usual spots on the table.

However, when a pronoun refers to more than one word joined by *or*, then the word closest to the pronoun determines its form:

> Either the teacher <u>or</u> the *tutors* eat their lunches in the classroom.
>
> Either the tutors <u>or</u> the *teacher* eats her lunch in the classroom.

Today many people try to avoid gender bias by writing sentences like the following:

> If anyone wants help with the assignment, he or she can visit me in my office.
>
> If anybody calls, tell him or her that I'll be back soon.
>
> Somebody has left his or her pager in the classroom.

But those sentences are wordy and awkward. Therefore some people, especially in conversation, turn them into sentences that are not grammatically correct.

> If anyone wants help with the assignment, they can visit me in my office.
>
> If anybody calls, tell them that I'll be back soon.
>
> Somebody has left their pager in the classroom.

Such ungrammatical sentences, however, are not necessary. It just takes a little thought to revise each sentence so that it avoids gender bias and is also grammatically correct:

> Anyone who wants help with the assignment can visit me in my office.
>
> Tell anybody who calls that I'll be back soon.
>
> Somebody has left a pager in the classroom.

Probably the best way to avoid the awkward *he or she* and *him or her* is to make the words plural. Instead of writing, "Each actor was in his or her proper place on stage," write, "All the actors were in their proper places on stage," thus avoiding gender bias and still having a grammatically correct sentence.

Pronoun Reference

A pronoun replaces a noun to avoid repetition, but sometimes the pronoun sounds as if it refers to the wrong word in a sentence, causing confusion. Be aware that when you write a sentence, *you* know what it means, but your reader may not. What does this sentence mean?

> The students tried to use the school's computers to access the Internet, but they were too slow, so they decided to go home.

Who or what was too slow, and who or what decided to go home? We don't know whether the two pronouns (both *they*) refer to the students or to the computers. One way to correct such a faulty reference is to use singular and plural nouns:

> The students tried to use a school computer to access the Internet, but it was too slow, so they decided to go home.

Here's another sentence with a faulty reference:

> Calvin told his father that he needed a haircut.

Who needed the haircut—Calvin or his father? One way to correct such a faulty reference is to use a direct quotation:

> Calvin told his father, "You need a haircut."
> Calvin said, "Dad, I need a haircut."

Or you could always rephrase the sentence completely:

> Calvin noticed his father's hair was sticking out in odd places, so he told his father to get a haircut.

Another kind of faulty reference is a *which* clause that appears to refer to a specific word, but it doesn't really.

> I wasn't able to finish all the problems on the exam, which makes me worried.

The word *which* seems to replace *exam,* but it isn't the exam that makes me worried. The sentence should read

> I am worried because I wasn't able to finish all the problems on the exam.

The pronoun *it* causes its own reference problems. Look at this sentence, for example:

> When replacing the ink cartridge in my printer, it broke, and I had to call the technician to come and fix it.

Did the printer or the cartridge break? Here is one possible correction:

> The new ink cartridge broke when I was putting it in my printer, and I had to call the technician for help.

E X E R C I S E S

Exercise 1

Underline the correct pronoun. Remember the trick of leaving out the extra name to help you decide which pronoun to use. Use the correct grammatical form even though an alternate form may be acceptable in conversation.

1. My sister and (I, me) went to a play last night.

2. I usually enjoy these trips to the theater more than (she, her).

3. This time, however, both (she and I, her and me) enjoyed it.

4. Since my sister is less of a reader than (I, me), she usually doesn't feel knowledgeable about theater.

5. Every time (she and I, her and me) have seen plays before, I have chosen what to see and where to sit.

6. The one who made the choices this time was (she, her).

7. She may not read as much as (I, me), but she sure picked a winner.

8. The cast seemed to be speaking directly to (she and I, her and me) in the front row, and the dialogue was moving and witty.

9. I guess I am still more of a theater-goer than (she, her), but I have learned to appreciate my sister's instincts.

10. In the future, I will leave the decisions of what to see and where to sit up to (she, her) and the box office.

Exercise 2

Underline the pronoun that agrees with the word the pronoun replaces. If the correct answer is *his or her/her or his*, revise the sentence to eliminate the need for this awkward expression. Check your answers as you go through the exercise.

1. The graduation ceremony was not without (its, their) problems.

2. Each of the dogs knows (its, their) trainer's commands.

3. Many of the older students had not rehearsed (his or her, their) speeches.

4. All of the prescription drugs have (its, their) own side effects.

5. Either the property owner or the tenants will win (her or his, their) case.

6. We like to hear our canary sing (its, their) beautiful song.

7. Everybody on the men's basketball team is doing well in (his, their) classes.

8. Everyone in the class sold (his or her, their) books back to the bookstore.

9. All of the participants at the convention left (her or his, their) business cards on a tray in the lounge.

10. Either the workers or the boss gets (his or her, their) way after a dispute.

Exercise 3

Underline the correct pronoun. Again, if the correct answer is *his or her/her or his*, revise the sentence to eliminate the need for this awkward expression.

1. The judge gave my fellow jurors and (I, me) very specific instructions.

2. (She and he, Her and him) are alike in many ways.

3. Marilyn Monroe was shorter than (I, me).

4. All of the children finished (his or her, their) projects before the open house.

5. Hotels and motels are not competitive in (its, their) pricing.

6. The one responsible for preparing the food was (I, me).

7. Each of the new teachers has (her or his, their) own set of books.

8. The mixed-doubles tennis teams will continue (his or her, their) tournament.

9. Everyone at the polling place had (her or his, their) own opinion and expressed it with (his or her, their) vote.

10. When it comes to plants, no one knows more than (he, him).

Exercise 4

Most—but not all—of the sentences in the next two sets aren't clear because we don't know what word the pronoun refers to. Revise such sentences, making the meaning clear. Since there are more ways than one to rewrite each sentence, yours may be as good as the ones at the back of the book. Just ask yourself whether the meaning is clear.

1. I finished printing my term paper, turned off my computer, and put it in my backpack.

2. Sandra told her mother that her car had a new dent in it.

3. They bought their textbooks early, which made them feel better.

4. Jeffrey's brother lets him take his new laptop to school.

5. When I put my shirt in the dryer, it shrunk.

6. The student told his counselor that he didn't understand him.

7. While we were counting the money from our garage sale, it blew away.

8. Our dog runs away all the time, which makes us angry.

9. Robert asked his friend why he wasn't invited to the party.

10. We shuffled the lottery tickets, and everybody chose one of them.

Exercise 5

1. The Hascoms planted some new bushes, but they were too short for them.

2. We sent him an arrangement of flowers, and it arrived the next day.

3. I signed the credit card slip, put my card back in my wallet, and handed it to the cashier.

4. When students work in groups, they get a lot of work done.

5. As he took the lenses out of the frames, they broke.

6. Whenever I put gas in my car, I get a headache from the smell of it.

7. Coupons help people save money on certain items that they buy.

8. Prospectors lived on the hope that they would find enough gold to make them rich.

9. Pearl's teacher asked her to copy her notes for another student.

10. Asked again to consider the rejected applications, the committee made its final decision.

PROOFREADING EXERCISE

The following paragraph contains errors in the use of pronouns. Find and correct the errors.

I told my friend Audrey a rumor at work the other day, and as soon as I did, I knew I would regret it. I forgot that Audrey is not as mature as me. Right before I told her the rumor, I said, "Now this is just between you and I, and you're not going to tell anyone, right?" She assured me that the only person she would talk to about it was me. I made the mistake of believing her. Later I saw she and another coworker laughing confidentially. The rumor was out, and I knew that the one responsible was me. Audrey and I are still coworkers, but her and I are no longer friends.

SENTENCE WRITING

Write ten sentences in which you describe similarities and/or differences between you and someone else. Then check that your pronouns are grammatically correct, that they agree with the words they replace, and that references to specific nouns are clear.

Avoiding Shifts in Person

To understand what "person" means when using pronouns, imagine a conversation between two people about a third person. The first person speaks using "I, me, my . . ."; the second person would be called "you"; and when the two of them talked of a third person, they would say "he, she, they . . . ." You'll never forget the idea of "person" if you remember it as a three-part conversation.

First person—*I, me, my, we, us, our*

Second person—*you, your*

Third person—*he, him, his, she, her, hers, they, them, their, one, anyone*

You may use all three of these groups of pronouns in a paper, but don't shift from one group to another without good reason.

Wrong: Few people know how to manage *their* time. *One* need not be an efficiency expert to realize that *one* could get a lot more done if *he* budgeted *his* time. Nor do *you* need to work very hard to get more organized.

Better: *Everyone* should know how to manage *his or her* time. *One* need not be an efficiency expert to realize that *a person* could get a lot more done if *one* budgeted *one's* time. Nor does *one* need to work very hard to get more organized. (Too many *one's* in a paragraph make it sound overly formal, and they lead to the necessity of avoiding sexism by using *s/he* or *he or she*, etc. Sentences can be revised to avoid using either *you* or *one*.)

Best: Many of *us* don't know how to manage *our* time. *We* need not be efficiency experts to realize that *we* could get a lot more done if *we* budgeted *our* time. Nor do *we* need to work very hard to get more organized.

Often students write *you* in a paper when they don't really mean *you, the reader.*

You wouldn't believe how many times I saw that movie.

Such sentences are always improved by getting rid of the *you.*

I saw that movie many times.

PROOFREADING EXERCISES

Which of the following student paragraphs shift *unnecessarily* between first-, second-, and third-person pronouns? In those that do, revise the sentences to eliminate such shifting, thus making the entire paragraph read smoothly. (First, read the paragraphs to determine whether unnecessary shifting takes place. One of the paragraphs is correct.)

1. We have all seen images of astronauts floating in their space capsules, eating food from little silver freeze-dried cube-shaped pouches, and sipping Tang out of special straws made to function in the weightlessness of space. Now you can buy that same food and eat it yourself on earth. NASA has gone online with a site called thespacestore.com, and all one has to do is point and click and get these space munchies delivered to your door. If people want NASA souvenirs, they can purchase them at the same site.

Source: Newsweek, July 16, 2001

2. People who drive need to be more aware of pedestrians. We can't always gauge what someone walking down the street will do. You might think that all pedestrians will keep walking forward in a crosswalk, but one might decide to turn back if he or she forgot something. You could run into him or her if that happens. A person's life could be affected in an instant. We all should slow down and be more considerate of others.

3. Scientists and others are working on several inventions that have not been perfected yet. Some of these developments seem like complete science fiction, but they're not. Each of them is in the process of becoming a real new technology. It's hard to imagine eating meat grown on plants. Scientists will feed the plants artificially made blood. Researchers are also working to produce animals (perhaps even humans) grown in artificial wombs. The most interesting development is selective amnesia (memory loss). Patients will be able to ask their doctors to erase painful memories as a mental-health tool. And, of course, computers will gain more and more personality traits to become more like human beings.

Source: The Futurist, August–September 1998

REVIEW OF SENTENCE STRUCTURE ERRORS

One sentence in each pair contains an error. Read both sentences carefully before you decide. Then write the letter of the *incorrect* sentence in the blank. Try to name the error and correct it if you can. You may find any of these errors:

awk	awkward phrasing
cliché	overused expression
dm	dangling modifier
frag	fragment
mm	misplaced modifier
pro	incorrect pronoun
pro agr	pronoun agreement error
pro ref	pronoun reference error
ro	run-on sentence
shift	shift in time or person
s/v agr	subject/verb agreement error
wordy	wordiness
//	not parallel

1. _____ A. I like crunchy peanut butter best.

   B. It is much more delicious in taste than the smooth peanut butter is.

2. _____ A. Writing essays is like pulling teeth for me.

   B. I plan to take a vocabulary class next semester.

3. _____ A. I've tried taking the bus to school and riding my bike.

   B. I like riding my bike because you don't have to wait around for it to pick you up.

4. _____ A. My friend and I visited the job fair at school.

   B. A recruiter for a delivery company gave my friend and I an application.

5. _____ A. This essay is the best I've ever written.

   B. It is interesting and full of details I cannot understand why I need to rewrite it.

6. _____ **A.** Everyone in the class had an amazed look on their faces.

   B. The teacher informed us that we all did well on the midterm.

7. _____ **A.** I want to finish my general education requirements early.

   B. I am taking four classes this semester I should have taken only three.

8. _____ **A.** I always plan my vacations so that they are relaxing, rejuvenating, and they must be fun too.

   B. The flowers arrived as buds and blossomed into roses.

9. _____ **A.** Our cat had kittens in the bottom drawer of my dresser.

   B. Each of the kittens are the same size.

10. _____ **A.** You have helped me in more ways than one; you're a real lifesaver.

    B. If I can ever help you, please ask.

11. _____ **A.** One of the puzzles is incomplete.

    B. One of its pieces are missing, so it can't be sold.

12. _____ **A.** Since our train was late due to the snowy weather.

    B. There were no rooms available when we finally arrived at the hotel.

13. _____ **A.** A flock of birds fly around those treetops every morning.

    B. Their squawking noises wake up the whole neighborhood.

14. _____ **A.** Some people simply hate to lose.

    B. Contestants must understand that you can't always win.

15. _____ **A.** Keeping his eyes tightly closed, the doctor gave the little boy his vaccination.

    B. After crying for a minute or two, he felt fine.

PROOFREADING EXERCISE

Can you find and correct the sentence structure errors in the following essay?

Let's Get Technical

In my child development classes, I'm learning about ways to keep girls interested in technology. Studies shows that girls and boys begin their school years equally interested in technology. After elementary school is the time that computers are less of an interest for girls. Because boys keep up with computers and other technology throughout their educations more than girls, they get ahead in these fields. Experts have come up with some suggestions for teachers and parents of girls to help them.

Girls need opportunities to experiment with computers. Girls spend time on computers, but they usually just do their assignments then they log off. Since computer games and programs are often aimed at boys. Parents and teachers need to buy computer products that will challenge girls not only in literature and art, but also in math, science, and business is important.

Another suggestion is to put computers in places where girls can socialize. One reason many boys stay interested in technology is that it is something he can do on his own. Girls tend to be more interested in working with others and to share activities. When computer terminals are placed close to one another, girls work at them for much longer periods of time.

Finally, parents and teachers need to be aware that nothing beats positive role models. Teach them about successful women in the fields of business, scientific, and technology. And the earlier we start interesting girls in these fields, the better.

Source: Technology & Learning, October 1998

PART 3

Punctuation and Capital Letters

Period, Question Mark, Exclamation Point, Semicolon, Colon, Dash

Every mark of punctuation should help the reader. Here are the rules for six marks of punctuation. The first three you have known for a long time and probably have no trouble with. The one about semicolons you learned when you studied independent clauses (p. 87). The ones about the colon and the dash may be less familiar.

Put a period (.) at the end of a sentence and after most abbreviations.

> The students elected Ms. Daniels to represent the class.
>
> Sept.   Mon.   in.   sq.   ft.   lbs.

Put a question mark (?) after a direct question but not after an indirect one.

> Will we be able to use our notes during the test? (direct)
>
> I wonder if we will be able to use our notes during the test. (indirect)

Put an exclamation point (!) after an expression that shows strong emotion. This mark is used mostly in dialogue or informal correspondence.

> I can't believe I did so well on my first exam!

Put a semicolon (;) between two independent clauses in a sentence unless they are joined by one of the connecting words *for, and, nor, but, or, yet, so.*

My mother cosigned for a loan; now I have my own car.

Some careers go in and out of fashion; however, people will always need teachers.

To be sure that you are using a semicolon correctly, see if a period and capital letter can be used in its place. If they can, you are putting the semicolon in the right spot.

My mother cosigned for a loan. Now I have my own car.

Some careers go in and out of fashion. However, people will always need teachers.

Put a colon (:) after a complete statement that introduces one of the following elements: a name, a list, a quotation, or an explanation.

The company announced its Employee-of-the-Month: Lee Jones. (The sentence before the colon introduces the name that follows it.)

That truck comes in the following colors: red, black, blue, and silver. (The complete statement before the colon introduces the list that follows it.)

That truck comes in red, black, blue, and silver. (Here the list is simply part of the sentence. There is no complete statement used to introduce the list and set it off from the rest of the sentence.)

Thoreau had this to say about time: "Time is but the stream I go a-fishin in." (The writer introduces the quotation with a complete statement. Therefore, a colon comes between them.)

Thoreau said, "Time is but the stream I go a-fishin in." (Here the writer leads directly into the quotation; therefore, no colon—just a comma—comes between them.)

Use dashes (—) to isolate inserted information, to signal an abrupt change of thought, or to emphasize what follows.

Lee Jones—March's Employee-of-the-Month—received his own special parking space.

I found out today—or was it yesterday?—that I have inherited a fortune.

We have exciting news for you—we're moving!

E X E R C I S E S

Add to these sentences the necessary punctuation (periods, question marks, exclamation points, semicolons, colons, and dashes). The commas used within the sentences are correct and do not need to be changed.

Exercise 1

1. My friend Kristine and I arrived early for work yesterday it was a very important day

2. We had worked late the night before perfecting our presentation

3. The boss had given us an opportunity to train our colleagues in the use of a new computer program

4. I wondered how the other workers would react when they heard that we had been chosen to teach them

5. Would they be pleased or annoyed

6. Kristine and I worked hard on the visual aid to accompany our workshop a slide show of sample screens from the program

7. Kristine thought our workshop should end with a test however, I didn't think that was a good idea

8. I knew that our fellow employees at least *some* of them would not want us to test them

9. By the time we ended our presentation, we both realized that I had been right

10. Now our co-workers see us as a couple of experts not a couple of know-it-alls

Exercise 2

1. Have you ever heard of Vinnie Ream

2. This young woman a very controversial figure in Washington, D.C. began her career as a sculptor in 1863 at the age of sixteen

3. Miss Ream was a student of the famous sculptor Clark Mills he is perhaps best-known for his statue of Andrew Jackson located across from the White House

4. Vinnie Ream started to work with Mills in his studio in the basement of the Capitol building soon members of Congress were volunteering to sit for Miss Ream, and she sculpted busts of them

5. Her fame and notoriety grew in the late 1860s that's when she was awarded a ten-thousand-dollar commission to create a life-size statue of Abraham Lincoln

6. Vinnie Ream had known Lincoln in fact, before his assassination, President Lincoln would allow Miss Ream to sit in his office within the White House and work on a bust of him as he carried out the business of running the country

7. Ream's intimate observation of Lincoln at work affected her design of Lincoln's posture and facial expression for her statue of him

8. Vinnie Ream's relationships and the works she produced were not accepted by everyone Ream's youth and physical beauty led to much of this harsh criticism

9. Some people questioned her motives others even questioned her abilities

10. Ream prospered in spite of the jealous accusations of others and often demonstrated her sculpting abilities in public to prove that she did her own work

Source: Smithsonian, August 2000

Exercise 3

1. Ralph Waldo Emerson gave us this famous bit of advice "Build a better mousetrap, and the world will beat a path to your door"

2. People have not stopped inventing mousetraps in fact, there are more U.S. patents for mousetraps than for any device over four thousand of them

3. Some are simple some are complicated, and some are just weird

4. Nearly fifty new patents for machines to kill mice are awarded every year perhaps thanks to Mr Emerson's advice

5. The most enduring mousetrap was designed by John Mast it is the one most of us picture when we think of a mousetrap a piece of wood with a spring-loaded bar that snaps down on the mouse just as it takes the bait

6. John Mast's creation received Patent #744,379 in 1903 since then no other patented mousetrap has done a better job

7. There is a long list of technologies that other inventions have used to trap mice electricity, sonar, lasers, super glues, etc

8. One patented mousetrap was built in the shape of a multilevel house with several stairways however, its elaborate design made it impractical and expensive

9. In 1878, one person invented a mousetrap for travelers it was a box that was supposed to hold men's removable collars and at night catch mice, but it was not a success

10. Who would want to put an article of clothing back into a box used to trap a mouse

Source: American Heritage, October 1996

Exercise 4

1. People in Australia have been asking themselves a question why are some dolphins carrying big sponges around on their heads

2. First it was just one dolphin now several dolphins are doing it

3. Marine biologists all over the world have been trying to understand this unusual sponge-carrying behavior

4. They wonder about whether the sponges decrease the dolphins' ability to maneuver under water

5. If they do, then why would the dolphins sacrifice this ability

6. The dolphins might be using the sponges for a very important reason to help them find food

7. Some scientists think that the sponges may protect the dolphins' beaks in some way

8. The sponges might indicate position in the social order that's another explanation

9. Or the dolphins could be imitating each other a kind of dolphin "fad," in other words

10. Only one group of experts knows whether these sponges are hunting tools or just fashion statements that is the dolphins themselves

Source: Discover, March 1998

Exercise 5

1. I just read an article that connected two things that I would never have thought went together the Old West, with its miners and saloon life, and Shakespeare, with his poetry and politics

2. People who had traveled out West on the Oregon Trail brought their Shakespeare books and shared them with a willing audience the unruly population of the mining camps and tiny towns of the West

3. Mountain men like Jim Bridger paid others who could read to act out Shakespeare's plays then he memorized the speeches and performed them for others

4. Theaters staged productions of the tragedies of *Hamlet, Othello,* and *Romeo and Juliet* to the delight of the Western crowds however, if they weren't pleased with an actor, theatergoers threw vegetables as large as pumpkins at times to get the actor off the stage

5. Crowds likewise rewarded good acting, which was lively and not overly refined spectators in gold mining camps threw nuggets and bags of gold on stage if they liked a performance

6. Oral storytelling had always been popular in the West therefore, people of the time embraced Shakespeare's language without thinking of it as intellectual or sophisticated

7. In the mid-1800s, people across the country had strong opinions about how Shakespeare should be performed there was a riot at one New York City theater concerning a particularly snobby performance of *Macbeth*

8. The fight moved from the theater into the streets more than twenty people were killed, and a hundred were injured

9. The casting of characters in Western performances included everything from all-male casts in the mining camps to a female Juliet performing without a real Romeo a stuffed dummy played his part

10. There was even a little girl named Anna Maria Quinn just six years old who played Hamlet at the Metropolitan Theatre in San Francisco in 1854

Source: Smithsonian, August 1998

PROOFREADING EXERCISE

Can you find the punctuation errors in this student paragraph? They will all involve periods, question marks, exclamation points, semicolons, colons, and dashes. Any commas used within the sentences are correct and should not be changed.

I wonder why the swimming pool on campus doesn't have a covered area for spectators? I'm certain—that the pool area is—an uncomfortable place for people to be unless they're in the pool. I have friends on the swim team therefore, I know what I'm talking about! Those of us who watch the swim team at practice or competitions have to squint, wear loads of sunblock, and drink gallons of water just to cope with the heat and glare. Why doesn't the school install a canopy over the spectator benches. I have even considered taking up a collection from the other pool visitors, buying a canopy, and installing it myself.

SENTENCE WRITING

Write ten sentences of your own that use periods, question marks, exclamation points, semicolons, colons, and dashes correctly. Imitate the examples used in the explanations if necessary. Write about a policy in class, at school, or at work that you don't agree with, and explain how it should be changed.

Comma Rules 1, 2, and 3

Commas and other pieces of punctuation guide the reader through your sentence structures in the same way that signs guide drivers on the highway. Imagine what effects misplaced or incorrect road signs would have. Yet students often randomly place commas in their sentences. Try not to use a comma unless you know there is a need for it. Memorize this rhyme about comma use: *When in doubt, leave it out.*

Among all of the comma rules, six are most important. Learn these six rules, and your writing will be easier to read. You have already studied the first rule on pages 87–94.

1. **Put a comma before *for*, *and*, *nor*, *but*, *or*, *yet*, *so* (remember these seven words as the *fanboys*) when they connect two independent clauses.**

   The neighbors recently bought a minivan, and now they take short trips every weekend.

   We wrote our paragraphs in class today, but the teacher forgot to collect them.

   She was recently promoted, so she has moved to a better office.

If you use a comma alone between two independent clauses, the result is an error called a ***comma splice.***

   The cake looked delicious, it tasted good too. (comma splice)

   The cake looked delicious, and it tasted good too. (correct)

Before using a comma, be sure such words do connect two independent clauses. The following sentence is merely one independent clause with one subject and two verbs. Therefore, no comma should be used.

> The ice cream looked delicious and tasted good too.

2. Use a comma to separate three or more items in a series.

> Students in literature classes are reading short stories, poems, and plays.
>
> Today I did my laundry, washed my car, and cleaned my room.

Occasionally, writers leave out the comma before the *and* connecting the last two items in a series, but it is more common to use it to separate all of the items equally. Some words work together and don't need commas between them even though they do make up a kind of series.

> The team members wanted to wear their brand new green uniforms.
>
> The bright white sunlight made the room glow.

To see whether a comma is needed between words in a series, ask yourself whether *and* could be used naturally between them. It would sound all right to say *short stories and poems and plays;* therefore, commas are used. But it would not sound right to say *brand and new and green uniforms* or *bright and white sunlight;* therefore, no commas are used.

If an address or date is used in a sentence, put a comma after every item, including the last.

> My father was born on August 19, 1941, in Mesa, Arizona, and grew up there.
>
> Shelby lived in St. Louis, Missouri, for two years.

When only the month and year are used in a date, no commas are needed.

> My aunt graduated from Yale in May 1985.

3. Put a comma after an introductory expression (a word, a phrase, or a dependent clause) or before a comment or question tagged onto the end.

> Finally, he was able to get through to his insurance company.
>
> During her last performance, the actress fell and broke her foot.
>
> Once I have finished my homework, I will call you.
>
> He said he needed to ruminate, whatever that means.
>
> The new chairs aren't very comfortable, are they?

E X E R C I S E S

Add commas to the following sentences according to the first three comma rules. Some sentences may not need any commas, and some may need more than one. Any other punctuation already in the sentences is correct. Check your answers after the first set.

Exercise 1

1. I've been reading Helen Keller's book *The Story of My Life* and I have learned a lot more about her.
2. I originally thought that Keller was born deaf and blind but I was wrong.
3. When she was just under two years old Keller became ill with a terrible fever.
4. The family doctor believed that Keller was dying and prepared her family for the worst.
5. Not long after the doctor shared his fears with her family Keller recovered from her fever.
6. Unfortunately this sudden illness left Keller without the ability to see to hear or to speak.
7. The only tools that Keller had left were her sense of touch her active mind and her own curiosity.
8. With her teacher Anne Sullivan's constant assistance Keller eventually learned to read to write and to speak.
9. Keller was lucky to have so many people who loved and cared for her.
10. In my opinion Helen Keller was an amazing person and her story inspires me to do my best.

Exercise 2

1. Throughout human history people have imagined designed and patented a lot of silly contraptions.

2. I've just read about two of the silliest: one of them is a self-cooling rocking chair and the other is a locket to hold a person's used chewing gum.

3. The "Air-Cooled Rocking-Chair" was patented on July 6 1869 and the person sitting in the chair is the one who cools it.

4. Beneath the seat of the chair the designer installed a bellows like those used to blow air into a fireplace.

5. Along the back of the chair the patent calls for a flexible tube to rise above the sitting person's head.

6. As the person rocks on the seat the bellows sends blasts of air through the tube and over his head.

7. I don't think that I would like that do you?

8. The "Chewing-Gum Preserver" was patented on January 1 1889 to allow the gum chewer to carry used chewing gum in a safe sanitary and responsible way.

9. In the drawing that accompanies the description of this invention it looks a lot like a pocket watch.

10. The chewing-gum locket could be worn on a chain or it could be carried in a pocket.

Source: Absolutely Mad Inventions (Dover, 1970)

Exercise 3

1. Whenever I ask my friend Karen a computer-related question I end up regretting it.

2. Once she gets started Karen is unable to stop talking about computers.

3. When I needed her help the last time my printer wasn't working.

4. Instead of just solving the problem Karen went on and on about print settings and font choices that I could be using.

5. When she gets like this her face lights up and I feel bad for not wanting to hear the latest news on software upgrades e-mail programs and hardware improvements.

6. I feel guilty but I know that I am the normal one.

7. I even pointed her problem out to her by asking, "You can't control yourself can you?"

8. She just grinned and kept trying to fix my printer.

9. Karen always solves my problem so I should be grateful.

10. When I ask for Karen's help in the future I plan to listen and try to learn something.

Exercise 4

1. Scientists have been studying the human face and they have been able to identify five thousand distinct facial expressions.

2. Researchers at the University of California in San Francisco have identified and numbered every action of the human face.

3. Winking is action number forty-six and we do it with the facial muscle that surrounds the eye.

4. People around the world make the same basic expressions when they are happy surprised sad disgusted afraid or angry.

5. These six categories of facial expressions are universally understood but different societies have different rules about showing their emotions.

6. The smile is one of the most powerful expressions for it changes the way we feel.

7. If we give someone a real smile showing genuine happiness then our brains react by producing a feeling of pleasure.

8. If we give more of a polite imitation smile then our brains show no change.

9. Even babies have been shown to smile one way for strangers and another way for their mothers.

10. A smile also wins the long-distance record for facial expressions for it can be seen from as far away as several hundred feet.

Source: Psychology Today, October 1998

Exercise 5

1. Gold is amazing isn't it?

2. Unlike metals that change their appearance after contact with water oil and other substances gold maintains its shine and brilliant color under almost any circumstances.

3. When a miner named James Marshall found gold in the dark soil of California in 1848 the gold rush began.

4. The piece of gold that Marshall discovered was only about the size of a child's fingernail but it meant that there was more to be found.

5. Before the gold rush San Francisco was a small town called Yerba Buena.

6. The town underwent a name change and gained thousands of citizens in search of gold.

7. Gold is actually present all over the world but the biggest nugget to be found so far came from a location on the Potomac River.

8. This chunk of gold is as big as a yam and it is on display at the National Museum of Natural History.

9. Some people have become rich directly because of gold and some have become rich indirectly because of gold.

10. For example if it had not been for California's gold rush Levi Strauss would not have had any customers and the world would not have blue jeans.

Source: Smithsonian, July 1998

PROOFREADING EXERCISE

Apply the first three comma rules to the following paragraph:

When you belong to a large family holidays are a mixed blessing. They are certainly times to see one another but how do you choose where to go and whom to see? For example I have four sets of relatives living in different areas and they all want to get together for Thanksgiving. If I accept one group's invitation I disappoint the others. If I turn them all down and stay home with my immediate family I make all of my other relatives mad. I guess I will just have to invite the whole clan to spend Thanksgiving at my house won't I?

SENTENCE WRITING

Combine the following sets of sentences in different ways using all of the first three comma rules. You may need to reorder the details and change the phrasing.

I drive to school alone everyday.
I would consider carpooling.

My car alarm goes off.
I don't even look out the window anymore.

Melanie and Kurt are currently software developers.
They used to be dancers.
Now they both want to get back in shape.

My birthday is the on the fifth of May.
My wedding anniversary is on the fifth of May.
I have a special fondness for the fifth of May
I graduated from college on the fifth of May.

Comma Rules 4, 5, and 6

The next three comma rules all involve using pairs of commas to enclose what we like to call "scoopable" elements. Scoopable elements are certain words, phrases, and clauses that can be taken out of the middle of a sentence without affecting its meaning. Notice that the comma (**,**) is shaped somewhat like the tip of an ice cream scoop? Let this similarity help you remember to use commas to enclose *scoopable* elements. Two commas are used, one before and one after, to show where scoopable elements begin and where they end.

4. Put commas around the name of a person spoken to.

> Did you know, Danielle, that you left your backpack at the library?
>
> We regret to inform you, Mr. Davis, that your policy has been canceled.

5. Put commas around expressions that interrupt the flow of the sentence (such as *however, moreover, therefore, of course, by the way, on the other hand, I believe, I think*).

> I know, of course, that I have missed the deadline.
>
> They will try, therefore, to use the rest of their time wisely.
>
> Today's exam, I think, was only a practice test.

Read the previous examples *aloud*, and you'll hear how these expressions surrounded by commas interrupt the flow of the sentence. Sometimes such expressions flow smoothly into the sentence and don't need commas around them.

> Of course he checked to see if there were any rooms available.
>
> We therefore decided to stay out of it.
>
> I think you made the right decision.

Remember that when a word like *however* comes between two independent clauses, that word needs a semicolon before it. It may also have a comma after it, especially if there seems to be a pause between the word and the rest of the sentence. (See p. 87.)

> The bus was late; *however,* we still made it to the museum before it closed.
>
> I am improving my study habits; *furthermore,* I am getting better grades.
>
> She was interested in journalism; *therefore,* she took a job at a local newspaper.
>
> I spent hours studying for the test; *finally,* I felt prepared.

Thus, you've seen a word like *however* or *therefore* used in three ways:

1. as a "scoopable" word that interrupts the flow of the sentence (needs commas around it)

2. as a word that flows into the sentence (no commas needed)

3. as a connecting word between two independent clauses (semicolon before and often a comma after)

   6. Put commas around additional information that is not needed in a sentence.

Certain additional information is "scoopable" and should be surrounded by commas whenever the meaning would be clear without it. Look at the following sentence:

> Maxine Taylor, who organized the fund-raiser, will introduce the candidates.

The clause *who organized the fund-raiser* is not needed in the sentence. Without it, we still know exactly who the sentence is about and what she is going to do: "Maxine Taylor will introduce the candidates." Therefore, the additional information is surrounded by commas to show that it is scoopable. Now read the following sentence:

> The woman who organized the fund-raiser will introduce the candidates.

The clause *who organized the fund-raiser* is necessary in this sentence. Without it, the sentence would read as follows: "The woman will introduce the candidates." The reader would have no idea *which woman*. The clause *who organized the fund-raiser* cannot be left out because it identifies which woman. Therefore, the clause is not scoopable, and no commas are used around it. Here is another sample sentence:

> *Hamlet*, Shakespeare's famous play, has been made into a movie many times.

The additional information *Shakespeare's famous play* is scoopable. It could be left out, and we would still understand the meaning of the sentence: "*Hamlet* has been made into a movie many times." Therefore, the commas surround the scoopable information to show that it could be taken out. Here is the same sentence with the information reversed:

> Shakespeare's famous play *Hamlet* has been made into a movie many times.

Here the title of the play is necessary. Without it, the sentence would read as follows: "Shakespeare's famous play has been made into a movie many times." The reader would have no idea which of Shakespeare's famous plays has been made into a movie many times. Therefore, the title is not scoopable, and commas should not be used around it.

The trick in deciding whether additional information is scoopable or not is to remember, "If I can scoop it out and still understand the sentence, I'll put commas around it."

EXERCISES

Surround any "scoopable" elements with commas according to Comma Rules 4, 5, and 6. Any commas already in the sentences follow Comma Rules 1, 2, and 3. Some sentences may be correct. Check your answers after the first set.

Exercise 1

1. People who own cats know that these pets often bring their owners unwelcome surprises.

2. Cats bring dead mice or birds to their owners and expect them to be pleased.

3. Cats become confused when their owners react angrily not happily to these "presents."

4. Desmond Morris renowned animal expert explains this misunderstood behavior in his book *Catwatching*.

5. Morris explains that the cats who most frequently bring prey to their owners are female cats without kittens.

6. These cats have a strong instinct to teach their kittens how to hunt for food.

7. In the absence of kittens, these cats treat their owners as the next best thing kitten replacements.

8. The first step in the process of teaching "kittens" how to hunt and the one cat owners hate most is sharing the results of the hunt with them.

9. The owners' reaction which usually involves yelling and disappointment should include praise and lots of petting.

10. Cat owners who do understand their pets will be flattered next time they see what the cat dragged in.

Exercise 2

1. Paula who left at intermission missed the best part of the play.

2. Anyone who left at intermission missed the best part of the play.

3. Our teacher posted the results of the test that we took last week.

4. Our teacher posted the results of the midterm which we took last week.

5. The math teacher Mr. Simon looks a lot like the English teacher Mr. Simon.

6. Mr. Simon the math teacher looks a lot like Mr. Simon the English teacher.

7. My clothes dryer which has an automatic shut-off switch is safer than yours which doesn't.

8. An appliance that has an automatic shut-off switch is safer to use than one that doesn't.

9. Students who ask a lot of questions usually do well on their exams.

10. John and Brenda who ask a lot of questions usually do well on their exams.

Exercise 3

1. This year's photo directory I believe turned out a little better than last year's.

2. I believe this year's photo directory turned out a little better than last year's.

3. There were I think still a few problems.

4. I think there were still a few problems.

5. The employee whose picture is at the top of our page is my supervisor, but he's not listed at the bottom.

6. My supervisor whose picture is at the top of our page is wearing his name tag, but he's not listed at the bottom.

7. Ms. Tracy the photographer who took the pictures needed to help people with their poses.

8. The photographer who took the pictures needed to help people with their poses.

9. And no one it seems had time to look in a mirror.

10. And it seems that no one had time to look in a mirror.

Exercise 4

1. We hope of course that people will continue to vote in elections.

2. Of course we hope that people will continue to vote in elections.

3. The people who usually volunteer their house as a polling place may have to install new equipment.

4. The Fosters who usually volunteer their house as a polling place may have to install new equipment.

5. They may therefore decide not to participate in upcoming elections.

6. Therefore they may decide not to participate in upcoming elections.

7. The voting booth a small cubicle where each person casts a vote will probably become more high-tech.

8. The small cubicle where each person casts a vote will probably become more high-tech.

9. We trust that no one will attempt to influence our thoughts there.

10. No one we trust will attempt to influence our thoughts there.

Exercise 5

1. Jim Henson who created the Muppets began his television career in the mid-1950s.

2. He was it seems eager to be on TV, and there was an opening for some-one who worked with puppets.

3. Henson and a buddy of his quickly fabricated a few puppets including one called Pierre the French Rat, and they got the job.

4. Henson's next project *Sam and Friends* also starred puppets.

5. *Sam and Friends* was a live broadcast lasting only five minutes; however it was on two times a day and ran for six years.

6. Kermit the Frog the character which we now associate with *Sesame Street* was part of the cast of *Sam and Friends*.

7. Henson provided the voice and animated the movements of Kermit and a few others from the beginning, and he worked with Frank Oz who helped round out the cast of Muppet characters.

8. In 1969, the Muppets moved to *Sesame Street*; however they graduated to their own prime-time program *The Muppet Show* in the late 1970s.

9. At the high point of its popularity worldwide, more than 200 million people adults and children tuned in to a single broadcast of *The Muppet Show*.

10. Jim Henson continued as a highly creative force in television until his death from a sudden and severe case of pneumonia in 1990.

Source: Time, June 8, 1998

PROOFREADING EXERCISE

Surround any "scoopable" elements in the following paragraph with commas according to Comma Rules 4, 5, and 6.

Two types of punctuation internal punctuation and end punctuation can be used in writing. Internal punctuation is used within the sentence, and end punctuation is used at the end of a sentence. Commas the most important pieces of internal punctuation are used to separate or enclose information within sentences. Semicolons the next most important also have two main functions. Their primary function separating two independent clauses is also the most widely known. A lesser-known need for semicolons to separate items in a list already containing commas occurs rarely in college writing. Colons and dashes likewise have special uses within sentences. And of the three pieces of end punctuation—periods, question marks, and exclamation points—the period which signals the end of the majority of English sentences is obviously the most common.

SENTENCE WRITING

Combine the following sets of sentences in different ways according to Comma Rules 4, 5, and 6. Try to combine each set in a way that needs commas and in a way that doesn't need commas. In other words, try to make an element "scoopable" in one sentence and not "scoopable" in another. You may reorder the details and change the phrasing as you wish. Sample responses are provided in the Answers section.

Mrs. Miniver is a great old movie.
I have seen it several times.

I think.
You could make more money at a different job.

My friend Carla never takes notes.
She gets the highest grades in the class.
She is a natural born writer.

Review of the Comma

Six Comma Rules

1. Put a comma before *for, and, nor, but, or, yet, so* when they connect two independent clauses.

2. Put a comma between three or more items in a series.

3. Put a comma after an introductory expression or before a tag comment or question.

4. Put commas around the name of a person spoken to.

5. Put commas around words like *however* or *therefore* when they interrupt a sentence.

6. Put commas around unnecessary additional ("scoopable") information.

COMMA REVIEW EXERCISE

Add the missing commas, and identify which one of the six comma rules applies in the brackets at the *end* of each sentence. Each of the six sentences illustrates a different rule.

I am writing you this note Irene to ask you to do me a favor. [   ] When you get home from work tonight would you take the ham out of the freezer? [   ] I plan to get started on the beans the cole slaw and the potato salad as soon as I walk in the door after work. [   ] I will be so busy however that I might forget to thaw out the ham. [   ] It's the first time I've cooked all the food for the picnic by myself and I want everything to be perfect. [   ] The big enamel roasting pan which is in the back of the cupboard under the sink will be the best place to keep the ham as it thaws. [   ]

Thanks for your help.

SENTENCE WRITING

Write at least one sentence of your own to demonstrate each of the six comma rules.

Quotation Marks and Underlining/*Italics*

Put quotation marks around a direct quotation (the exact words of a speaker) but not around an indirect quotation.

> The officer said, "Please show me your driver's license." (a direct quotation)
>
> The officer asked to see my driver's license. (an indirect quotation)

If the speaker says more than one sentence, quotation marks are used before and after the entire speech.

> She said, "One of your brake lights is out. You need to take care of the problem right away."

If the quotation begins the sentence, the words telling who is speaking are set off with a comma unless the quotation ends with a question mark or an exclamation point.

> "I didn't even know it was broken," I said.
>
> "Do you have any questions?" she asked.
>
> "You mean I can go!" I shouted.
>
> "Yes, consider this just a warning," she said.

Notice that each of the previous quotations begins with a capital letter. But when a quotation is interrupted by an identifying phrase, the second part doesn't begin with a capital letter unless the second part is a new sentence.

> "If you knew how much time I spent on the essay," the student said, "you would give me an A."

> "A chef might work on a meal for days," the teacher replied. "That doesn't mean the results will taste good."

Put quotation marks around the titles of short stories, poems, songs, essays, TV program episodes, or other short works.

> I couldn't sleep after I read "The Lottery," a short story by Shirley Jackson.

> My favorite Woodie Guthrie song is "This Land Is Your Land."

> We had to read George Orwell's essay "A Hanging" for my speech class.

> Jerry Seinfeld's troubles in "The Puffy Shirt" episode are some of the funniest moments in TV history.

Underline titles of longer works such as books, newspapers, magazines, plays, record albums or CDs, movies, or the titles of TV or radio series.

> The Color Purple is a novel by Alice Walker.

> I read about the latest discovery of dinosaur footprints in Newsweek.

> Gone with the Wind was re-released in movie theaters in 1998.

> My mother listens to The Writer's Almanac on the radio every morning.

You may choose to *italicize* instead of underlining if your word processor gives you the option. Just be consistent throughout any paper in which you use underlining or italics.

> *The Color Purple* is a novel by Alice Walker.

> I read about the latest discovery of dinosaur footprints in *Newsweek.*

> *Gone with the Wind* was re-released in movie theaters in 1998.

> My mother listens to *The Writer's Almanac* on the radio every morning.

E X E R C I S E S

Correctly punctuate quotations and titles in the following sentences by adding quotation marks or underlining (*italics*).

Exercise 1

1. The Brady Bunch is still a popular television series.

2. The greater part of our happiness or misery depends on our dispositions, said Martha Washington, not on our circumstances.

3. Do I have to do all of the housework by myself? my roommate asked.

4. Last night we watched the movie Wag the Dog on DVD.

5. Oscar Wilde wrote the play The Importance of Being Earnest, the novel The Picture of Dorian Gray, the poem The Ballad of Reading Gaol, and the children's story The Selfish Giant.

6. No one can make you feel inferior without your consent, Eleanor Roosevelt once said.

7. The class period can't be over! said the student, I haven't even started my concluding paragraph yet.

8. I ran into my cousin in the library reading the latest issue of Smithsonian magazine.

9. We were asked to read Amy Tan's essay Fish Cheeks as homework for Wednesday's class.

10. The movie version of The Joy Luck Club was just as sad as the book.

Exercise 2

1. The Raven is a poem by Edgar Allan Poe.

2. Once you complete your test, the teacher said, please bring it up to my desk.

3. I have a subscription to several magazines, including The New Yorker.

4. Everything exists in limited quantities, Pablo Picasso perceived, even happiness.

5. How many times, she asked, are you going to mention the price we paid for dinner?

6. After Babe Ruth's death, his wife remarked, I don't even have an auto-graphed ball. You don't ask your husband for an autographed ball. He'd probably think you were nuts.

7. Sophocles, the Greek playwright, wrote the tragedy Oedipus Rex in the fifth century BC.

8. When you go by on a train, everything looks beautiful. But if you stop, Edward Hopper explained, it becomes drab.

9. There is a Mexican proverb that says, Whoever sells land sells his mother.

10. When Fiorello La Guardia, who was just over five feet tall, was asked what it felt like to be short, he answered, Like a dime among pennies.

Exercise 3

1. In his book Catwatching, Desmond Morris has this to say about their preferences: Cats hate doors.

2. Phil Hartman was the voice of Troy McClure and many other memo-rable characters on the animated TV series The Simpsons.

3. Hold fast to your dreams, wrote Langston Hughes, for if dreams die, then life is like a broken winged bird that cannot fly.

4. Langston Hughes wrote of his childhood in a short narrative entitled Salvation; it is part of his larger autobiography The Big Sea.

5. Joan Didion describes her relationship with migraine headaches in her essay In Bed.

6. Where can I buy some poster board? he asked.

7. There is a school-supply store around the corner, his friend replied, but I don't think that it's open this late.

8. Sylvia asked the other students if they had seen the Alfred Hitchcock movie called The Birds.

9. I don't remember, James answered.

10. It's not something you could ever forget! she yelled.

Exercise 4

1. Kurt Vonnegut, in his short story Harrison Bergeron, describes his main character's appearance as Halloween and hardware.

2. Now he belongs to the ages! cried Edwin M. Stanton after Abraham Lincoln's assassination.

3. In her book The Mysterious Affair at Styles, Agatha Christie wrote that Every murderer is probably somebody's old friend.

4. Swear not by the moon, says Juliet to Romeo.

5. John F. Kennedy told the U.S. Congress, The human mind is our fundamental resource.

6. Abraham Lincoln stated that Public opinion in this country is everything.

7. Writers are always selling somebody out, Joan Didion observed.

8. The expression All animals are equal, but some animals are more equal than others can be found in George Orwell's novel Animal Farm.

9. A Swahili proverb warns that To the person who seizes two things, one always slips from his grasp!

10. Groucho Marx once remarked, I wouldn't want to belong to any club that would accept me as a member.

Exercise 5

1. Ovid reminded us that We can learn even from our enemies.

2. We know what a person thinks not when he tells us what he thinks, said Isaac Bashevis Singer, but by his actions.

3. The Spanish proverb El pez muere por la boca translated means The fish dies because it opens its mouth.

4. Ask yourself whether you are happy, and you cease to be so, John Stuart Mill wrote.

5. A Russian proverb states, Without a shepherd, sheep are not a flock.

6. William Faulkner felt that Some things you must always be unable to bear.

7. St. Jerome had the following insight: The friendship that can cease has never been real.

8. Oscar Wilde found that In this world there are only two tragedies. One is not getting what one wants, and the other is getting it.

9. Henry Ford warned, You can't build a reputation on what you're going to do.

10. Choose a job you love, Confucius suggested, and you will never have to work a day in your life.

PARAGRAPH EXERCISE

Correctly punctuate quotations and titles in the following paragraph by adding quotation marks or underlining (*italics*). Some quotations have been shortened with the use of ellipses (. . .).

I admire the way that Helen Keller describes her feelings in her autobiography, The Story of My Life. Being totally blind and deaf, Keller tries to explain how she can experience something like moonlight. She writes, I cannot, it is true, see the moon climb up the sky behind the pines and steal softly across the heavens. But, she continues, I know she is there, and . . . I feel the shimmer of her garments as she passes. Keller could *feel* light rather than see it. She explains that, when a certain combination of air and light strike her, A luminous warmth seems to enfold me. . . . It is like the kiss of warm lips on my face.

SENTENCE WRITING

Write ten sentences that list and discuss your favorite songs, TV shows, characters' expressions, movies, books, and so on. Be sure to punctuate quotations and titles correctly. Refer to the rules at the beginning of this section if necessary.

Capital Letters

1. Capitalize the first word of every sentence.

Peaches taste best when they are cold.

A piece of fruit is an amazing object.

2. Capitalize the first word of every direct quotation.

She said, "I've never worked so hard before."

"I have finished most of my homework," she said, "but I still have a lot to do." (The *but* is not capitalized because it does not begin a new sentence.)

"I love my speech class," she said. "Maybe I'll change my major." (*Maybe* is capitalized because it begins a new sentence.)

3. Capitalize the first, last, and every important word in a title. Don't capitalize prepositions (such as *in*, *of*, *at*, *with*), short connecting words, the *to* in front of a verb, or *a*, *an*, or *the*.

I saw a copy of Darwin's *The Origin of Species* at a yard sale.

The class enjoyed the essay "How to Write a Rotten Poem with Almost No Effort."

Shakespeare in Love is a film based on Shakespeare's writing of the play *Romeo and Juliet.*

4. Capitalize specific names of people, places, languages, races, and nationalities.

Rev. Jesse Jackson	China	Cesar Chavez
Ireland	Spanish	Japanese
Ryan White	Philadelphia	Main Street

5. Capitalize names of months, days of the week, and special days, but not the seasons.

March	Fourth of July	spring
Tuesday	Easter	winter
Valentine's Day	Labor Day	fall

6. **Capitalize a title of relationship if it takes the place of the person's name. If** *my* **(or** *your*, *her*, *his*, *our*, *their*) **is in front of the word, a capital is not used.**

I think Mom wrote to him.	*but*	I think my mom wrote to him.
We visited Aunt Sophie.	*but*	We visited our aunt.
They spoke with Grandpa.	*but*	They spoke with their grandpa.

7. **Capitalize names of particular people or things, but not general terms.**

I admire Professor Washborne.	*but*	I admire my professor.
We saw the famous Potomac River.	*but*	We saw the famous river.
Are you from the South?	*but*	Is your house south of the mountains?
I will take Philosophy 4 and English 100.	*but*	I will take philosophy and English.
She graduated from Sutter High School.	*but*	She graduated from high school.
They live at 119 Forest St.	*but*	They live on a beautiful street.
We enjoyed the Monterey Bay Aquarium.	*but*	We enjoyed the aquarium.

EXERCISES

Add all of the necessary capital letters to the sentences that follow.

Exercise 1

1. many consider *the diary of anne frank* to be one of the most important books of the twentieth century.

2. anne frank wrote her famous diary during the nazi occupation of holland in world war ii.

3. the building in amsterdam where the frank family and several others hid during the two years before their capture is now a museum and has been recently renovated.

4. visitors to the anne frank house can stand before her desk and see pictures of movie stars like greta garbo on her wall.

5. they can climb the stairs hidden behind a bookcase that led to the annex where anne lived with her mother, edith; her father, otto; and her sister, margot.

6. one of the others hiding with the franks was peter van pels, who was roughly the same age as anne.

7. anne writes of her relationship with peter in her diary.

8. visitors to the museum can enter the room where peter gave anne her first kiss just a few months before the nazis discovered their hiding place in 1944.

9. anne's family and peter's were both sent to concentration camps in germany.

10. only anne's father lived to see the anne frank house open as a museum for the first time on may 3, 1960.

Source: Smithsonian, October 2001

Exercise 2

1. dad and i have both decided to take college classes next fall.

2. fortunately, in los angeles we live near several colleges and universities.

3. classes at the community colleges usually begin in late august or early september.

4. within twenty minutes, we could drive to los angeles valley college, los angeles city college, glendale community college, or pasadena city college.

5. i want to take credit classes, and my dad wants to sign up for community education classes.

6. for instance, i will enroll in the academic courses necessary to transfer to a university.

7. these include english, math, science, and history classes.

8. my father, on the other hand, wants to take noncredit classes with titles like "learn to play keyboards," "web pages made easy," and "be your own real estate agent."

9. dad already has a great job, so he can take classes just for fun.

10. i know that if i want to go to one of the university of california campuses later, i will have to be serious from the start.

Exercise 3

1. i grew up watching *the wizard of oz* once a year on tv before video stores like blockbuster even rented movies to watch at home.

2. i especially remember enjoying it with my brother and sisters when we lived on topeka drive.

3. mom would remind us early in the day to get all of our homework done.

4. "if your homework isn't finished," she'd say, "you can't see the munchkins!"

5. my favorite part has always been when dorothy's house drops on one of the wicked witches, and her feet shrivel up under the house.

6. the wicked witch of the west wants revenge after that, but dorothy and toto get help from glinda, the good witch of the north.

7. glinda tells dorothy about the emerald city and the wizard of oz.

8. on their way, toto and dorothy meet the scarecrow, the tin man, and the cowardly lion.

9. together they conquer the witch and meet professor marvel the real man who has been pretending to be a wizard.

10. The ruby slippers give dorothy the power to get back to kansas and to her aunt em and uncle henry.

Exercise 4

1. oscar wilde was an irish-born writer who lived and wrote in england for much of his life during the late 1800s.
2. he was famous for his refined ideas about art and literature.
3. while still a young man, wilde traveled to america.
4. contrary to what many people expected, he was well received in rough mining towns such as leadville, colorado.
5. he gave one particularly long speech to the miners who lived in leadville.
6. wilde spoke on the following topic: "the practical application of the aesthetic theory to exterior and interior house decoration, with observations on dress and personal ornament."
7. during his stay in leadville, wilde had gained the miners' respect by visiting them down in the mines and by proving that he could drink as much whiskey as they could without getting drunk.
8. wilde wrote about one incident that took place in leadville.
9. before giving a lecture he called *the ethics of art,* wilde was told that two criminals accused of murder had been found in town.
10. earlier that evening on the same stage where wilde was about to give his speech, the two men were convicted and executed by leadville officials.

Source: Saloons of the Old West (Knopf, 1979)

Exercise 5

1. the southern writer known as flannery o'connor was born with the name mary flannery o'connor.
2. o'connor lived much of her life in milledgeville, georgia.

3. she attended peabody high school, georgia state college for women (currently georgia college), and the state university of iowa (currently the university of iowa).

4. while at college in georgia, o'connor edited the campus newspaper, *the colonnade,* and its literary magazine, *the corinthian.*

5. when she began publishing her writing, o'connor left off her first name, mary.

6. students in literature classes study o'connor's short stories, including "revelation," "good country people," "a good man is hard to find," and "the life you save may be your own."

7. o'connor's stories received the o. henry award many times.

8. and organizations such as the ford foundation and the national institute of arts and letters awarded o'connor with grants to support her writing.

9. she also wrote the novels *wise blood* and *the violent bear it away.*

10. in 1962, notre dame's st. mary's college made flannery o'connor an honorary doctor of letters.

Source: Flannery O'Connor: Her Life, Library and Book Reviews (Edwin Mellon, 1980)

REVIEW OF PUNCTUATION AND CAPITAL LETTERS

Punctuate these sentences. They include all the rules for punctuation and capitalization you have learned. Compare your answers carefully with those at the back of the book. Sentences may require several pieces of punctuation or capital letters.

1. the golden gate bridge is the most famous landmark in san francisco

2. have you ever read gary sotos narrative essay the pie

3. we traveled to many european cities with our high school band it was an experience we'll never forget

4. how much would you pay for a script from the first star wars movie

5. we received your resumé ms clark and will contact you if we have any openings

6. the participant who guesses the correct number of gumballs will win the gigantic gumball machine

7. prof mitchell teaches the beginning french class

8. whenever i go there i leave something behind then i have to drive back and get it

9. we brought the food but we forgot the plates the cutlery and the plastic cups

10. roy scheider came up with the famous line we're gonna need a bigger boat in the movie jaws

11. i love to read the cartoons in the newspaper it's my favorite thing to do on sundays

12. packing for a short trip seems easy however it's not

13. our english instructor made us memorize the following rhyme about commas when in doubt leave them out

14. i wonder if i needed to bring my mathematics book with me today

15. i love lucy is the only tv series that my whole family thinks is funny

COMPREHENSIVE TEST

In these sentences you'll find all the errors that have been discussed in the entire text. Try to name the error in the blank before each sentence, and then correct the error if you can. You may find any of the following errors:

awk	awkward phrasing
apos	apostrophe
c	comma needed
cap	capitalization
cliché	overused expression
cs	comma splice
dm	dangling modifier
frag	fragment
mm	misplaced modifier
p	punctuation
pro	incorrect pronoun
pro agr	pronoun agreement
pro ref	pronoun reference
ro	run-on sentence
shift	shift in time or person
sp	misspelled word
s/v agr	subject/verb agreement
wordy	wordiness
ww	wrong word
//	not parallel

A perfect—or almost perfect—score will mean you've mastered the first part of the text.

1. _____ The girls put down the suitcases, and they walked away.

2. _____ I hope that my application is excepted.

3. _____ The solution was as clear as a bell; I don't know why we didn't see it.

4. _____ My family took a trip to the san diego zoo.

5. _____ The instructor gave my friend and I extra credit for attending the play.

6. _____ Everyone was allowed to revise their essays.

7. _____ The countertops were clean but the floors needed mopping.

8. _____ Taking a long vacation, our bus broke down in Wichita.

9. _____ She told Ms. Kepler that she lost her textbook.

10. _____ The box was totally empty when we opened it and looked inside of it.

11. _____ I wonder if I will finish my project by the due date?

12. _____ The mens' team challenged the womens' team.

13. _____ Her first child was born at the age of thirty.

14. _____ The hall has been reserved, however, they haven't chosen a caterer yet.

15. _____ We wore our ribbons as symbols of hope, solidarity, and because we were committed to the cause.

16. _____ I start a new journal page whenever I finished an entry.

17. _____ Your going to need a new car soon.

18. _____ Because the party was so loud and the neighbors called the police.

19. _____ A bouquet of roses were delivered to our office today.

20. _____ Each of the dogs at the kennel has their own distinct personality.

P A R T 4

Writing

Aside from the basics of word choice, spelling, sentence structure, and punctuation, what else do you need to understand to write better? Just as sentences are built according to accepted patterns, so are other "structures" of English—paragraphs and essays, for example.

Think of writing as including levels of structures, beginning small with words connecting to form phrases, clauses, and sentences. Then sentences connect to form paragraphs and essays. Each level has its own set of "blueprints." To communicate clearly in writing, words must be chosen and spelled correctly. Sentences must have a subject, a verb, and a complete thought. Paragraphs must be indented and contain a main idea supported with sufficient detail. Essays explore a valuable topic in several coherent paragraphs, usually including an introduction, a body, and a conclusion.

Not everyone approaches writing as structure, however. You can write better without thinking about structure at all. A good place to start might be to write what you care about and care about what you write. You can make an amazing amount of progress by simply being *genuine*, being who you are naturally. No one has to tell you to be yourself when you speak, but you might need encouragement to be yourself in your writing.

Writing is almost never done without a reason. The reason may come from an experience, such as receiving an unfair parking ticket, or from a requirement in a class. And when you are asked to write, you often receive guidance in the form of an assignment: tell a story to prove a point, paint a picture with your words, summarize an article, compare two subjects, share what you know about something, explain why you agree with or disagree with a statement or an idea.

Learning to write well is important, one of the most important things you will do in your education. Confidence is the key. The Writing sections will help you build confidence, whether you are expressing your own ideas or summarizing and responding to the ideas of others. Like the Sentence Structure sections, the Writing sections are best taken in order. However, each one discusses an aspect of writing that you can review on its own at any time.

What Is the Least You Should Know about Writing?

"Unlike medicine or the other sciences," William Zinsser points out, "writing has no new discoveries to spring on us. We're in no danger of reading in our morning newspaper that a breakthrough has been made in how to write [clearly]. . . . We may be given new technologies like the word processor to ease the burdens of composition, but on the whole we know what we need to know."

One thing that's certain is that you learn to write b*y writing*—not by reading long discussions about writing. Therefore, the explanations and instructions in these sections are as brief as they can be, followed by samples from student and professional writers.

Understanding the basic structures and learning the essential skills covered in these sections will help you become a better writer.

Basic Structures	Writing Skills
I. The Paragraph	**III.** Writing in Your Own Voice
II. The Essay	**IV.** Finding a Topic
	V. Organizing Ideas
	VI. Supporting with Details
	VII. Revising Your Papers
	VIII. Presenting Your Work
	IX. Writing about What You Read

Basic Structures

I. The Paragraph

A paragraph is unlike any other structure in English. Visually, it has its own profile: the first line is indented about five spaces, and sentences continue to fill the space between both margins until the paragraph ends (which may be in the middle of the line):

_____

_____

_____

_____

_____ .

As a beginning writer, you may forget to indent your paragraphs, or you may break off in the middle of a line within a paragraph, especially when writing in class. You must remember to indent whenever you begin a new paragraph and fill the space between the margins until it ends. (Note: In business writing, paragraphs are not indented but double-spaced in between.)

Defining a Paragraph

A typical paragraph develops one idea, usually phrased in a topic sentence from which all the other sentences in the paragraph radiate. The topic sentence does not need to begin the paragraph, but it most often does, and the other sentences support it with specific details. (For more on topic sentences and organizing paragraphs, see p. 229.) Paragraphs usually contain several sentences, though no set number is required. A paragraph can stand alone, but more commonly paragraphs are part of a larger composition, an essay. There are different kinds of paragraphs, based on the jobs they are supposed to do.

Types of Paragraphs

Sample Paragraphs in an Essay

Introductory paragraphs begin essays. They provide background information about the essay's topic and usually include the thesis statement or main idea of the essay. (See p. 227 for information on how to write a thesis statement.) Here is the introductory paragraph of a student essay entitled "A Cure for My Premature Old Age":

> Most people would love to live in a quiet neighborhood. I have heard that some people even camp out in front of a house they are planning to buy just to see if the block is as quiet as they have been told. Maybe I am unusual, but not long ago I felt that my community was too quiet. It was a problem for me, but I didn't get much sympathy when I told people about it. I learned that, from the problems in our lives, we become who we are.

In this opening paragraph, the student leads up to the main idea that "we become who we are" as a result of the challenges in our lives with background information about the "problem" of living in a quiet neighborhood.

Body paragraphs are those in the middle of essays. Each body paragraph contains a topic sentence and presents detailed information about one subtopic or idea that relates directly to the essay's thesis. (See p. 229 for more information on organizing body paragraphs.) Here are the body paragraphs of the same essay:

> The silence of my neighborhood affected me. Everyday I woke up to an alarm clock of quiet. There were no birds chirping, no cars passing by, nothing noisy around to comfort me. I lived then (and still do) in a cul-de-sac next to a home for senior citizens. Even the ambulances that came to transport the old folks never used their sirens. I often felt lonely and spent time looking

out the window at the bushes and the badly painted fence. I too was becoming old, but I was only nineteen. I found myself actually whispering at times.

There was no easy solution to my problem. My grandmother hated loud sounds, and she would never consider moving. We didn't even watch television because the blaring commercials upset her. I wanted to get out of the house with friends and visit noisy places, but my grandmother needed me to help her while my parents were at work. I didn't mind spending time with her, and she did teach me to make an incredible spaghetti sauce.

One day, I finally discovered a remedy for my problem. I took my grandmother to visit her friend Irene at the nursing home next door, and—no, I didn't leave her there. I started reading out loud to both of them. At first I read from the newspaper, but then someone suggested that I read a short story instead. As I read them the story, I realized that I had been silent for so long that I loved to hear my own voice, to act out the characters' personalities, and to live through the actions of the characters. Grandma and Irene loved it, too.

Notice that each of the three body paragraphs discusses a single aspect of the student's response to the problem—the ways it affected him, the lack of a simple solution, and finally the "cure."

Concluding paragraphs are the final paragraphs in essays. They bring the discussion to a close and share the writer's final thoughts on the subject. (See p. 229 for more about concluding paragraphs.) Here is the conclusion of the sample essay:

Now I am in my first year of college, and I've chosen English as a major. My grandmother spends three days a week visiting Irene next door. After school, I read them the essays I write for my classes, and they give me advice on how to make them better. I also work on campus, making recordings of books for visually impaired students. And I will be playing the part of Mercutio in our theater department's production of *Romeo and Juliet*. I never imagined that the solution to my problem would turn out to be the beginning of my adult life.

In this concluding paragraph, the student describes his transformation from depressed "aging" teen to promising student and aspiring actor—all as a result of living in a quiet cul-de-sac and caring for his grandmother.

Sample of a Paragraph Alone

Single-paragraph writing assignments may be given in class or as homework. They test the your understanding of the unique structure of a paragraph. They may ask you to answer a single question, perhaps following a reading, or to provide details about a limited topic. Look at this student paragraph, the result of a homework assignment asking students to report on a technological development in the news:

I learned on the evening news last night that in the future we will still be reading books, magazines, and newspapers made of paper, but the words and pictures will be printed with electronic ink. This special ink will turn a piece of paper into something like a computer screen. So the information on the page will change completely when new data is sent to it through a kind of pager device. The same sheets of electronic paper that had yesterday's news printed on them will be able to be cleared so that today's news is printed on them. The ink will work like the cards that crowds of people in sports stadiums hold and turn over in patterns to display a message or a picture. Each tiny bit of the ink will have a white and a black side that flips one way or the other, forming letters and pictures on the page. Paper and books using electronic ink will be here soon, and I can't wait.

These shorter writing assignments help students practice presenting information within the limited structure of a paragraph.

The assignments in the upcoming Writing Skills section will sometimes ask you to write paragraphs. Remember that you may review the previous pages as often as you wish until you understand the unique structure of the paragraph.

II. The Essay

Like the paragraph, an essay has its own profile, usually including a title and several paragraphs.

Title

_____
_____
_____
_____
_____ .
_____
_____
_____
_____
_____
_____ .
_____
_____
_____
_____
_____ .
_____
_____

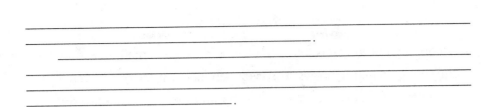

While the paragraph is the single building block of text used in almost all forms of writing (in essays, magazine articles, letters, novels, newspaper stories, and so on), an essay is a larger, more complex structure.

The Five-Paragraph Essay and Beyond

The student essay analyzed on pages 214–215 illustrates the different kinds of paragraphs within essays. Many people like to include five paragraphs in an essay: an introductory paragraph, three body paragraphs, and a concluding paragraph. Three is a comfortable number of body paragraphs—it is not two, which makes an essay seem like a comparison even when it isn't; and it is not four, which may be too many subtopics for the beginning writer to organize clearly.

However, an essay can include any number of paragraphs. As you become more comfortable with the flow of your ideas and gain confidence in your ability to express yourself, you are free to create essays of many different shapes and sizes. As with many skills, learning about writing begins with structure and then expands to include all possibilities.

Defining an Essay

There is no such thing as a typical essay. Essays may be serious or humorous, but the best of them are thought-provoking and—of course—informative. Try looking up the word *essay* in a dictionary right now. Some words used to define what an essay is might need to be explained themselves:

An essay is *prose* (meaning it is written in the ordinary language of sentences and paragraphs).

An essay is *nonfiction* (meaning it deals with real people, factual information, actual opinions and events).

An essay is a *composition* (meaning it is created in parts that make up the whole, several paragraphs that explore a single topic).

An essay is *personal* (meaning it shares the writer's unique perspective, even if only in the choice of topic, method of analysis, and details).

An essay is *analytical* and *instructive* (meaning it examines the workings of a subject and shares the results with the reader).

A Sample Essay

For an example of a piece of writing that fits the above definition, read the following essay by George Beiswinger about how, if you know someone *very* well, you can communicate almost without words.

Verbal Shorthand

I don't know why it is, but people who have been married a long time tend to cut corners when it comes to spoken language. In fact, if it weren't for pronouns, I don't think many of us could communicate at all. A single word may convey several meanings, thoughts or requests, but somehow each partner knows exactly what the other is saying at any given time.

My wife and I are guilty of using such verbal shorthand. For example, the other evening I asked her if she would please hand me the thing. She knew immediately that I wanted the TV remote.

If she asks me to turn it down, I know she means the TV, if it's on. Otherwise, she's talking about the thermostat. See what I mean? "It" covers many bases. My wife may say, "Please put it back together when you are through." I understand she is referring to the newspaper.

"It's about time for it to come," I might proclaim. This could mean the mail, the paper, the bus, or the cab we called, depending on the time and context. While in the laundry room, she might remark, "We've got to get a new one before long." "Yes," I reply. "It's given us many years of service." We both mean the washing machine. If she calls from the laundry room and inquires, "Is it on yet?" she means, Are the commercials over and is the program starting?

She may say: "You would think he would be cold out there without a coat." If she is looking out our north window, I know she means Harry next door. If the south window, it's neighbor Bob. But when she asks, "Has he been out yet?" she means Earl, our dog.

When I exclaim, "I've had it for now!" my wife knows that I'm frustrated with whatever project I've been working on and am ready for a nap. When she says, "You'd better do something for that," I know that she has heard me sneeze. When she's in another room and admonishes, "That will spoil your appetite," she's heard the rustle of my candy-bar wrapper.

If I head toward the garage, she may say, "Don't forget to fill it up." She means the car. But if I'm in the backyard and she says the same thing, I know she means the birdbath. When she says, "I think you can do better than that," I have either just finished mowing the lawn, trimming the hedge or (in winter) shoveling the sidewalk and driveway.

When my wife proffered a box of assorted chocolates the other evening and asked which I preferred, I said, "The one in the corner." I got the one I wanted. I didn't have to say, "the chocolate, nougat and caramel-covered macadamia nut cluster." She knew.

And so it goes. Somehow we manage to subsist on this sparse diet of words. Tonight, after the dinner dishes had been washed, dried, and put back in the cabinets, she asked sweetly if I would carry out the garbage. I was a bit taken aback. The first noun today, and it's garbage.

Source: Originally appeared in *Smithsonian* (August 2001). Reprinted with permission.

Now that you have learned more about the basic structures of the paragraph and the essay, you are ready to practice the skills necessary to write them.

Writing Skills

III. Writing in Your Own Voice

All writing "speaks" on paper. And the person "listening" is the reader. Some beginning writers forget that writing and reading are two-way methods of communication, just like spoken conversations between two people. When you write, your reader listens; when you read, you also listen.

When speaking, you express a personality in your choice of phrases, your movements, your tone of voice. Family and friends probably recognize your voice messages on their answering machines without your having to identify yourself. Would they also be able to recognize your writing? They would if you extended your "voice" into your writing.

Writing should not sound like talking, necessarily, but it should have a *personality* that comes from the way you decide to approach a topic, to develop it with details, to say it your way.

The beginning of this book discusses the difference between spoken English, which follows the looser patterns of *speaking*, and Standard Written English, which follows accepted patterns of writing. Don't think that the only way to add "voice" to your writing is to use the patterns of spoken English. Remember that Standard Written English does not have to be dull or sound academic. Look at this example of Standard Written English that has a distinct voice, part of the book *The Dachshund*, by Ann Carey:

> The Dachshund is a sturdy dog. Even the Miniature is not a fragile animal. Small is not a word in the Dachshund's vocabulary. This hound is also persistent. He'll bark at the garbage until you remove it. He will jump on the furniture no matter how many times you tell him *"No!"*—unless you remain firm and do not give in. Being opinionated, he will test you. Being sly, he will do it if he thinks you're not around. Being intelligent, he will get down when he hears you coming or if you are forceful in your command to "Get off the sofa!" To be honest, it is easier to cover the chair or the sofa or keep him out of any room you don't want him to claim as his own.

Carey's description of the Dachshund's personality illustrates Standard Written English at its best—from its solid sentence structures to its precise use of words. But more importantly, Carey's clear voice speaks to us and involves us in her world, in her admiration of Dachshunds. You can involve your reader, too, by writing in your own voice. Here is an example of a student response to a brief assignment to write about a problem at school or at work.

> At a few minutes past three every Monday through Friday, a whirlwind of activity disturbs the stillness of the grocery store where I work. A loud group of teenagers enters like the cast of an imaginary play, all talking to each other as if no other people existed around them. They walk around, make their way up and down the candy and snack food aisles, and finally reach the registers. Usually only one of them has any money, and for a few seconds, the rest go quiet and hope this friend will pay for all their sweet and salty treats. After bankrolling the rowdy bunch, the one with the money leads the others out the automatic doors, and the store returns to normal.

Notice that both the professional and the student writers tell stories (narration) and paint pictures (description) in the sample paragraphs. Narration and description require practice, but once you master them, you will gain a stronger voice and will be able to add interest and clarity to even the most challenging academic writing assignments.

Narration

Narrative writing tells the reader a story, and since most of us like to tell stories, it is a good place to begin writing in your own voice. An effective narration allows readers to experience an event with the writer. Since we all see the world differently and feel unique emotions, the purpose of narration is to take readers with us through an experience. As a result, the writer gains a better understanding of what happened, and readers get to live other lives momentarily.

Listen to the "voice" of this student writer telling the story of a difficult lesson she learned while in high school:

A Piercing Disappointment

My mom and I have always been close. She has never done the things other parents do to turn their kids against them. She has never talked down to me and has always respected the choices I make about the places I go and the people I see. If she doesn't like something I'm doing, she tells me straight out and lets me take it from there. About a year and a half ago while I was still in high school, I played a joke on my mom that almost ruined our good relationship.

I wanted a nose ring, but my mom wanted me to wait until I was living on my own to make such a big decision. She said she didn't like the look of nose rings. I felt it was unfair to make her look at one if she didn't want to, so I agreed to put it off.

One day I was at the mall with my friends, and we found a store that sold fake nose rings. I thought it would be funny to play a trick on my mom and see her reaction. She takes jokes pretty well, I thought, and I bragged about how "cool" my mom was about these things to my friends. I bought the fake nose ring and even added a little lip liner around the "hole" so it would look as if I just had my nose pierced. Then I went home to show Mom.

As I walked in the door of our house, I smelled vegetable lasagna, our favorite dinner, cooking in the kitchen. I hesitated as I heard my mom's voice greet me with the usual "Hi, Hun!" Part of me—the good part—wanted to yank the silly thing off my nose and give my mom the biggest hug, but the bad part went on with the charade. I really felt like one of those cartoon characters with the little angel on one shoulder and the

little devil on the other one, and the devil was
winning.

I didn't even make it all the way into the kitchen
before my mom spotted the glint of silver where it
hadn't been before. Her expression sank like a ship
going down in a storm. I'll never forget the way her
eyes turned instantly glassy and red. I smiled and said,
"You like it?" She didn't say anything. She just turned
around and went back to the lettuce she was tearing up
into a bowl. "It's fake," I said. She turned around
again. Her angry look was even worse than the sad one
before. I slipped the ring off and apologized repeatedly
as we ate the lasagna that had been, but would never
again be, our favorite meal.

By playing this one stupid trick on my mom, I
learned that the trust between us was like a balloon
that kept inflating. And the bigger it got, the easier
it was to pierce. Then we had to start all over again.

Description

Descriptive writing paints word pictures with details that appeal to the reader's five
senses—sight, sound, touch, taste, and smell. The writer of description often uses
comparisons to help readers picture one thing by imagining something else, just as
the writer of "A Piercing Disappointment" compared her mother's expression to a
"ship going down in a storm" and the previous student writer compared the noisy
group of teenagers to "the cast of an imaginary play."

Here is another example of clear description, from the book *Lillian
Woodward's Moss Landing*, in which Woodward describes the effects of a winter
sunset on her boatyard at Moss Landing, California. As we read her description, we
can feel the cold, hear the buzzer, enjoy the birds, and watch the sun make its way
to the top of the masts.

Freezing mornings, bright days, and cold evenings is the pattern
of this New Year's week. Every time the buzzer rings on the dock, we
say, "Who could want anything when it's so cold?" But we are glad they
do. It takes us out of the warm office into the brisk beauty of the out-
doors to see, around the crescent of the bay, deep blue mountains
standing clearly against a paler blue sky.

Cold days don't hinder flights of seagulls and pelicans, propelled
by strong northwest winds. They swoop and climb and dive as effort-

lessly as they do in mid-summer. We shiver inwardly as they land in the chilly water, but they look contented with their lot.

In the second week of winter I stood on the dock at closing time. It seemed that already I noticed a minute more of daylight. That particular evening the sun wrought a miracle to the masts and poles of the fishing boats tied side by side. It turned them to gold. The encroaching darkness crept up the hulls and cabins and top spires until only the masts and poles stood briefly in that golden light.

Darkness came and the whole scene turned gray. It was a lovely, almost eerie, scene witnessed before but always just a bit different. Whoever declares Moss Landing an ugly place, and there are some, has not been present at such moments of beauty.

You may have noticed that all of the examples in this section use both narration and description. In fact, most effective writing—even a good resumé or biology lab report—calls for clear storytelling and vivid word pictures to engage the reader.

Writing Assignments

The following two assignments will help you develop your voice as a writer. For now, don't worry about topic sentences or thesis statements or any of the things we'll consider later. Narration and description have their own logical structures. A story has a beginning, a middle, and an end. And we describe things from top to bottom, side to side, and so on.

Assignment 1
NARRATION: FAMOUS SAYINGS

The following is a list of well-known expressions. No doubt you have had an experience that proves at least one of these to be true. Write a short essay that tells a story from your own life that relates to one of these sayings. (See if you can tell which of the sayings fits the experience narrated in the student essay "A Piercing Disappointment" on p. 221.) You might want to identify the expression you have chosen in your introductory paragraph. Then tell the beginning, middle, and end of the story. Be sure to use vivid details to bring the story to life. Finish with a brief concluding paragraph in which you share your final thoughts on the experience.

Truth is stranger than fiction.

The grass is always greener on the other side of the fence.

If at first you don't succeed . . . try, try again.

Money can't buy happiness.

We learn best from our mistakes.

He (or she) who hesitates is lost.

Assignment 2
DESCRIPTION: A PICTURE WORTH 250 WORDS?

Describe a picture that means a lot to you. It could be a favorite family photo, a well-known news image, a famous drawing or painting, or a moment from a popular movie or TV commercial. Your goal is to make the reader *visualize* the picture. Try to use details and comparisons that appeal to the reader's senses in some way. Look back at the examples for inspiration. Be sure the reader knows—from your choice of details—what the picture means to you.

IV. Finding a Topic

You will most often be given a topic to write about, perhaps based on a reading assignment. However, when the assignment of a paper calls for you to choose your own topic without any further assistance, try to go immediately to your interests.

Look to Your Interests

If the topic of your paper is something you know about and—more important—something you *care* about, then the whole process of writing will be smoother and more enjoyable for you. If you collect coins, if you can draw, or even if you just enjoy going to the movies, bring that knowledge and enthusiasm into your papers.

Take a moment to think about and jot down a few of your interests now (no matter how unrelated to school they may seem), and then save the list for use later when deciding what to write about. One student's list of interests might look like this:

> instant messaging with friends online
> playing poker on weekends
> skiing in the mountains in winter
> detailing a new car

Another student's list might be very different:

> playing the piano
> going to concerts
> watching old musicals on video
> making cards out of old wallpaper

While still another student might list the following interests:

> going to the horse races
> reading for my book club
> traveling in the summer
> buying lottery tickets

These students have listed several worthy topics for papers. And because they are personal interests, the students have the details needed to support them. With a general topic to start with, you can use several ways to gather the details you will need to support it in a paragraph or an essay.

Focused Free Writing (or Brainstorming)

Free writing is a good way to begin. When you are assigned a paper, try writing for ten minutes, putting down all your thoughts on one subject—playing the piano, for example. Don't stop to think about organization, sentence structures, capitalization, or spelling–just let details flow onto the page. Free writing will help you see what material you have and will help you figure out what aspects of the subject to write about.

Here is an example:

> Whenever I play the piano I fill great! My mind racing along with the notes, I like the faster songs better. They take me away from my troubles at the same time getting out the nervousness that my troubles cause me to feel. A slow song gets me impatient and I lose track. I can never remember the names of the composers after my piano teacher teaches me a piece. Sometimes my teacher does ear training with me and asks me who wrote one, and I can never remember. I think that I will really be a "good" musician when I can tell one writer's pieces from anothers.

Now the result of this free-writing session is certainly not ready to be typed and turned in as a paragraph. However, it does begin to show why the student prefers playing fast songs to slow songs and why she does not yet consider herself a "good musician." She could use the free writing as the first step in writing a paragraph or essay that compares fast and slow pieces of music or that defines "good musician" and identifies the qualities that one must have.

Clustering

Clustering is another way of putting ideas on paper before you begin to write an actual draft. A cluster is more visual than free writing. You could cluster the topic of "going to the horse races," for instance, by putting it in a circle in the center of a piece of paper and then drawing lines to new circles as ideas or details occur to you. The idea is to free your mind from the limits of sentences and paragraphs to generate pure details and ideas. When you are finished clustering, you can see where you want to go with a topic.

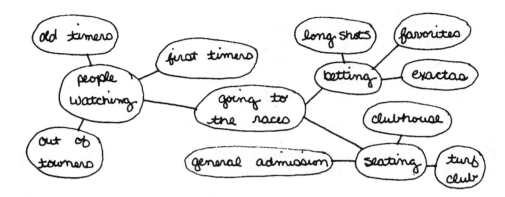

This cluster shows that the student has found three general aspects of attending the horse races: the variety of seating, types of bets, and groups of people to watch. This cluster might lead to another where the student chooses one aspect—groups of people to watch, for instance—and thinks of more details about them.

Talking with Other Students

It may help to talk to others when deciding on a topic. Many teachers break their classes up into groups at the beginning of an assignment. Talking with other students helps you realize that you see things just a little differently. Value the difference—it will help your written voice that we discussed earlier emerge.

Assignment 3
LIST YOUR INTERESTS

Make a list of four or five of your own interests. Be sure that they are as specific as the examples listed on p. 224. Keep the list for later assignments.

Assignment 4
DO SOME FREE WRITING

Choose one of your interests, and do some focused free writing about it. Write for ten minutes with that topic in mind but without stopping. Don't worry about anything such as spelling or sentence structures while you are free writing. The results are meant to help you find out what you have to say about the topic *before* you start to write a paper about it. Save the results for a later assignment.

Assignment 5
TRY CLUSTERING IDEAS

Choose another of your interests. Put it in the center of a piece of paper, and draw a cluster of details and ideas relating to it following the sample on page 226. Take the cluster as far as it will go. Then choose one aspect to cluster again on its own. This way you will arrive at specific, interesting details and ideas—not just the first ones that come to mind. Save the results of all your efforts.

V. Organizing Ideas

Most important to keep in mind, no matter what you are writing, is the idea you want to get across to your reader. Whether you are writing a paragraph or an essay, you must have in mind a single idea that you want to express. In a paragraph, such an idea is called a topic sentence; in an essay it's called a thesis statement, but they mean the same thing—an idea you want to get across. We will begin with a discussion of thesis statements.

Thesis Statements

Let's choose one of the students' interests listed on page 224 as a general topic. "Instant messaging with friends online" by itself doesn't make any point. What about it? Why do you like it? What does it do for you? What point about instant messaging would you like to present to your reader? You might write

Instant messaging with friends online is a good way to keep in touch.

But this is a vague statement, not worth developing. You might move into more specific territory and write

I have improved my reading and writing skills by instant messaging with friends online.

Now you have said something specific. *When you write in one sentence the point you want to present to your reader, you have written a thesis statement.*

All good writers have a thesis in mind when they begin to write, or the thesis may well evolve as they write. Whether they are writing essays, novels, poems, or plays, they eventually have in mind an idea they want to present to the reader. They may develop it in various ways, but behind whatever they write is their ruling thought, their reason for writing, their thesis.

For any writing assignment, after you have done some free writing or clustering to explore your topic, the next step is to write a thesis statement. As you write your thesis statement, keep two rules in mind:

1. A thesis statement must be a sentence *with a subject and a verb* (not merely a topic).

2. A thesis statement must be *an idea that you can explain or defend* (not simply a statement of fact).

Exercise 1
THESIS OR FACT?

Which of the following are merely topics or facts, and which are thesis statements that you could explain or defend? In front of each one that could be a thesis statement, write THESIS. In front of each one that is a fact, write FACT. Check your answers with those at the back of the book.

1. _____ It took me a long time to plan my wedding.
2. _____ Getting my first car took away my freedom.
3. _____ A robot of some kind could easily do my job.
4. _____ Hawaii has many volcanoes.
5. _____ Scientists have learned a lot of new facts about dinosaurs.
6. _____ So far, killer bees have not been as big a problem as predicted.
7. _____ I have finally learned the secrets to applying for a scholarship.
8. _____ Some people can only tell the time using digital clocks and watches.
9. _____ Chain-letter type e-mails are extremely annoying.
10. _____ Sharks have no bones in their bodies.

Assignment 6
WRITE A THESIS STATEMENT

Use your free-writing or clustering results from Assignments 4 and 5 (pp. 226–227) and write at least one thesis statement based on one of your interests. Be sure that the thesis you write is phrased as a complete thought that can be defended or explained in an essay.

Organizing an Essay

Once you have written a good thesis and explored your topic through discussion with others or by free writing and clustering, you are ready to organize your essay.

First you need an introductory paragraph. It should catch your reader's interest, provide necessary background information, and either include or suggest your thesis statement. (See p. 214 and p. 221 for two examples of student writers' introductory paragraphs.) In your introductory paragraph, you may also list supporting points, but a more effective way is to let them unfold paragraph by paragraph rather than to give them all away in the beginning of the essay. Even if your supporting points don't appear in your introduction, your reader will easily spot them later if your paper is clearly organized.

Your second paragraph will present your first supporting point—everything about it and nothing more.

Your next paragraph will be about your second supporting point—all about it and nothing more.

Each additional paragraph will develop another supporting point.

Finally, you'll need a concluding paragraph. In a short paper, it isn't necessary to restate your points. Your conclusion may be brief; even a single sentence to round out the paper may do the job. Remember that the main purpose of a concluding paragraph is to bring the paper to a close by sharing your final thoughts on the subject. (See p. 215 and p. 222 for two examples of successful concluding paragraphs.)

Learning to write a brief organized essay of this kind will help you to distinguish between the parts of an essay. Then when you're ready to write a longer paper, you'll be able to organize it clearly and be more creative in its design and content.

Topic Sentences

A topic sentence does for a paragraph what a thesis statement does for an essay—it states the main idea. Like thesis statements, topic sentences must be phrased as complete thoughts to be proven or developed through the presentation of details. But the topic sentence introduces an idea or subtopic that is the right size to cover in a paragraph. The topic sentence doesn't have to be the first sentence in a paragraph. It may come at the end or even in the middle, but putting it first is most common.

Each body paragraph should contain only one main idea, and no detail or example should be in a paragraph if it doesn't support the topic sentence or help to transition from one paragraph to another. (See p. 214 and pp. 221–222 for more examples of effective body paragraphs within essays and of paragraphs alone.)

Organizing Body Paragraphs (or Single Paragraphs)

A single paragraph or a body paragraph within an essay is organized in the same way as an entire essay only on a smaller scale. Here's the way you learned to organize an essay:

Thesis: stated or suggested in introductory paragraph

First supporting paragraph

Second supporting paragraph
Additional supporting paragraphs
Concluding paragraph

And here's the way to organize a paragraph:

Topic sentence
First supporting detail or example
Second supporting detail or example
Additional supporting details or examples
Concluding or transitional sentence

You should have several details to support each topic sentence. If you find that you have little to say after writing the topic sentence, ask yourself what details or examples will make your reader believe that the topic sentence is true for you.

Transitional Expressions

Transitional expressions within a paragraph and between paragraphs in an essay help the reader move from one detail or example to the next and from one supporting point to the next. When first learning to organize an essay, you might start each supporting paragraph in a paper with a transitional expression. Later, if they sound too repetitious, take these individual words out and replace them with more detailed prepositional phrases or dependent clauses, thereby improving your sentence variety.

Here are several transitions to show addition:

Also
Furthermore
Another (example, point, step, etc. . . .)
In addition

Here are some that show sequence:

First	One reason	One example
Second	Another reason	Another example
Finally	Most important	In conclusion

Here are those that show comparison or contrast:

Similarly	In the same way	In comparison
However	On the other hand	In contrast

Exercise 2
ADDING TRANSITIONAL EXPRESSIONS

Place the transitional expressions from the following list into the blanks in the following paragraph to make it read smoothly. Check your answers with those in the back of the book.

Therefore   Finally   Next   First of all

When I moved into my own apartment for the first time last month, I discovered the many hidden expenses of entering "the real world." _____, I had no idea that utility companies needed a security deposit from anyone who hasn't rented before. Each utility required a thirty dollar to fifty dollar deposit. _____, my start-up costs just for gas, electricity, and phone used up all the money I had saved for furnishings. _____, I found out how expensive it was to supply a kitchen with the basic staples of food and cleaning supplies. My initial trip to the grocery store cost $125, and I hadn't even bought my curtains at that point. _____, I was able to budget my money and keep a little aside for any other unexpected expenses of living on my own.

Assignment 7
CAN YOU COMMUNICATE WITHOUT WORDS?

In his essay called "Verbal Shorthand" on page 218, George Beiswinger illustrates the idea that if you know someone well enough, communication is possible using very few words. Write a long paragraph or a short essay in which you briefly answer the question "Do you know anyone well enough so that you don't need words to communicate?" Your answer to the question will be your main idea, and the reasons and details that support it should be based on your own experiences. Try free writing, clustering, or discussing the topic with other students before you begin to write.

VI. Supporting with Details

Now you're ready to support your main ideas with subtopics and specific details. That is, you'll think of ways to convince your reader that what you say in your thesis is true. How could you convince your reader that instant messaging with friends online has improved your reading and writing skills? You might write

> My reading and writing skills have improved since I began instant messaging with friends online. (because)

1. The computer won't find my friends online if I use sloppy spelling and punctuation.

2. I read and write much faster on screen than I ever did on paper.

3. I write messages to friends and family, but I never wrote real letters to them before.

NOTE - Sometimes if you imagine a *because* at the end of your thesis statement, it will help you write your reasons or subtopics clearly and in parallel form.

Types of Support

The subtopics developing a thesis and the details presented in a paragraph are not always *reasons*. Supporting points may take many forms based on the purpose of the essay or paragraph. They may be

> *examples* (in an illustration)
>
> *steps* (in a how-to or process paper)
>
> *types or kinds* (in a classification)
>
> *meanings* (in a definition)
>
> *similarities and/or differences* (in a comparison/contrast)
>
> *effects* (in a cause-and-effect analysis).

Whatever they are, supporting points should develop the main idea expressed in the thesis or topic sentence and prove it to be true.

Here is the final draft of a student essay on the problem of not being able to trust her instincts. Notice how the body paragraphs present examples of the student's indecision. And all of the details within the body paragraphs support her topic sentences.

Indecision

As far back as I can remember, I've always been fickle-minded. At first, my mind would settle on one decision. Then suddenly, in a snap, I would change it. I have trouble with everything from choosing birthday presents for my friends to deciding what to eat for dinner every night. My problem of indecision is worst at school, where I have never trusted my instincts.

For instance, whenever I take multiple-choice tests, I get two points lower than an *A* because of last-minute changes. I get the right answer first, yet I frequently hear this inner voice tell me to change it when I review my answers. It feels as though I'm being torn between my left hand's urge to erase my first answer and my right hand trying to stop the other one from doing it. Then this weird voice orders me to change the answer anyway.

The sad part comes after the test. I open my notes and scan for the right answer. Then I realize that once again I have wasted my energy, my eraser, and most of all the point or points on the test. Next is the indescribable feeling of a "lump" in my throat and pressure on my chest when the tests are given back. I usually get *B*'s just because of erasures. This has happened in my anatomy, history, and psychology classes. I guess something in me is afraid of getting *A*'s.

The same problem of indecision occurred last week outside of school. We were assigned to purchase a basal thermometer for an experiment in my anatomy class. So I went to the pharmacy near my house, and I found two—one just like the sample the teacher showed us in class and another brand with the same information on the label. Once more my hands fought with my brain. Incredibly, I chose the off brand. I came home and tried it. The mercury read my temperature, but the silver line didn't

> go down when I shook the thermometer afterward. Once
> again I should have trusted my instincts and bought the
> one the teacher showed us. The following day, I had to
> take an extra trip on the bus just to exchange it.
>
> After this incident, I have resolved to value my
> first judgments. I know that if I trust my initial
> decisions, I will be trusting myself. I will still go
> through my test papers a second time, but I won't change
> a thing unless I know an answer is one hundred percent
> wrong. With this plan, I may become an *A* student yet.

(Note: See p. 235 for a rough draft of this essay, before its final revisions.)

Learning to support your main ideas with vivid details is perhaps the most important thing you can accomplish in this course. Many writing problems are not really *writing* problems but *thinking* problems. Whether you're writing a term paper or merely an answer to a test question, if you take enough time to think, you'll be able to write a clear thesis statement and support it with paragraphs loaded with meaningful details.

Assignment 8
WRITE AN ESSAY ON ONE OF YOUR INTERESTS

Return to the thesis statement you wrote about one of your interests for Assignment 6 on p. 228. Now write a short essay to support it. You can explain the allure of your interest, its drawbacks or its benefits (such as the one about instant messaging improving the student's reading and writing skills). Don't forget to use any free writing or clustering you may have done on the topic beforehand.

Assignment 9
MAKING DECISIONS

Like the student writer of "Indecision," many of us have trouble making decisions. We may make them too quickly, too slowly, or be unable to make them at all. How we make decisions directly affects our lives and the lives of the people close to us. Write an essay about how well you make important decisions. You could discuss a particular decision you've made and its effect on you and those around you. Or you could describe the habits involved in your own method of decision-making. Do these habits work for you or not? Start by freewriting, clustering, or whatever prewriting technique you choose in order to generate ideas and specific details.

VII. Revising Your Papers

Great writers don't just sit down and write a final draft. They write and revise. You may have heard the expression, "Easy writing makes hard reading." True, it is *easier* to turn in a piece of writing the first time it lands on paper. But you and your reader will probably be disappointed by the results. Try to think of revision as an opportunity instead of a chore, as a necessity instead of a choice.

Whenever possible, you should write a paper several days before the first draft is due. Let it sit for a while. When you reread it, you'll see ways to improve the organization or to add more details to a weak paragraph. After revising the paper, put it away for another day, and try again to improve it. Save all of your drafts along the way to see the progress that you've made or possibly to return to an area left out in later drafts but which fits in again after revision.

Don't call any paper finished until you have worked it through several times. Revising is one of the best ways to improve your writing.

Take a look at an early draft of the student essay you read on page 233 on the problem of indecision. Notice that the student has revised her rough draft by crossing out some parts, correcting word forms, and adding new phrasing or reminders for later improvement.

Indecision

* give more background

As far back as I can remember, I've always been fickle-minded. At first, my mind would settle on one decision. Then suddenly, in a snap, I would change it. * I have never trusted my instincts.

For instance, whenever I ~~have~~ take tests ~~like scantrons or~~ (multiple-choice), I get two points lower than ~~the grade I~~ an "A" ~~want~~ because of last minute changes. I ~~always~~ get the right answer ~~on my~~ first ~~choice~~, yet I frequently hear this inner voice say to change it when I ~~go back and~~ review my answers. It ~~always~~ feels ~~like~~ as though I'm being torn

between by left hand's urge to erase my first answer, and
my right ~~holding~~ [hand trying to keep] my left hand ~~to keep~~ from doing it. Then
comes the ~~wierd~~ [weird] voice that orders me to ~~do erase it~~ [change the answer]
anyway.

The sad part comes after the test. I open my notes [Then]
and scan ~~for the the question and~~ the right answer. I
realize that ~~I went through all that trouble only to find~~ [once again]
~~out~~ I wasted my energy, eraser, ~~temptation~~, and most of
all the point or points on the test.

[same paragraph] Next ~~comes~~ [is] the indescribable [feeling of a] "lump" ~~sensation~~ in my
throat and [pressure on my] chest when the ~~papers~~ [tests] are given back. I
usually get B's just because of erasures. This has
happened in a ~~lot of~~ [my] subjects, like [a] Anatomy, History, [and]
Psychology, ~~and a lot more.~~ [classes.] I guess something in me is [of indecision] afraid of getting A's.

The same problem [is] occurred last week. We were assigned [outside of school]
to purchase a basal thermometer for an experiment in my
anatomy class. So I went to the pharmacy near my house,
and I found two—one just like the ~~one~~ [sample] the teacher showed
us in class and another ~~one a little different but~~ [brand] with
the same information on the label. Once more my hands
fought with my brain. [Incredibly] I chose the ~~new one~~ [off brand]. I came home
and tried it. The mercury read my temperature, but ~~it~~ [the silver line]
didn't go down when I shook ~~it~~ [the thermometer afterwards]. Again, I should have
trusted my instincts and ~~got~~ [bought] the one the teacher showed
us. The following day, I had to take an extra trip on the
bus just to exchange it.

After this incident, I [have] resolve[d] to ~~trust~~ [value] my first
judgments. I know that if I trust my initial decisions, I
will be trusting myself. I will still go through my test
papers a second time, but I won't change a thing unless I
know an answer is one hundre[d] percent wrong. With this
plan, I ~~hope things will turn out better.~~ [may become an A student yet.]

Can you see why each change was made? Analyzing the reasons for the changes will help you improve your own revision skills.

Assignment 10

WHAT DOES IT TAKE TO BE A LEADER?

You've read about many leaders in this text—from presidents and first ladies who have led the nation to activists who have led the fight to save trees or eliminate drunkenness. What qualities do you think a leader needs to be successful? Think of one or more leaders that you admire (past or present) and isolate the individual qualities that make them examples of strong leaders.

Write a rough draft of the paper and then set it aside. When you finish writing about what it takes to be a leader, reread your paper to see what improvements you can make to your rough draft. Use the following checklist to help guide you through this or any other revision.

Revision Checklist

Here's a checklist of revision questions. If the answer to any of these questions is no, revise that part of your paper until you're satisfied that the answer is yes.

1. Does the introductory paragraph introduce the topic clearly and suggest or include a thesis statement that the paper will explain or defend?

2. Does each of the other paragraphs support the thesis statement?

3. Does each body paragraph contain a clear topic sentence and focus on only one supporting point?

4. Do the body paragraphs contain enough details, and are transitional expressions well used?

5. Do the final thoughts expressed in the concluding paragraph bring the paper to a smooth close?

6. Does your (the writer's) voice come through?

7. Do the sentences read smoothly and appear to be correct?

8. Are words well-chosen and are spelling and punctuation consistent and correct?

Exchanging Papers

The preceding checklist can also be used if you exchange papers with another student in your class. Since you both have written a response to the same assignment, you will understand what the other writer has been going through and learn from the differences between the two papers.

Proofreading Aloud

Finally, you should read your finished paper *aloud*. If you read it silently, you will see what you *think* is there, but you are sure to miss some errors. Read your paper aloud slowly, pointing to each word as you read it to catch omissions and errors in spelling and punctuation. Reading a paper to yourself this way may take fifteen minutes to half an hour, but it will be time well spent. There are even word-processing programs that will "speak" your text in a computer's voice. Using your computer to read your paper to you can be fun as well as helpful. If you don't like the way something sounds, don't be afraid to change it! Make it a rule to read each of your papers *aloud* before handing it in.

Here are four additional writing assignments to help you practice the skills of writing and revising.

Assignment 11
WHAT'S IN A NAME?

Write about your name, any part or all of it. Are there any special stories behind your name? Do you know its meaning, if any? Are you named after anyone special? How do you feel about your name—would you ever consider changing it? Organize your responses to these questions into the structure of a brief essay.

Assignment 12
"CLOTHES MAKE THE MAN"

We are all judged at times by the clothes we wear. Some people think of clothes as simply practical coverings and never consider their effect. Others treat clothes as an avenue for creative expression and craft their outfits as carefully as costumes. Which of these two categories do you fall into, and why? Write a thesis statement that you then support with detailed body paragraphs.

Assignment 13
A MOVIE OR TV SHOW THAT HAS MADE AN IMPRESSION

Choose a movie or TV show that has made a strong impression on your life. Write a brief overview of the characters and the storyline, and then explain why it has had such a strong effect. Think back over all the stages of your life to find one that has really made a difference. Be sure to use plenty of details.

Assignment 14
MAKING "SENSE" OF IT ALL

Helen Keller lost her ability to see and hear due to illness when she was a toddler, but (by using her other senses) she seems to have had experiences as rich as anyone else's. Read the short paragraph about Helen Keller's description of moonlight in the Paragraph Exercise on page 202; then answer the following question: Which of your own senses—sight, sound, touch, taste, smell—do you rely on the most? Write a short paper in which you explain with examples from your own experiences.

VIII. Presenting Your Work

Part of the success of a paper could depend on how it looks. The same paper written sloppily or typed neatly might even receive different grades. It is human nature to respond positively when a paper has been presented with care. Here are some general guidelines to follow.

Paper Formats

Your paper should be typed or written on a computer, double-spaced, or copied neatly in ink on 8 1/2-by-11-inch paper on one side only. A 1-inch margin should be left around the text on all sides for your instructor's comments. The beginning of each paragraph should be indented 5 spaces.

Most instructors have a particular format for presenting your name and the course material on your papers. Always follow such instructions carefully.

Titles

You should spend some time thinking of a good title. Just as you're more likely to read a magazine article with an interesting title, so your readers will be more eager to read your paper if you give it a good title. Which of these titles from student papers would make you want to read further?

An Embarrassing Experience   Super Salad?

Falling into The Gap   Buying Clothes Can Be Depressing

Hunting: The Best Sport of All?   Got Elk?

Remember these three rules about titles:

1. Only the first letter of the important words in a title should be capitalized.

A Night at the Races

2. Don't put quotation marks around your own titles unless they include a quotation or title of an article, short story, or poem within them.

"To Be or Not to Be" Is Not for Me

3. Don't underline (or *italicize*) your own titles unless they include the title of a book, play, movie, or magazine within them.

Still Stuck on *Titanic*

A wise person once said, "Haste is the assassin of elegance." Instead of rushing to finish a paper and turn it in, take the time to give your writing the polish it deserves.

IX. Writing about What You Read

Reading and writing are related skills. The more you read, the better you will write. When you are asked to prepare for a writing assignment by reading a newspaper story, a magazine article, a professional essay, or a book, there are many ways to respond in writing. Among them, you may be asked to write your reaction to a reading assignment or a summary of a reading assignment.

Writing a Reaction

Reading assignments become writing assignments when your teacher asks you to share your opinion about the subject matter or to relate the topic to your own experiences. In a paragraph, you would have enough space to offer only the most immediate impressions about the topic. However, in an essay you could share your personal reactions, as well as your opinions on the value of the writer's ideas and support. Of course, the first step is always to read the selection carefully, looking up unfamiliar words in a dictionary.

Sample Reaction Paragraph

Here is a sample paragraph-length response following several readings about controversial court cases in history: "Choose any one of the cases we have read about and explain your reaction to it." This student chose the case of Julius and Ethel Rosenberg, who were executed in 1953 after being accused and found guilty of espionage, specifically of passing America's atomic bomb secrets to Russian agents. They were the first civilians in America to be put to death for spying.

> When I first read about the execution of the Rosenbergs, I couldn't believe it really happened. They were a young married couple with two small children. I had always thought that America respected families above everything else. All I could think about was that the poor little boys had

to say good-bye to their mom and dad in prison, knowing exactly what time both of their parents were going to be killed. It was strange that officials cared enough about the couple not to execute them at the holiest time of their Sabbath but then killed them just the same. I know that what the Rosenbergs supposedly did was wrong, but I believe that killing them for it was worse.

If this had been an essay-length assignment, the student would have included more details about the case. Perhaps he would have compared it with another case to broaden the discussion or would have explored more in-depth the reasons why he believed executing the Rosenbergs was wrong.

Assignment 15
WRITE A REACTION PARAGRAPH

The following is an excerpt from a book entitled *Backtalk: 4 Steps to Ending Rude Behavior in Your Kids,* by Dr. Audrey Ricker and Dr. Carolyn Crowder. Write a paragraph in which you respond thoughtfully to Ricker and Crowder's topic and to the details they use to support it.

Here are some common examples of backtalk that are often unrecognized in the beginning. We've listed them in age categories.

Up to age three: (Yes, backtalk that early!) "Bad mommy," "I don't like you," and "No!"

Age four to six: "I hate you," "Shut up," "That's mine, don't touch it," and "You can't make me." "As if!" is also gaining popularity, according to some parents.

Age six to eight: "You're stupid!" or "I'm not doing that!"

Age eight to eleven: "Oh, give me a break!" "That sucks!" Plus a lot of eye-rolling and huffing and sighing. "All the other kids get to do it!"

Age twelve to fourteen: "Mom" (or Dad), "you know absolutely nothing about music" (or video games or clothes or anything else the child cares about). "You have to take me to the mall" (or do anything else the child demands). "You call this edible?"

Age fifteen or older: "I'm stressed [tired, bummed out, overworked, etc.], okay?"

The content of these messages is not important—the tone and attitude are. Like darts dipped in poison, these messages and others like them are meant to immobilize the target instantly. The receiver of these comments feels humiliated, angry, and paralyzed with guilt, all at the same time. The parent can't figure out what to do, and so does nothing or uses the same tactics on the child. . . . Those who react with anger bring more angry backtalk their way, which starts a cycle that ends only when one participant or the other gets exhausted or leaves the room.

Before starting your reaction paragraph, *read the selection again carefully.* **Be sure to use a dictionary to look up any words you don't know. You can also use the free-writing and clustering techniques explained on pages 225–228. Or your instructor may want you to discuss the reading in groups.**

Coming to Your Own Conclusions

Often you will be asked to come to your own conclusions based on a reading that simply reports information. In other words, you have to think about and write about what it all means.

Read the following excerpt from a book published in 1907 and written by Elbert Hubbard. Hubbard begins the book, titled *Little Journeys*, by telling the story of how he lost his first manuscript on a train and had to start all over again.

> The printers were ready to take the work in hand, but I begged them to allow me two more days for careful revision; and as I was just starting away to give a lecture at Janesville, Wisconsin, I took the manuscript with me, intending to do the final work of revision on the train.
>
> All went well on the journey, the lecture had been given with no special tokens of disapproval on part of the audience, and I was on board the early morning train that leaves for Chicago. As my mind is fairly clear in the early hours, I began at work retouching the good MS. [manuscript]. We were nearing Beloit when I bethought me to go into the Buffet Car for a moment.
>
> When I returned the MS. was not to be seen. I looked in various seats, and under the seats, asked my neighbors, enquired of the brakeman and then hunted up the porter and asked him if he had seen my manuscript. He did not at first understand what I meant by the term "manuscript," but finally enquired if I referred to a pile of dirty, dog-eared sheets of paper, all marked up and down and over and criss-cross, ev-ry-which-way.
>
> I assured him that he understood the case.
>
> He then informed me that he had "chucked the stuff," that is to say, he had tossed it out of the window, as he was cleaning up his car, just as he always did before reaching Chicago.
>
> I made a frantic reach for the bell cord, but was restrained. A sympathetic passenger came forward and explained that five miles back he had seen the sheets of my precious MS. sailing across the prairie. We were going at the rate of a mile a minute and the wind was blowing fiercely, so there was really no need of backing the train up to regain the lost goods.
>
> [The porter said that he hoped the papers weren't important] as I stood sort of dazed, gazing into vacancy.

I shook myself into partial sanity. "Oh, they were of no value, I was just looking for them so as to throw them out the window myself," I answered. [And the train pulled into the Chicago station.]

Assignment 16
WHAT ARE YOUR CONCLUSIONS?

What aspects of this nearly hundred-year-old piece of writing reveal its age? One way to begin is to consider how you think the experience and people's reactions might be different if they had occurred today.

WRITING 100-WORD SUMMARIES

One of the best ways to learn to read carefully and to write concisely is to write 100-word summaries. Writing 100 words sounds easy, but actually it isn't. Writing 200- or 300- or 500-word summaries isn't too difficult, but condensing all the main ideas of an essay or article into 100 words is a time-consuming task—not to be undertaken in the last hour before class.

A summary presents only the main ideas of a reading, *without including any reactions to it*. A summary tests your ability to read, understand, and *rephrase* the ideas contained in an essay, article, or book.

If you work at writing summaries conscientiously, you'll improve both your reading and your writing. You'll improve your reading by learning to spot main ideas and your writing by learning to construct a concise, clear, smooth paragraph. Furthermore, your skills will carry over into your reading and writing for other courses.

Sample 100-Word Summary

First, read the following excerpt from the book *Lillian Woodward's Moss Landing.* It will be followed by a sample 100-word summary.

June

Anyone who has been seasick in even the slightest degree knows that it is a most unhappy condition. If the experience has been severe enough, the victim can scarcely bear to stand on a dock, while boarding a boat is enough to bring on all the symptoms. In that grave state, you think you are going to die, miserably hoping that you will. Several times in our years at Moss Landing, men have bought boats never imagining such torture would overtake them. At least two of these men made only one trip and never set foot aboard their boats again. "I'd give the boat away before I'd suffer like that again," said one fellow turning slightly green at the recollection.

But one man we know conquered the malady to such an extent he is now a successful fisherman. Once the season has started, he is afflicted no more. For five nights before he makes his first trip and while the boat is "on the hook" in Monterey Bay, he sleeps aboard getting used to the motion.

"That first night is pretty bad," he said. "I'm leaning over the side more time than I'm in the bunk. And that's just a gentle roll, mind you, no big waves or turbulence. The second night is a little better. I sleep about half the time and since I know I'm improving every hour, I'm happy as each one passes.

"Night number three is fairly comfortable. I go to bed late and get up early. By that time I can even look down and see the water rippling around and watch other boats rocking at their moorings. I'm able to eat a piece of toast, shave myself and whistle a little. I really think I'd be able to go out on the fourth night, but I throw it in for good measure, just to make sure, you know. Things are going great now, I sleep like a baby the whole night through and the next day I make final preparations for the opening season.

"That last night I'm happy as a king," the fellow continued. "I go on my boat, hit the sack and sleep until daybreak when all the boats file out of the bay in a long line ready for another fishing year. 'I've made it again,' I say to myself. From then on all through the long months and over the stormy seas, I don't have even a slight queasiness. This is my own program worked out just for me. Might not suit another fellow at all," he said.

"And the next year?" I asked.

His face fell.

"The next year," he said with a grimace, "The next year I do the whole bloody bit over again."

Here is a sample 100-word summary of the article:

> Seasickness is an awful illness with terrible symptoms. Once some people experience it, they completely avoid boats—and sometimes the ocean itself—so that they'll never feel seasick again. Others believe that seasickness can be cured by gradual exposure to a boat's movements on the water. In the beginning, the person feels stomach upset and wooziness as severely as ever. But soon the person gets used to the sea's effects. Eventually, the sufferer feels the same level of comfort on a boat or on land. However, this cure for seasickness wears off if the person avoids a boat for long.

Assignment 17
WRITE A 100-WORD SUMMARY

Your aim in writing your summary should be to give someone who has not read the article a clear idea of it. First, read the following excerpt from Sal Marino's article "Straight Talk," and then follow the instructions given after it.

Straight Talk

Why should you read my columns? What qualifies me to give you advice? Modesty tells me not to answer. But ego tells me to pour it on. So here goes.

In the prehistoric days when I went to college, my four-year full-tuition scholarship totaled $1,000, or $250 a year. To help pay for my room and board ($60 per month), I labored as a student assistant, washed dishes, and waited tables. I was paid 35 cents an hour. . . . I was a college student before air conditioning, before television, before penicillin, and before Big Macs.

Today, I'm so old I can remember when grass was mowed instead of smoked. When Coke was a soft drink. And pot was something you cooked in. We bought candy for pennies, ice cream cones for nickels, and went to the movies for dimes. Nobody had ever heard of credit cards, or computers, or even highways, let alone electronic superhighways. Hardware was something you bought in a corner store—and software wasn't even a word.

I have a tremendous respect for words. We are all word-dependent. We are the beneficiaries (or the victims) of the words we write, speak, hear, and read. Using the words we know has become more important than knowing the words we use. For every word at our disposal, there are a multiplicity of alternatives. Something cannot only be big, it can also be large, immense, vast, capacious, huge, bulky, massive, or whopping. . . .

To a writer, this abundance of words can be a virtue. And yet, a critic could argue that English is an untidy language, cluttered with a plethora of needless words. Jules Feiffer once drew a cartoon in which the down-on-his-heels character observed that he was first called poor, then needy, then deprived, then underprivileged, and then disadvantaged. He concluded that although he still didn't have a dime, he sure had acquired an impressive vocabulary.

It is possible to load products on a truck and deliver them to a customer without any change in the products. But it is impossible to load ideas on a page, or radio, or television and guarantee they will be received as delivered. In communicating, we code our ideas into words. We then transmit the words to our readers or listeners. The receiver must now decode the words back into ideas. What the decoded words convey is often totally different from what the sender intended. Let me give you an example:

The village blacksmith hired an apprentice. He gave the young man these instructions: "When I take the horseshoe out of the fire, I'll lay it on the anvil. Then, when I nod my head, hit it with a hammer." The apprentice did what he thought he had been told to do. Now he's the village blacksmith.

Today, more than ever before, readers should question their information sources. I, for one, intend to do just that. . . . I want media that deliver usefulness instead of uselessness. I want news sources that are fair with their views rather than first with the news, that care more about being right than wrong.

Source: Reprinted with permission from *Industry Week*, May 4, 1998. Copyright, Penton Media, Inc., Cleveland, Ohio.

A good way to begin the summary of an article is to figure out the thesis statement, the main idea the author wants to get across to the reader. Write that idea down now *before reading further.*

How honest are you with yourself? Did you write that thesis statement? If you didn't, *write it now* before you read further.

You probably wrote something like this:

Times have changed, and our use of words has changed with them.

Using that main idea as your first sentence, summarize the article by choosing the most important points. *Be sure to put them in your own words.* Your rough draft may be 150 words or more.

Now cut it down by including only essential points and by getting rid of wordiness. Keep within the 100-word limit. You may have a few words less but not one word more. (And every word counts—even *a, and,* and *the.*) By forcing yourself to keep within the 100 words, you'll get to the kernel of the author's thought and understand the article better.

When you have written the best summary you can, then and only then compare it with the summary on page 325. If you look at the model sooner, you'll cheat yourself of the opportunity to learn to write summaries because, once you read the model, it will be almost impossible not to make yours similar. So do your own thinking and writing, and then compare.

Summary Checklist

Even though your summary is different from the model, it may be just as good. If you're not sure how yours compares, answer these questions:

1. Did you include the same main ideas *without* adding your own reactions or opinions?

2. Did you leave out all unnecessary words and examples?

3. Did you rephrase the writer's ideas, not just recopy them?

4. Does the summary read smoothly?

5. Would someone who had not read the article get a clear idea of it from your summary?

Assignment 18

WRITE A REACTION OR A 100-WORD SUMMARY

Respond to Dominique Browning's editorial "Wandering Home" in any of the three ways we've discussed—in a reaction paragraph, a 100-word summary, or an essay. If you plan to respond with an essay, briefly summarize Browning's main ideas about the places and states of mind that we humans call "home" in your introductory paragraph. Then elaborate on your reactions and your own concept of "home" in your body paragraphs. Save your final thoughts for your concluding paragraph.

Wandering Home

Every morning for weeks this spring I was awakened at five by the gentle, persistent cooing of a dove. Such a soft, lovely song, yet each day it was able to penetrate my dreams and lure me from my bed onto the balcony. I would search through the treetops for a glimpse of her until the damp chill sent me back indoors, and then finally one day I spotted her. She had built a nest on the trellis right over my door, wedged in amid a looping tangle of wisteria. I didn't dare go out onto the balcony again, for fear of disturbing her. Several days later the cooing stopped, and I suppose she became serious about laying and hatching her eggs, or why else would she sit so still and silent in her new home?

Nesting. Why do we do it, why does it matter? Why do we care so much? This has been on my mind lately, because I recently met a real wanderer, someone who is defiantly, dogmatically, devotedly nomadic. He isn't selfishly drifting; homeless by choice, he has spent the past 20 years living all over the world, doing good. Home for him is a provisional thing. I was so struck by the marked contrast to the way my friends and I have hunkered down, sent out roots, gathered treasure, gotten anchored. Maybe got stuck, who knows? I have always thought of making a home as one of those basic desires, but why should it be?

It is too easy to say home is where the heart is, where your loved ones sleep. Your loved ones can go with you, wherever you roam, and your loved ones can just as well be scattered to all corners of the world. We grow up (most of us) and ruthlessly leave behind the first homes of our childhood. And we often leave with the thought that the home we make for ourselves will be markedly different from the one made by our parents.

Some of us end up finding home in the town where we were raised. Some of us have ancestral homes, where generations of the family have been raised—places dear enough to draw everyone back. Some of us simply choose a place, or, if we are lucky, we feel the place chooses us. For some of us, a home is as large as a country—"I'm at home in France," one friend will say, or "I felt like I had come home when I got to Ireland"—and for others, a home is as small as the four walls of a room. Some of us move restlessly from house to house; others are restless within the house, rearranging the furniture, circling toward some approximation of beauty, serenity. And then some of us are so settled that our bodies creak to leave the sofa.

Maybe home is one of those subjects over which much of the world is divided: those who care about it passionately and those who don't give it a second thought. Maybe some of us are the fixed points of the compass; we're home, so others can twirl in circles around the globe. Some of us need the foundation of a home because our thoughts, dreams, emotions are constantly wheeling, wandering. And for some of us, there is the great adventure of making a home—you know, that thing about the world in a grain of sand or, dare I say, a smear of paint, a dab of plaster, the twinkle of a chandelier, the gleam of that old pearwood commode. The adamant wanderer finally confessed to having a warehouse full of stuff collected over the years, so even a nomad isn't immune to fantasies of home, however delayed the gratification of making one might turn out to be.

As for the dove: after a few quiet weeks, I noticed on the ground beneath her nest what I first took to be a bright curl of Styrofoam and of course turned out to be the fragment of an eggshell. One down. One untimely flight, one tiny lost soul. But still the dove sits, home for the time being.

Answers

SPELLING

WORDS OFTEN CONFUSED, SET 1 (PP. 9–14)

Exercise 1

1. It's, its, a
2. chose, do, an
3. Due, new, already
4. fill, clothes
5. its, a

6. knew
7. Conscious
8. clothes, have
9. complement, its
10. break

Exercise 2

1. advice, accepted, our
2. are
3. an, desserts
4. course, chose, course, dessert
5. hear, feel

6. conscience, knew
7. effect, complemented
8. fourth, course, all ready
9. break
10. have

Exercise 3

1. our, an, are
2. It's, feel
3. clothes, know
4. due, do
5. conscious, an, effect, our

6. break, conscience
7. course, an, dessert, feel
8. advice, forth, conscious
9. it's
10. know, no, already, chose

Exercise 4

1. its, chose, an
2. an
3. Its, it's
4. conscious, a
5. effect, due

6. accept, clothes
7. fill
8. new, complement
9. course, cloths, coarse, it's
10. course, fill, our, clothes, cloths

Exercise 5

1. already
2. know, its
3. It's, an, have
4. a, conscience
5. accept

6. an
7. chose, accept, desert
8. clothes
9. except
10. due, break, it's, our

Proofreading Exercise

My cat had six kittens last week, and they were all strong and active ~~accept~~ *except* the littlest one born last—it was the runt. ~~It's~~ *Its* head and body were much smaller than those of ~~it's~~ *its* brother and sisters. We named her first and called her Sweet Pea because we were ~~all ready~~ *already* starting to ~~fill~~ *feel* that she was special. At first, the other kittens wouldn't let Sweet Pea eat, and we could ~~here~~ *hear* her cry for milk. It's almost as if the others were trying to get rid of her. We didn't know what to do, so we called the vet to get some ~~advise~~ *advice*. He told us that we could make sure Sweet Pea got enough milk by taking the others out of the box after they seemed full and that eventually Sweet Pea would be ~~excepted~~ *accepted* by the others. The plan worked. By the second day, Sweet Pea was part of the family. We could ~~of~~ *have* lost ~~are~~ *our* favorite kitten if we hadn't received such good advice.

WORDS OFTEN CONFUSED, SET 2 (PP. 19–24)

Exercise 1

1. through
2. women, than
3. whose, who's
4. past, their
5. whether, they're, their

6. woman, wear
7. quite, they're
8. principle, you're, then
9. whether, right, personal
10. There, lose, than, there

Exercise 2

1. There, piece
2. where, past
3. Two, they're, their
4. passed
5. who's, their
6. quite
7. whose, personal
8. led, to, were, were
9. led, to
10. weather, to

Exercise 3

1. where, your
2. two, piece
3. to
4. where
5. loose, than
6. two
7. quite, wear, your, piece
8. you're
9. their, peace, quiet
10. personal, you're

Exercise 4

1. your
2. You're, right, they're, quite
3. through, to, right
4. Their, wear, loose, there
5. to, quite, to, peace
6. than, their
7. who's, they're
8. piece
9. two
10. their, there

Exercise 5

1. where
2. were, wear, write, their
3. were, women
4. whether, principal
5. personnel
6. led, through, past
7. their, quiet, through
8. threw, lose
9. Then, loose, piece
10. whose, were

Proofreading Exercise

When I was in high school, I ~~past~~ *passed* all my classes but didn't learn as much as I wanted ~~too~~ *to*. All of my teachers did ~~they're~~ *their* best, and the ~~princi-ple~~ *principal* was an enthusiastic ~~women~~ *woman* ~~who's~~ *whose* love of education was contagious. ~~Their~~ *There* was no shortage of school spirit; I just wasn't paying enough attention to make the hard information stick. Since I ~~lead~~ *led* a carefree life at the time, I goofed off more ~~then~~ *than* I should have. If I had those high school years to live over again, I would listen in class, do my homework carefully, and make sure that I knew all of the ~~write~~ *right* answers on tests and that I didn't just forget the answers once the test was over.

THE EIGHT PARTS OF SPEECH (PP. 27–30)

Exercise 1

     ADJ.   N.   V.   N.
1. Business owners hire employees.

        N.   V.   ADV. CONJ. V.   N.
2. Employees work hard and earn money.

   PREP. N.   ADJ.   N.   V.   N.   PREP.   N.
3. At holidays, nice bosses offer bonuses to workers.

     ADJ.   N.   ADV. V.   N.   PREP.   N.
4. Business owners often show appreciation to customers.

       ADJ.   N.   V.   ADJ.   N.
5. A prosperous business is a wonderful accomplishment.

   PRO. V.   ADJ.   N.   CONJ. ADJ. N.
6. It reveals good planning and good luck.

       N.   V.   ADJ.   N.
7. Businesspeople speak a special language.

   PRO.   V.   N.   PREP.   N. CONJ.   N.
8. They know the difference between a dozen and a gross.

     N.   V.   N.
9. A dozen equals twelve.

     N. V. ADJ.   N.
10. A gross is twelve dozen.

Exercise 2

     N.   V.   N. CONJ. N.
1. Plants need water and sunlight.

    ADV.   ADJ. N. V.   ADV.
2. Sometimes house plants die unexpectedly.

    ADV.   N.   V. PRO. ADV. ADJ. N. CONJ. ADV. ADJ.   N.
3. Often people give them too much water or not enough water.

   PRO. V.   N.   PREP.   ADJ.   N.   ADV.
4. I saw an experiment on a television show once.

   PRO. V.   ADJ.   N.
5. It involved two plants.

        ADJ.   N.   V.   ADJ.   N.   PREP.   N.   CONJ.   N.
6. The same woman raised both plants with water and sunlight.

       N.   V. PREP. ADJ.   ADJ.   N.
7. The plants grew in two different rooms.

   PRO.   V.   PREP. ADJ. N. CONJ. V.   ADJ.   N. PREP.   PRO.
8. She yelled at one plant but said sweet things to the other.

      ADV.   ADJ.   N.   V.   ADV.
9. The verbally praised plant grew beautifully.

      ADV.   ADJ.   N.   V.
10. The verbally abused plant died.

Exercise 3

    ADJ.   ADJ.   N.   V.   ADJ.   N.
1. Wild Quaker parrots are interesting birds.

   PRO.   ADV.   V.   PREP.   N.
2. They originally came from Argentina.

   PRO. V. ADJ.   N.   PREP.   N.   PREP.   N.
3. They are noisy inhabitants of neighborhoods across the country.

    ADJ.   N.   V. PREP. ADJ.   N. PREP.   N. PREP. ADJ. N.
4. These birds live in large nests at the top of tall trees.

    ADV.   ADJ.   N.   V.   N.
5. Only Quaker parrots build nests.

    ADJ.   N.   V.   ADJ.   N.
6. These nests have three compartments.

     ADJ. N.   V.   N.   PREP.   N.
7. The back part offers protection for the eggs.

    ADJ.   N.   V.   N.
8. The middle section houses the adults.

    N. PREP.   ADJ.   N.   V.   N.   PREP.   N.
9. Parrots in the front compartment guard the entrance to the nest.

    ADJ.   N.   V.   ADJ.   N. PREP. N.
10. Some people raise Quaker parrots as pets.

Exercise 4

         N.   V.   PREP.   N.   CONJ. V. PREP. N.
1. The *Titanic* collided with an iceberg and sank in 1912.

         N.   V.   ADJ.   N.
2. Robert Baboian is a corrosion expert.

  PRO. V.   ADJ.   N.   PREP.   N.
3. He has a unique theory about the disaster.

       N.   V.   PREP.   ADJ.   N. PREP.   N.
4. Baboian believes in an additional cause for the sinking.

    N.   V.   N. PREP.   ADJ. N. CONJ.   N.   V.   N.
5. Rust weakened the rivets in the ship's hull because the builders made an error.

       N.   V.   ADJ.   N. PREP. N. PREP.   N.
6. Builders used one kind of metal for the rivets.

  PRO.   V.   ADJ.   N. PREP. N. PREP.   N.
7. They used another kind of metal for the hull.

  ADV. PRO.   V.   PREP. ADJ. N. PREP.   N.   PREP.   N.
8. Then they worked for one year on the interior of the ship.

     N.   V.   PREP.   N. PREP. ADJ. N.
9. The ship floated in the water for that year.

    PREP.   ADJ.   N.   N.   V.   ADJ.   N.
10. Before the fateful voyage, a photograph shows rust damage.

Exercise 5

  PRO. ADV.   V.   ADJ.   N.   PREP.   ADJ.   N.
1. I recently read some facts about movie kisses.

        ADJ. PRO.   V.   PREP. N. PREP.   N.   PREP. N.
2. The first one occurs in a film by Thomas Edison in 1896.

      N. PREP. ADJ. ADJ. N. V.   N.
3. The title of that short film is *The Kiss*.

   ADJ.   ADJ.   N.   V.   N. PREP. N.
4. A longer movie kiss holds the record for time.

  PREP. ADJ.   N.   N.   V.   N.   PREP. ADJ. ADJ.   N.
5. In a 1941 film, Jane Wyman kisses Regis Toomey for three full minutes.

      N.   V.   PREP. ADJ.   N. PREP. ADJ. N.   CONJ. PRO. ADV.   V.   PRO.
6. Mae West flirts with many men in her movies although she never kisses one

 PREP. PRO.
 of them.

       N.   V.   N.   PREP. ADJ.   N. PREP. PRO.

7. *Don Juan* (1926) is a movie with many kisses in it.

           N.   V.   ADV. ADJ.   N.   PREP. PRO.

8. John Barrymore delivers nearly two hundred of them.

  PREP. ADJ.   N.   ADJ. N.   V. PREP. ADJ.   N.   PREP. N.

9. In that movie, one kiss occurs for each minute of film.

   INTER. PRO. V.   ADJ.   N. PREP. N.

10. Gee, I love trivial facts like these.

Paragraph Exercise

           N. V. ADV. ADV.   ADJ.   N.   PREP. N. PREP.   N.   N. CONJ. N. V.

        Birds are not usually a good match with rats. In the wild, birds and rats are

ADJ.   N.   PREP.   N.   PREP.   ADJ.   N.   N. V. ADJ. N. CONJ.

natural enemies. In survival of the biggest (animal), rats eat small birds and

ADJ.   N.   ADJ.   N.   V. PREP. N. ADV. ADV. CONJ. PREP. ADJ.   N.   ADJ. N. V.

bird eggs. Large birds prey on rats as well. So, as a general rule, most birds are

   ADJ. CONJ. ADV.   ADJ.   PREP.   N.

nervous and even frightened around rats.

CONTRACTIONS (PP. 32–37)

Exercise 1

  1. who's

  2. That's

  3. wasn't

  4. wasn't

  5. didn't

  6. didn't, would've

  7. couldn't

  8. It's

  9. isn't

  10. wouldn't

Exercise 2

  1. aren't

  2. they're

  3. it's

  4. we've

  5. no contractions

  6. It's

  7. no contractions

  8. no contractions

  9. they're

  10. Let's

Exercise 3

1. aren't, they're
2. they've
3. They're, you're
4. we've, they're
5. They're

6. they're
7. There's, who's, they've
8. shouldn't
9. doesn't, it's
10. that's

Exercise 4

1. I'm, you've
2. weren't
3. she's, he's, they're, who's
4. that's
5. no contractions

6. That's, we've, she's, wouldn't
7. wasn't
8. didn't, she's
9. he's
10. doesn't, she's

Exercise 5

1. I've, hasn't
2. they'd
3. it's (obvious), wouldn't
4. it's, they're
5. that's, there's

6. wouldn't
7. wasn't, it's
8. don't, wouldn't, that's
9. wouldn't
10. should've, wouldn't, that's

Proofreading Exercise

Jokes can ~~effect~~ *affect* people differently. No ~~too~~ *two* individuals have the same sense of humor. ~~Thats~~ *That's* why it may be risky to tell jokes at work or to people ~~youv'e~~ *you've* just met. I had a friend once ~~who's~~ *whose* timing and delivery were perfect. Jake could tell a joke to a person getting a root canal, and the person would ~~of~~ *have* laughed. It ~~was'nt~~ *wasn't* the actual jokes that were so funny; it was the way Jake told them. I remember one of the short ones. Jake would ask, "What sits at the bottom of the ocean and shakes?" ~~Hed~~ *He'd* tilt his head to the side a bit and look the person in the eye while waiting for an answer. Just as the person was about to respond with a stupid guess, Jake would blurt out, "A nervous wreck." The look on Jake's face was as funny as the punch line, and I think that must be the secret of a good comedian—he or ~~shes~~ *she's* funnier ~~then~~ *than* the jokes themselves.

POSSESSIVES (PP. 39–44)

Exercise 4

1. Manning's
2. critic's, Columbia Pictures'
3. Manning's, *Knight's*
4. writer's
5. Manning's

6. studio's
7. Manning's
8. public's
9. no possessives
10. films'

Exercise 5

1. zipper's
2. no possessives
3. people's
4. zipper's
5. Judson's, mechanism's

6. Sundback's
7. public's
8. person's
9. America's, jeans' (zippers)
10. world's

Proofreading Exercise

The Calderons are members of a family that has lived next door to me for 20 years. I have grown up with the ~~Calderon's~~ *Calderons'* daughter, Kim. My family is bigger than ~~her's~~ *hers*. When I go to her house, ~~Kims~~ *Kim's* favorite pastime is putting together jigsaw puzzles. We always start off by separating a ~~puzzles~~ *puzzle's* pieces into different categories. She makes piles of edge pieces, sky pieces, flower pieces, and so on. Then I start putting the edge ~~piece's~~ *pieces* together to form the border. The Calderons' son, Simon, usually shows up just in time to put the last piece in the puzzle.

REVIEW OF CONTRACTIONS AND POSSESSIVES (PP. 44–46)

1. I've, Lucy's
2. show's, today's
3. Lucy's, Ethel's
4. can't, it's

5. it'll

6. Lucy and Ethel's, agent's

7. factory's, woman's, candies'

8. Lucy's, can't, hasn't

9. don't

10. Ricky and Fred's, haven't, Lucy and Ethel's, it's

Going to the Globe

I was very fortunate to attend a high school where there's an English teacher, Ms. Evans, who absolutely loves Shakespeare. Ever since she'd heard that a new Globe Theater had been built in London, she said, "I'm going to see it now that it's finished, and I'll take a group of students with me."

Shakespeare's original Globe Theater had been destroyed by a fire in 1613 during a performance of one of his plays, and it hadn't been rebuilt until recently. I'm one of the lucky students who accompanied Ms. Evans on her first trip to the new Globe.

When we arrived in London, Ms. Evans' excitement rubbed off on all of us. We found the Globe's location across the Thames River from another of London's most famous landmarks—Big Ben.

The theater's outside was just as beautiful as its inside, and it smelled like freshly cut lumber. In fact, that's what it's almost entirely made of. There's not a nail used in the whole outer frame structure. The huge wooden beams visible from the outside are held in place with more than 6,000 wooden pegs, just as Shakespeare's craftsmen would've done.

We didn't get to see a performance at the Globe, but the tour guide's description of one of them made it possible to imagine an audience's excitement, an actor's challenges, and a playwright's satisfaction at the rebuilding of his Globe Theater.

RULE FOR DOUBLING A FINAL LETTER (PP. 48–49)

Exercise 1

1. steaming	**6.** wedding
2. expelling	**7.** stressing
3. sipping	**8.** flopping
4. suffering	**9.** spinning
5. warring	**10.** differing

Exercise 2

1. shopping
2. offering
3. wrapping
4. nailing
5. knitting

6. omitting
7. honoring
8. bragging
9. marking
10. hopping

Exercise 3

1. getting
2. trusting
3. tripping
4. planning
5. benefiting

6. missing
7. reading
8. occurring
9. skimming
10. screaming

Exercise 4

1. creeping
2. subtracting
3. abandoning
4. drooping
5. happening

6. weeding
7. fogging
8. dropping
9. referring
10. submitting

Exercise 5

1. interpreting
2. preferring
3. betting
4. stooping
5. flipping

6. inferring
7. guessing
8. bugging
9. jogging
10. building

PROGRESS TEST (P. 50)

1. B. should *have* worked
2. B. break

3. B. children's

4. A. whether

5. A. It's

6. B. advice

7. B. complemented

8. B. Equipping

9. A. complimented

10. A. its

SENTENCE STRUCTURE

FINDING SUBJECTS AND VERBS (PP. 61–64)

Exercise 1

1. Human beings are creatures of habit.

2. They visit predictable places and do predictable things.

3. In their work, scientists study such behavior.

4. George Karev is a member of the Bulgarian Academy of Sciences.

5. Karev studied the habits of people in movie theaters.

6. Karev's results about moviegoers make a lot of sense.

7. Most moviegoers prefer seats on the right side of the theater and always sit there.

8. Therefore, their left eye sees most of the movie.

9. The left eye generally reports to the right hemisphere of the brain.

10. The right hemisphere connects people with their own feelings and with the emotions of others.

Exercise 2

1. Traffic reports on the radio and TV affect people's lives.

2. But such reports are not always available.

3. On the road, drivers without radios miss important warnings.

4. There are many possible results.

5. Sometimes a bad <u>accident</u> or a construction <u>site</u> <u>slows</u> traffic to a halt.

6. At such times, <u>drivers</u> and their <u>passengers</u> <u>sit</u> in traffic jams for hours.

7. <u>Police</u> and transportation <u>officials</u> often <u>provide</u> detours in these cases.

8. Informed <u>drivers</u> <u>avoid</u> wasted hours through the use of such detours.

9. Traffic <u>reports</u> on the radio <u>are</u> invaluable.

10. <u>They</u> <u>help</u> drivers out of many difficult situations.

Exercise 3

1. There <u>is</u> a long-standing <u>tradition</u> in lunch rooms.

2. <u>Children</u> <u>get</u> peanut butter-and-jelly sandwiches in their lunchboxes.

3. The PB&J <u>sandwich</u> <u>seems</u> an almost fool-proof choice for a kid's lunch.

4. Most <u>kids</u> <u>love</u> the sight, smell, and taste of this combination of salty peanut butter, sweet jelly, and soft bread.

5. But <u>peanuts</u> <u>are</u> dangerous to children with peanut allergies.

6. Most <u>youngsters</u> <u>eat</u> peanuts and <u>feel</u> fine.

7. A mildly allergic <u>child</u> <u>reacts</u> with watery eyes and hives.

8. In extreme cases, <u>children</u> with peanut allergies <u>die</u>.

9. So there <u>are</u> peanut-free <u>zones</u> in some schools.

10. With each new academic year, <u>schools</u> <u>increase</u> their awareness of risks such as peanut allergies.

Exercise 4

1. <u>I</u> never <u>knew</u> much about curses and magic spells.

2. According to *Smithsonian* magazine, the <u>Greeks</u> and <u>Romans</u> <u>used</u> them all the time.

3. There <u>were</u> <u>magicians</u> for hire back then.

4. These <u>magicians</u> <u>made</u> money through their knowledge of the art of cursing.

5. Some ancient <u>citizens</u> <u>took</u> revenge on their enemies with special curses for failure.

6. <u>Others</u> <u><u>wanted</u></u> only love and <u><u>placed</u></u> spells on the objects of their desire.

7. The <u>magicians</u> <u><u>wrote</u></u> the commissioned curses or love spells on lead tablets.

8. Then <u>they</u> <u><u>positioned</u></u> these curse tablets near their intended victims.

9. <u>Archeologists</u> <u><u>found</u></u> one 1,700-year-old curse tablet over the starting gate of an ancient race course.

10. <u>It</u> <u><u>named</u></u> the horses and drivers of specific chariots and <u><u>itemized</u></u> the specifics of the curse.

Exercise 5

1. Plastic snow <u>domes</u> <u><u>are</u></u> popular souvenir items.

2. <u>They</u> <u><u>are</u></u> clear domes usually on white oval bases.

3. <u>People</u> <u><u>display</u></u> these water-filled objects or <u><u>use</u></u> them as paperweights.

4. Inside <u><u>are</u></u> tiny <u>replicas</u> of famous tourist attractions like the Eiffel Tower or Big Ben.

5. <u>Snow</u> or <u>glitter</u> <u><u>mixes</u></u> with the water for a snowstorm effect.

6. These <u>souvenirs</u> often <u><u>hold</u></u> startling combinations.

7. In a snow dome, even the <u>Bahamas</u> <u><u>has</u></u> blizzards.

8. There <u><u>is</u></u> also a Los Angeles <u>dome</u> with smog instead of snow.

9. Snow dome <u>collectors</u> <u><u>regard</u></u> them as valuable objects.

10. <u>Others</u> <u><u>treat</u></u> them as mere trinkets.

Paragraph Exercise

<u>Al Levis</u> <u><u>invented</u></u> the popular snack Slim Jims. <u>Slim Jims</u> <u><u>are</u></u> stick-shaped meat snacks. <u>Levis</u> <u><u>was</u></u> a high-school dropout but eventually <u><u>made</u></u> a fortune from his snack product. <u>Slim Jims</u> originally <u><u>came</u></u> in jars full of vinegar. In the 1940s and 50s, bar <u>customers</u> <u><u>ate</u></u> Slim Jims with their cocktails. Then Levis's <u>company</u> offered Slim Jims in individual packages. <u>People</u> <u><u>ate</u></u> them on camping trips and at sporting events. <u>Levis</u> <u><u>sold</u></u> his invention in the late 1960s but <u><u>continued</u></u> his good work. Before his death in March of 2001, <u>Levis</u> <u><u>donated</u></u> millions of dollars to worthy causes.

LOCATING PREPOSITIONAL PHRASES (PP. 67–70)

Exercise 1

1. (In February) (of 2001), a powerful <u>earthquake</u> <u><u>struck</u></u> Seattle, Washington, and its surrounding communities.

2. <u>One</u> (of those communities) <u><u>was</u></u> Port Townsend.

3. (At Mind Over Matter), a Port Townsend specialty store, the <u>shaking</u> (of the earth) <u><u>caused</u></u> more than just damage.

4. A favorite <u>display</u> (at the store) <u><u>was</u></u> a pendulum (with sand) (beneath it).

5. (With its powerful shaking), the <u>earthquake</u> <u><u>moved</u></u> the pendulum and <u><u>drew</u></u> a picture (in the shape) (of a rose).

6. <u>Jason Ward</u>, the store's owner, <u><u>noticed</u></u> the unique drawing (in the sand) right (after the quake).

7. (During some earthquakes), the <u>ground</u> <u><u>moves</u></u> back and forth (in one direction).

8. (In the Seattle quake), the <u>ground</u> <u><u>shook</u></u> (in many directions).

9. <u>Ward</u> and <u>others</u> <u><u>marveled</u></u> (at the beauty) (of the quake's design) and <u><u>planned</u></u> a casting (of it).

10. But Ward's <u>son</u> <u><u>knocked</u></u> the sand tray (by mistake) and <u><u>erased</u></u> nature's handiwork.

Exercise 2

1. The many <u>cases</u> (of food poisoning) (in America) each year <u><u>alarm</u></u> people.

2. Some food <u>scientists</u> <u><u>point</u></u> (to food irradiation) (as one possible solution).

3. The <u>irradiation</u> (of food) <u><u>kills</u></u> bacteria (through exposure) (to gamma rays).

4. (With irradiation), <u>farmers</u> <u><u>spray</u></u> fewer pesticides (on their crops).

5. And irradiated <u>food</u> <u><u>lasts</u></u> longer (on the shelf) or (in the refrigerator).

6. However, many <u>scientists</u> and <u>consumers</u> <u><u>worry</u></u> (about the risks) (of food irradiation).

7. <u>Irradiation</u> <u><u>reduces</u></u> vitamins and <u><u>changes</u></u> nutrients (in the food).

8. The radioactive <u>materials</u> (at the irradiation plants) <u><u>are</u></u> also potentially dangerous.

9. <u>Critics</u> <u><u>predict</u></u> accidents (in the transportation and use) (of these radioactive substances).

10. (In the United States), the <u>controversy</u> (about food irradiation) <u><u>continues</u></u>.

Exercise 3

1. *<u>Romeo and Juliet</u>* <u><u>is</u></u> many people's favorite play (by William Shakespeare).

2. The Bard's love <u>story</u> <u><u>remains</u></u> one (of the most famous) (in the world).

3. Many <u>movies</u> <u><u>use</u></u> aspects (of this story) (as part) (of their plots).

4. One <u>thing</u> (about the story) <u><u>surprises</u></u> people.

5. Both <u>Romeo</u> and <u>Juliet</u> <u><u>have</u></u> other love interests (at some point) (in the play).

6. <u>Romeo</u> <u><u>has</u></u> his eyes (on Rosaline) (before Juliet).

7. And <u>Juliet</u> <u><u>accepts</u></u> Paris's marriage proposal (against her will).

8. But (before her unwanted wedding day), <u>Juliet</u> <u><u>elopes</u></u> (with Romeo) (in secret).

9. <u>Friar Lawrence</u> <u><u>helps</u></u> the newlyweds (with a plan) (for their escape) (without anyone's notice).

10. However, the complicated <u>timing</u> (of his plan) <u><u>has</u></u> tragic results (on the lives) (of Romeo and Juliet).

Exercise 4

1. (For a change) (of pace), <u>I</u> <u><u>shopped</u></u> (for my Mother's Day gift) (at an antique mall).

2. <u>I</u> <u><u>found</u></u> old Bakelite jewelry (in every shade) (of yellow, brown, red, blue, and green).

3. There <u><u>were</u></u> even <u>linens</u> (from all the way) back (to the pioneer days).

4. One <u>booth</u> <u><u>sold</u></u> only drinking glasses (with advertising slogans and cartoon characters) (on them).

5. Another <u>stocked</u> old metal banks (with elaborate mechanisms) (for children's pennies).

6. (In the back corner) (of the mall), <u>I</u> <u>found</u> a light blue pitcher (with a dark blue design).

7. My <u>mother</u> <u>had</u> one (like it) (in the early years) (of my childhood).

8. My <u>sisters</u> and <u>I</u> <u>liked</u> to drink punch (from it) (on hot days) (in the summer). [*To drink* is a *verbal*, not a prepositional phrase or the real verb in the sentence.]

9. <u>I</u> <u>checked</u> the price (on the tag) (underneath the pitcher's handle).

10. But (at a moment) (like that), my <u>mind</u> <u>was</u> not on money.

Exercise 5

1. (Over the weekend), <u>I</u> <u>watched</u> a hilarious old movie, *Genevieve,* (on late-night television).

2. The whole <u>story</u> <u>takes</u> place (in the countryside) (of England).

3. <u>It</u> <u>is</u> a black-and-white movie (from the 1930s or 1940s).

4. The <u>clothes</u> and <u>manners</u> (of the characters) (in *Genevieve*) <u>are</u> very proper and old-fashioned.

5. Two young <u>couples</u> <u>enter</u> their cars (in a road rally) (for fun).

6. <u>They</u> <u>participate</u> (in the race) strictly (for adventure).

7. <u>Genevieve</u> <u>is</u> the name (of the main couple's car).

8. (During the road rally), the two couples' polite <u>manners</u> <u>disappear</u> (in the rush) (for the finish line).

9. Predictably, <u>they</u> <u>began</u> to fight (with each other) and to sabotage each other's cars. [*To fight* and *to sabotage* are *verbals*, not prepositional phrases or real verbs in the sentence.]

10. But (like all good comedies), <u>Genevieve</u> and its <u>ending</u> <u>hold</u> a surprise (for everyone).

Paragraph Exercise

Meteors are visitors (from outer space). They hit our atmosphere (at tremendous speeds)—perhaps 90,000 miles (per hour). Friction (with the air) (of the upper atmosphere) heats them (to incandescence), and most (of them) vaporize (into gases) or disintegrate (into harmless dust) . . . (within 30 miles) (of the earth's surface). Thus our atmosphere protects us. Millions (of meteors), most (of them) smaller than grains (of sand), hit our atmosphere every day. Very few ever reach the ground.

UNDERSTANDING DEPENDENT CLAUSES (PP. 74–78)

Exercise 1

1. People who need glasses often wear contact lenses.

2. Clear contact lenses maintain a person's appearance because they fit over the eye and have no frames.

3. But there are contact lenses that change a person's eye color.

4. Someone who has green eyes makes them blue or brown with colored contact lenses.

5. Now even people who don't need glasses change their eye color with contact lenses.

6. Colored lenses are fashion statements that are especially popular with young people.

7. Unless a doctor fits them, contact lenses that people buy or trade with friends invite injuries.

8. Ill-fitting lenses squeeze or scratch the eyes as they move around under the eyelids.

9. After a scratch occurs, germs easily infect the eyes' surface.

10. Such infections sometimes lead to damage that is permanent.

Exercise 2

1. I am not very talkative in school.

2. Whenever my teacher asks a question in class, I get nervous.

3. If I know the answer, I usually look straight ahead.

4. When I forget the answer, I check my shoes or a note in my notebook.

5. Usually, the teacher chooses someone else before I finish my fidgeting.

6. Obviously, when I take a speech class, I talk sometimes.

7. In my last speech class, we all demonstrated some sort of process.

8. The speech that I gave explained how I make crepes.

9. Since I work at a French restaurant, I borrowed a crepe pan for my demonstration.

10. The crepes cooked so quickly that the teacher and students passed the plates around before I said anything at all.

Exercise 3

1. Many people remember when microwave ovens first arrived in stores.

2. People worried about whether they were safe or not.

3. Before they had the microwave oven, people cooked all food with direct heat.

4. At first, microwave ovens were strange because they heated only the food.

5. And microwave ovens cooked food so much faster than ordinary ovens did.

6. Eventually, people welcomed the convenience that microwave ovens offered.

7. Since they are fast and cool, microwave ovens work well almost anywhere.

8. People who are on a budget bring lunch from home and heat it up at work or school.

9. Now that microwave ovens are here, people even make popcorn without a pan.

10. As each new technology arrives, people wonder how they ever lived without it.

Exercise 4

1. Since we all want perfect documents, nearly everyone uses correction fluid or tape sometimes.

2. Bette Nesmith invented Liquid Paper or, as she first called it, "Mistake Out."

3. After the young bank secretary noticed that sign painters always painted over their errors instead of erasing them, she had an idea.

4. Nesmith started filling up small bottles with white paint, which she used for her typing mistakes.

5. As soon as her friends saw how well Nesmith's paint worked, they all wanted their own bottles.

6. Once she realized that the idea was a success, she developed a liquid that was more than just paint.

7. She patented her formula and called it Liquid Paper.

8. She took the product to a big corporation.

9. After IBM rejected Nesmith's invention, she formed The Liquid Paper Company herself and earned a large fortune.

10. Michael Nesmith, who is Bette Nesmith's son, helped his mother in her business even after he became a member of the famous group The Monkees.

Exercise 5

1. When I first heard the expression "white elephant," I didn't know what it meant.

2. Yesterday I finally learned what "white elephant" means.

3. A white elephant is an unwanted object that is difficult to get rid of.

4. Most white elephants are gifts that friends or relatives give us.

5. As I read the story behind the expression, I understood it better.

6. The ruler of an ancient land received any white elephants born in his country; it was a custom that sometimes came in handy.

7. The ruler then gave the white elephants as presents to people who angered him.

8. The elephants ate so much and were so costly that they ruined the lives of the people who received them as "gifts."

9. That is why we now use the term for objects that cause us to feel responsible and burdened.

10. Whenever I give a present, I choose it carefully so that it is not a white elephant.

Paragraph Exercise

I do not remember when I first realized that I was different from other people; but I knew it before my teacher came to me. I had noticed that my mother and my friends did not use signs as I did when they wanted anything done, but talked with their mouths. Sometimes I stood between two persons who were conversing and touched their lips. I could not understand, and was vexed. I moved my lips and gesticulated frantically without result. This made me so angry at times that I kicked and screamed until I was exhausted.

I think [that] I knew when I was naughty, for I knew that it hurt Ella, my nurse, to kick her, and when my fit of temper was over I had a feeling akin to regret. But I cannot remember any instance in which this feeling prevented me from repeating the naughtiness when I failed to get what I wanted.

CORRECTING FRAGMENTS (PP. 81–85)

Exercise 1

Possible revisions to make the fragments into sentences are *italicized*.

1. Duct tape has many uses. (sentence)

2. *Duct tape* holds objects together firmly. (fragment)

3. *It also* patches holes in backpacks and tents. (fragment)

4. People are very creative with duct tape. (sentence)

5. Books *have been* written about the unique uses for it. (fragment)

6. *The makers of Duck Brand duct tape hold a yearly contest.* (fragment)

7. High school prom couples make their outfits entirely from duct tape. (sentence)

8. Strips of duct tape *form* tuxedos, cummerbunds, gowns, hats, and corsages. (fragment)

9. A $2,500 prize *goes* to the couple with the best use of duct tape and another $2,500 *goes* to their high school. (fragment)

10. Hundreds of couples from across the country participate in this contest every year. (sentence)

Exercise 2

Changes used to make the fragments into sentences are *italicized*.

1. The largest of the dinosaurs were probably vegetarians. (sentence)

2. Tyrannosaurus rex *was* a meat-eater or carnivore. (fragment)

3. *T. Rex was* supposedly the biggest of the carnivorous dinosaurs. (fragment)

4. In 1995, scientists discovered the remains of a bigger carnivore than T. Rex. (sentence)

5. *This big carnivorous dinosaur lived* in Africa ninety million years ago. (fragment)

6. Scientists named it Carcharodontosaurus saharicus. (sentence)

7. *Carcharodontosaurus saharicus means* having shark-like teeth and living in the Sahara Desert. (fragment)

8. It was almost fifty feet long and weighed eight tons. (sentence)

9. *Its* skull *was* five and a half feet in length. (fragment)

10. T. Rex may have been smaller but will always have an easier name to remember. (sentence)

Exercise 3

Answers may vary, but here are some possible revisions.

1. We shopped all day at the mall. We were looking for the perfect suitcases for our cruise this summer.

2. We knew of a specialty store with hard and soft luggage, large and small sizes, and lots of accessories to choose from.

3. Walking from store to store and getting tired, we gave up after a while and sat down.

4. Resting on a bench for a few minutes, we enjoyed ourselves by "people-watching."

5. We could not believe the crowds at the mall on a weekday. They were in every shop and at the food court, too.

6. Crowding the walkways and window shopping, human beings circulated in every direction.

7. Teenagers gathered in groups, laughed at each other, and ignored the shoppers.

8. Pairs of older people used the mall as an exercise facility and walked briskly around the balconies.

9. We finally resumed our search and found the perfect luggage at a little store near the elevators at the end of the mall.

10. Because of all the interesting people and the final outcome, our shopping trip was a complete success.

Exercise 4

Answers may vary, but here are some possible revisions.

1. Thrift stores, yard sales, and flea markets are popular places to shop because they sell items that aren't available anywhere else as cheaply.

2. Also, most thrift stores benefit charities, which use the profits to help people in need. (The comma before *which* indicates that the clause contains unessential information.)

3. Although the styles of clothing and furniture found in thrift stores are often five to thirty years old, many people prefer these vintage designs.

4. For instance, thrift stores sell old shelving units made of solid wood or thick metal, which are much more substantial than modern ones made of cheap wood or plastic. (The comma before *which* indicates that the clause contains unessential information.)

5. There are also famous stories of people becoming rich because they shopped at yard sales and flea markets.

6. One man bought a framed picture for a few dollars at a flea market since he liked the frame itself but not the picture.

7. When he removed the picture from the frame at home, he found one of the original copies of the "Declaration of Independence."

8. At a yard sale, a woman bought a small table which she later discovered was worth half a million dollars.

9. Of course, collectors always shop at these places, where they hope to find treasures like rare cookie jars, pens, paintings, records, toys, and other objects of value. (The comma before *where* indicates that the clause contains unessential information.)

10. In a way, shopping at thrift stores, yard sales, and flea markets is a kind of recycling, which is something that benefits everyone. (The comma before *which* indicates that the clause contains unessential information.)

Exercise 5

Answers may vary, but here are some possible revisions. (Additions are in *italics*.)

1. *The referees watched* as the players walked off the field.

2. She was a tough comedienne with a painful past.

3. Luckily, a relative saw the amnesia victim's story on the news.

4. If cars could fly, *traffic would not be a problem.*

5. Tragically, Mozart died at an early age.

6. We had no fire insurance at the time.

7. Since that car costs too much, *I'll buy a less expensive one.*

8. Finally, I asked someone for directions to the museum.

9. The government protects endangered species.

10. *No one knows* where the technology of cloning will be in ten years.

Proofreading Paragraph

Here is one possible revision to eliminate the five fragments.

Shark attacks have been on the rise. We've all heard the heartbreaking news stories of people on their honeymoons or children playing in only a few feet of water being attacked by sharks. Movies like *Jaws* make us wary and scared when we watch them. But their effects fade over time, and we forget about the risks of entering the habitats of dangerous animals. Experts try to convince us that sharks and other powerful species are not targeting human beings on purpose. To a shark, a person is no different from a seal or a sea turtle. Facts such as these prompt many of us to think twice before we take a dip in the ocean.

CORRECTING RUN-ON SENTENCES (PP. 89–93)

Exercise 1

Your answers may differ depending on how you choose to separate the two clauses.

1. Nearly everyone yawns, but few understand the dynamics of yawning.

2. The sentence is correct.

3. The sentence is correct.

4. The sentence is correct.

5. Groups of people do similar things, for they are acting somewhat like herds of animals.

6. The sentence is correct.

7. The yawning helps the group act as one, so it minimizes conflict.

8. There are a few misconceptions about yawns. One of them has to do with oxygen levels.

9. The sentence is correct.

10. Surprisingly, studies show no changes in yawning patterns due to levels of oxygen; in fact, research subjects inhaling pure oxygen yawned the same number of times as those breathing normally.

Exercise 2

Your answers may differ depending on how you choose to separate the two clauses.

1. I am writing a research paper on Margaret Fuller. She is a famous American writer and philosopher from the early 1800s.

2. The sentence is correct.

3. Historians call this famous group of people the "Concord Circle," for they lived in and around Concord, Massachusetts.

4. Fuller's father chose to educate her himself; therefore, they had a very close and intense relationship.

5. She read Latin at the age of six and became extremely well-educated, but her famous neighbors found the mixture of her intellect and her lively personality puzzling.

6. Fuller wrote a book called *Woman in the Nineteenth Century.* After that, she moved to Italy.

7. She married an Italian named Giovanni Ossoli; they had a son and planned to return to America.

8. Some of her acquaintances back in America frowned on her marriage to a younger and less intelligent man, so they dreaded her return.

9. Fuller had nightmares of drowning in a shipwreck; she wrote of these fears in letters to her mother and others.

10. In 1850, Margaret Fuller, her husband, and their son died. Their ship sank in a storm just a few hundred yards off the coast of America.

Exercise 3

Your answers may differ since various words can be used to begin dependent clauses.

1. On summer evenings, people around the world enjoy the sight of little lights that are flying around in the air.

2. Although most people know the glowing insects as fireflies, they are also called lightning bugs and glowworms.

3. Glowworms are unique since they don't fly.

4. The term *fireflies* is a little misleading because they are not technically flies.

5. Lightning bugs are beetles that have special substances in their bodies.

6. The substances that make them glow are luciferin and luciferase.

7. When the luciferin and luciferase combine with oxygen, they produce a greenish light.

8. The light can be so intense that people in some countries use caged fireflies as lamps.

9. The sentence is correct.

10. Incredibly, even though groups of fireflies blink out of order at first, they seem to coordinate their blinking within a few minutes.

Exercise 4

Your answers may differ since various words can be used to begin dependent clauses.

1. The sentence is correct.

2. The calls are made by companies whose salespeople try to interest us in the newest calling plan or credit card offer.

3. They don't call during the day when nobody is home.

4. I feel sorry for some of the salespeople since they're just doing their job.

5. When my father tells them to call during business hours, they hang up right away.

6. The sentence is correct.

7. When my mother answers, she is too polite, so they just keep talking.

8. Although we try to ignore the ringing, it drives us all crazy.

9. The sentence is correct.

10. Since we never buy anything over the phone, maybe these companies will all get the message and leave us alone.

Exercise 5

Your answers may differ depending on how you chose to connect the clauses.

1. In 2001, American businessman Dennis Tito did something that no one had done before.

2. Tito became the world's first tourist in space when he paid twenty million dollars for a ride to the International Space Station.

3. Tito wanted the United States to take him into space, but NASA said no.

4. NASA declined Tito's offer; however, Russian space officials accepted it gladly.

5. In early May 2001, Tito boarded a Russian Soyuz rocket, and he blasted off into outer space.

6. Tito could talk to the cosmonauts on board because he studied Russian for six months before his trip.

7. Dennis Tito's first-of-its-kind vacation was just the beginning of civilian travel into outer space; more and more individuals will want to follow Tito's example.

8. There will be travel agents who will specialize in space travel.

9. Other countries besides Russia will welcome the income from such trips; for example, China may soon have the ability to take people into space.

10. In 2001, NASA chose not to let Tito on one of its space shuttles; however, if future space programs are funded through space tourism, NASA may not have a choice.

REVIEW OF FRAGMENTS AND RUN-ON SENTENCES (P. 94)

Your revisions may differ depending on how you chose to correct the errors.

In April of 2001, a writer named Terry Ryan published a book about her mother. She titled the book *The Prize Winner of Defiance: How My Mother Raised 10 Kids on 25 Words or Less*. Ryan had already written two poetry books and was busy writing a comic strip for a San Francisco newspaper when she decided to tell her mom's story. Terry's mother, Evelyn Ryan, was a remarkable woman who entered contest after contest in the 1950s and won most of them. In those days, companies sponsored competitions and gave prizes to the writers of the best slogan, poem, or jingle about their product. Evelyn Ryan was such a naturally good writer that she won countless prizes, ranging from small appliances to large cash awards. She earned them all through skill and perseverance. Terry Ryan especially remembers her mother's organizational skills and generosity. Evelyn Ryan, her daughter explains, was also motivated by her circumstances as the wife of an alcoholic. She did it all for her family; winning such contests was her way of staying at home, supporting ten children, and keeping the family together.

IDENTIFYING VERB PHRASES (PP. 96–100)

Exercise 1

1. Shopping (for holiday items) has taken a turn (for the worse) (in recent years).

2. Before one holiday has arrived, another holiday's decorations line the shelves (of stores).

3. (In early July), (for instance), shoppers will not find banners to celebrate Independence Day.

4. Instead, they will see Halloween items already (for sale).

5. And (by October), store owners will have placed turkeys and pilgrims (in full view).

6. (Of course), Kwanza, Hanukah, and Christmas sales begin (in September) (on their own special aisle).

7. What <u>can</u> <u>people</u> <u>do</u> (about this trend)?

8. <u>Shoppers</u> <u>could</u> <u>protest</u> and <u>boycott</u> early displays.

9. <u>They</u> <u>could</u> <u>tell</u> store managers (about their concerns).

10. But <u>they</u> <u>might</u> just <u>miss</u> the chance to buy that cute little bunny (at the spring sale) (in January).

Exercise 2

1. (On December 16, 2000), the London stage <u>production</u> (of Agatha Christie's play *The Mousetrap*) <u>marked</u> a milestone.

2. (On that night), <u>actors</u> <u>were</u> <u>performing</u> Christie's play (for the twenty-thousandth time).

3. (In fact), *The Mousetrap* <u>broke</u> the record (as the world's longest running play).

4. The <u>play</u> <u>opened</u> (in London) (on November 25, 1952), and <u>had</u> <u>been</u> <u>running</u> continually ever since.

5. More than ten million <u>people</u> <u>had</u> <u>attended</u> the London performances.

6. There <u>are</u> other interesting <u>facts</u> (about this production).

7. Two <u>pieces</u> (of the original set)—the clock and the armchair—<u>had</u> <u>survived</u> (on stage) (for half a century).

8. The <u>cast</u>, however, <u>had</u> <u>changed</u> more often.

9. Some <u>actors</u> <u>had</u> <u>remained</u> (in the show) (for years) while <u>others</u> <u>had</u> <u>played</u> parts (for only a short time).

10. One <u>actress</u> <u>understudied</u> (for over six thousand performances), but <u>she</u> <u>was</u> <u>needed</u> (on stage) only seventy-two times.

Exercise 3

1. <u>Felix</u> <u>Hoffmann</u>, a chemist, <u>was</u> <u>trying</u> to ease his own father's pain when <u>he</u> <u>discovered</u> aspirin (in 1897).

2. Although <u>aspirin</u> <u>can</u> <u>cause</u> side effects, each year <u>people</u> (around the world) <u>give</u> themselves fifty billion doses (of the popular pain killer).

3. But different <u>countries</u> <u>take</u> this medicine (in different ways).

4. The <u>British</u> <u>like</u> to dissolve aspirin powder (in water).

5. The <u>French</u> <u>have</u> <u>insisted</u> that slow-release <u>methods</u> <u>work</u> best.

6. <u>Italians</u> <u>prefer</u> aspirin drinks (with a little fizz).

7. And <u>Americans</u> <u>have</u> always <u>chosen</u> to take their aspirin (in pill form).

8. However <u>it</u> <u>is taken</u>, <u>aspirin</u> <u>continues</u> to surprise researchers (with benefits) (to human health).

9. <u>It</u> <u>has been found</u> to benefit people susceptible (to heart attack, colon cancer, and Alzheimer's disease).

10. Where <u>would</u> <u>we</u> <u>be</u> (without aspirin)?

Exercise 4

1. <u>I</u> <u>have</u> just <u>read</u> (about the life) (of Philo T. Farnsworth).

2. Thirteen-year-old <u>Philo T. Farnsworth</u> <u>was plowing</u> a field (in 1922) when <u>he</u> <u>visualized</u> the concept <u>that</u> <u>led</u> (to television) as <u>we</u> <u>know</u> it.

3. <u>Others</u> <u>were working</u> (on the idea) (of sending images) (through the air), but <u>Farnsworth</u> actually <u>solved</u> the problem (in that open field).

4. <u>He</u> <u>looked</u> (at the rows) that the <u>plow</u> <u>had made</u> (in the earth).

5. And <u>he</u> <u>reasoned</u> that <u>images</u> <u>could be broken</u> down (into rows) and <u>sent</u> line (by line) (through the air) and (onto a screen).

6. Farnsworth's <u>idea</u> <u>made</u> television a reality, but historically <u>he</u> <u>has</u> not <u>been</u> fully <u>recognized</u> (for this and his other accomplishments).

7. (In 1957), <u>he</u> <u>was featured</u> (as a guest) (on *I've Got a Secret,*) a television show <u>that</u> <u>presented</u> mystery contestants.

8. The <u>panelists</u> (on the show) <u>were supposed</u> to guess the guest's secret, which the <u>audience</u> <u>was shown</u> so that <u>everyone</u> <u>knew</u> the answer (except the people) asking the questions.

9. <u>They</u> <u>asked</u> if <u>he</u> <u>had invented</u> something painful, and <u>he</u> <u>replied</u> that <u>he</u> <u>had</u>; the <u>panelists</u> never <u>guessed</u> that <u>he</u> <u>was</u> the inventor (of television).

10. <u>Farnsworth</u> <u>did receive</u> a box (of cigarettes) and eighty dollars (for being) (on the show).

Exercise 5

1. <u>I</u> <u>like</u> to walk (around the park) (with my two little dogs) (in the early evenings).

2. The <u>three</u> (of us) <u>have enjoyed</u> this ritual (for several years) now.

3. (On Friday evening), <u>we</u> <u>were</u> just <u>passing</u> the duck pond, and a big <u>dog</u> (with no owner) <u>ran</u> over (to us).

4. It was obviously looking (for other dogs) to play with.

5. Yip and Yap have never barked so loudly before.

6. I had originally named them (for their distinct barking noises).

7. But lately I had not heard these short, ear-splitting sounds very often.

8. The big dog was shocked (by the fierceness) (of my little dogs' reply) and quickly ran to find other friends.

9. Even I could not believe it.

10. I will never worry (about their safety) (around big dogs) again.

Review Exercise

While computer and digital technology are slowly taking over most (of the animation industry), *The Simpsons* remains 100 percent hand-painted. Did you get that—100 percent *hand-painted*! If you consider that it takes anywhere (from fifteen to twenty-four pieces) (of art) (for every second) that you see (on the screen) and that the show is anywhere (from twenty-two to twenty-three minutes) long—we are talking somewhere (between 18,900 and 33,220 hand-painted cels) (per episode)! This attention (to detail) and the continual use (of actual artists) (instead of computers) makes *The Simpsons* the leader (in this rapidly emerging industry).

The painting is done (in Korea) or, quite frankly, it would never happen. It would be too expensive. . . .

When the shipment first arrives (in Korea), the exposure sheets [are] translated (into Korean). Then the work is divided up and distributed (to the staff). They have exactly the same character and background model sheets as we do and all the tools [that] they need to do the job. There, a team (of unsung heroes) draws all the in-between poses and copies them (to cels), and then another team flips them over and, using the paint (by number) instructions (of the color department), paints what we see (on some future Sunday evening).

USING STANDARD ENGLISH VERBS (PP. 102–106)

Exercise 1

1. walk, walked
2. is, was
3. have, had
4. do, did
5. needs, needed

6. am, was
7. has, had
8. are, were
9. does, did
10. works, worked

Exercise 2

1. is, was
2. do, did
3. have, had
4. asks, asked
5. have, had

6. learn, learned
7. are, were
8. does, did
9. plays, played
10. am, was

Exercise 3

1. started, like
2. offers
3. are, have
4. finished, needed
5. run, do

6. advise, comfort
7. enjoy, are
8. completed, expected
9. have
10. thank

Exercise 4

1. do, don't
2. am, is
3. need, explains
4. help, does
5. works, hope

6. did, dropped
7. was, do
8. work, check
9. learn, learns
10. expect, don't

Exercise 5

1. The sentence is correct.

2. Fifty of us and one teacher *rehearsed* the musical for three months.

3. We *were* all very excited about opening night.

4. Before the curtain went up, we *joined* hands and wished each other luck.

5. We *discovered* that audiences love musicals.

6. Once we *were* performing, their reactions *settled* all our nerves.

7. The sentence is correct.

8. The sentence is correct.

9. After the first performance, all of us in the show *celebrated* at our teacher's house.

10. She *ordered* a cake that was shaped like the "Wells Fargo Wagon," and we all loved it.

Proofreading Paragraph

Everyday as we drive though our neighborhoods on the way to school or to work, we see things that *need* to be fixed. Many of them cause us only a little bit of trouble, so we forget them until we face them again. Every morning, drivers in my neighborhood *have* to deal with a truck that someone *parks* right at the corner of our street. It *blocks* our view as we try to turn onto the main avenue. We need to move out past the truck into the oncoming lane of traffic just to make a left turn. One day last week, I *turned* too soon, and a car almost hit me. This truck *doesn't* need to be parked in such a dangerous place.

USING REGULAR AND IRREGULAR VERBS (PP. 112–116)

Exercise 1

1. looked

2. look

3. looking

4. look

5. looked

6. look

7. looked

8. looking

9. looks

10. look

Exercise 2

1. drive, driven

2. thinking, thought

3. take, takes

4. told, telling

5. wrote, written

6. knew, know

7. teach, taught

8. torn, tearing

9. ridden, rode

10. made, make

Exercise 3

1. were, heard
2. seen, begun
3. flown, eaten
4. got, did
5. take, eating

6. written, coming, lost
7. swore, felt
8. bought, paid
9. getting, thought
10. saw, told, lay

Exercise 4

1. used, supposed
2. catch, came, heard
3. were, left
4. read, draw, build
5. felt, drew

6. did, slept
7. knew, spent
8. went, were
9. woke, stayed
10. forget, spent, were

Exercise 5

1. laid, lying, felt
2. know (or knew), been
3. broke, had
4. became, thought
5. was

6. read, frightened
7. kept, shook
8. worked, rose, snuck
9. left, go
10. lose, stung

PROGRESS TEST (P. 117)

1. B.   run-on sentence (parking areas for bikes, but they are)
2. B.   fragment (*The officials were* concerned . . .)
3. A.   incorrect verb form (Everyday, she *writes* . . .)
4. A.   fragment (*Combine A and B:* Whenever I hand in late assignments, my teachers reduce the grades.)
5. B.   incorrect verb form (was *supposed*)
6. A.   unnecessary comma (He has saved his money and is finally taking . . .)
7. B.   missing comma to prevent misreading (When she left, everyone . . .)
8. B.   run-on sentence (We ate sushi; it was delicious.)

9. A. incorrect verb form (Those two employees *deserve* a raise.)

10. B. fragment (*I will transfer* just as soon as I pass my last math class.)

MAINTAINING SUBJECT/VERB AGREEMENT (PP. 120–124)

Exercise 1

1. is
2. was
3. knows, have
4. has
5. has, expect

6. are
7. were, have, hold
8. is
9. work
10. looks, remains

Exercise 2

1. is
2. surprise
3. aren't
4. is
5. shines

6. speak
7. talk
8. is
9. enjoys
10. waits

Exercise 3

1. has
2. have, have
3. love
4. makes
5. says

6. thinks
7. is, haven't
8. has
9. looks
10. knows

Exercise 4

1. have
2. is
3. is
4. is, is
5. are

6. has
7. represent
8. are
9. comes
10. shine

Exercise 5

1. has	**6.** get
2. is	**7.** have
3. is	**8.** have
4. visits	**9.** get
5. travel	**10.** are

Proofreading Exercise

My teachers for this school year are really interesting. Each of their personalities *is* different. Some of them *require* us to be on time every day and follow directions to the letter. Others *treat* students almost as casual friends. The expectations of my geography teacher *are* higher than I expected. Students in that class *have* to do just what the teacher says, or they risk failing. Most of my other professors *take* a more lenient approach. But two of them *have* an odd grading technique, at least it seems odd to me. These two teachers *want* us to turn in all of our papers over the Internet. We can't turn in any handwritten work. I guess there *are* good reasons behind their demands. My friends says that turning in work over the Internet makes the teachers' jobs easier because it *eliminates* the possibility of plagiarizing.

AVOIDING SHIFTS IN TIME (PP. 126–127)

Proofreading Exercises

1. I am taking an art history class right now. Everyday, we watch slide shows of great pieces of art throughout history. We memorize each piece of art, its time period, and the artist who created it. I enjoy these slide shows, but I have trouble remembering the facts about them. I always get swept away by the beautiful paintings, drawings, and sculptures and forget to take notes that I can study from at home.

2. The paragraph is correct.

3. I loved traveling by train. The rocking motion made me so calm, and the clackety-clack of the railroad ties as we rode over them sounded like a heartbeat to me. I also enjoyed walking down the aisles of all the cars and looking at the different passengers. Whole families sat together, with children facing their parents. I noticed the kids liked to ride backward more than the adults. The food that we ate in the dining car was expensive, but it was always fancy and delicious. My favorite part of the train was the observation car. It was made of glass from the seats up so that we could see everything that we passed along the way.

RECOGNIZING VERBAL PHRASES (PP. 129-133)

Exercise 1

   1. Many people <u>dislike</u> [speaking in front of strangers].

   2. That <u>is</u> why there <u>is</u> an almost universal fear of [giving speeches].

   3. [Feeling insecure and {exposed}], people <u>get</u> dry mouths and sweaty hands.

   4. Note cards <u>become</u> useless, [rearranging themselves in the worst possible order].

   5. [To combat this problem], people <u>try</u> [to memorize a speech], only [to forget the whole thing] as the audience <u>stares</u> back at them expectantly.

   6. And when they <u>do remember</u> parts of it, the microphone <u>decides</u> [to quit at the punch line of their best joke].

   7. [Embarrassed] and [humiliated], they <u>struggle</u> [to regain their composure].

   8. Then the audience usually <u>begins</u> [to sympathize with and encourage the speaker].

   9. Finally [used to the spotlight], the speaker <u>relaxes</u> and <u>finds</u> the courage [to finish].

   10. No one <u>expects</u> [giving a speech] [to get any easier].

Exercise 2

   1. I <u>have learned</u> how [to manage my time] when I <u>am</u> not <u>working</u>.

   2. I <u>like</u> [to go to the movies on Friday nights].

   3. [Watching a good film] <u>takes</u> me away from the stress of my job.

   4. I especially <u>enjoy</u> [eating buttery popcorn] and [drinking a cold soda].

   5. It <u>is</u> the perfect way for me [to begin the weekend].

   6. I <u>get</u> [to escape from deadlines and the pressure {to succeed}].

   7. I <u>indulge</u> myself and <u>try</u> [to give myself a break]—nobody <u>is</u> perfect, and everybody <u>has</u> setbacks.

   8. All day Saturday I <u>enjoy</u> [lounging around the house in my weekend clothes].

   9. I <u>do</u> a little [gardening] and <u>try</u> [to relax my mind].

   10. By Sunday evening, after [resting for two days], I <u>am</u> ready [to start my busy week all over again].

Exercise 3

1. [Choosing a major] <u>is</u> one of the most important decisions for students.

2. Many students <u>take</u> a long time [to decide about their majors].

3. But they <u>fear</u> [wasting time on the wrong major] more than indecision.

4. They <u>spend</u> several semesters as undecided majors [taking general education classes].

5. [Distracted by class work], students <u>can forget</u> [to pay attention to their interests].

6. Finally, a particular subject area <u>will attract</u> them [to study it further].

7. One student <u>might find</u> happiness in [doing a psychology experiment].

8. [Writing a poem in an English class] <u>may be</u> the assignment [to make another decide].

9. [Attracted by telescopes], a student <u>might choose</u> [to major in astronomy].

10. [Finding a major] <u>takes</u> time and patience.

Exercise 4

1. Astronaut Shannon Lucid <u>blasted</u> off in March of 1996 [to join the cosmonauts on Mir space station].

2. Lucid, a woman in her fifties, <u>thrived</u> in her weightless environment, [setting a record for the longest trip in space by an American].

3. One of the dangers of [living without gravity] <u>is</u> that bones and muscles <u>deteriorate</u> rapidly without exercise.

4. During her time aboard Mir, Lucid <u>kept</u> in shape by [exercising on a specially {designed} treadmill and bicycle].

5. Part of her mission <u>required</u> her [to conduct various experiments].

6. NASA <u>designed</u> these experiments [to study the effects of weightlessness]; they <u>included</u> [burning candles], [growing crystals], and [incubating quail eggs] in zero gravity.

7. Lucid <u>took</u> along books [to keep her busy] between experiments and [exercising].

8. When she <u>ran</u> out of [reading] material, Lucid's daughter <u>helped</u> by [sending a new book up on a cargo ship] [carrying other supplies to Mir from Earth].

9. Chocolate <u>turned</u> out [to be in short supply] aboard the space station while Lucid <u>was</u> there.

10. [Waiting for her] when she <u>landed</u> after [being in space for 188 days] <u>was</u> a gift from President Clinton—it <u>was</u> a gigantic box of M&M's [wrapped in gold paper].

Exercise 5

1. We <u>have</u> all <u>seen</u> stage shows where magicians try [to hypnotize people] [beginning with the suggestion], "You <u>are getting</u> very sleepy . . . ."

2. Then they <u>order</u> their [hypnotized] subjects [to cluck like chickens] or [to cry like babies].

3. Hypnotists <u>can</u> even <u>convince</u> subjects [to feel very cold] even if the room <u>is</u> actually warm.

4. More important, [hallucinating on command] and the ability [to control pain] <u>have been achieved</u> through hypnosis.

5. Now researchers <u>are studying</u> the brains of supposedly [hypnotized] people [to see if there is such a thing as a real hypnotic state].

6. [Measuring the {altered} blood flow to different locations in the brain] <u>allows</u> scientists [to visualize the effects of hypnosis].

7. And studies <u>show</u> that these effects <u>can</u> indeed <u>be measured</u> by changes in the brains of [hypnotized] subjects.

8. [To identify people] only [pretending to be hypnotized], scientists secretly <u>filmed</u> all participants while only an audiotape <u>made</u> suggestions to the subjects.

9. Subjects genuinely able [to be hypnotized] <u>responded</u> to either the audiotape or the hypnotist himself.

10. Those who <u>did</u> not <u>respond</u> unless a hypnotist <u>was</u> in the room <u>were judged</u> [to be faking the effects of hypnosis], and their brain measurements <u>revealed</u> less change than the others.

Paragraph Exercise

[Born in May of 1860 in Savannah, Georgia], Ellen Axson <u>was</u> a sensitive and [refined] woman with a talent for [painting] and an interest in music and literature. She <u>married</u> Woodrow Wilson on June 24, 1885.

   Mrs. Wilson <u>spent</u> much of her brief time in the White House [painting] and [drawing] in an attic studio. She <u>had worked</u> previously as a professional painter, but as first lady she <u>donated</u> her work [to be auctioned for charity]. As an outgrowth of her own interest in art, Mrs. Wilson <u>devoted</u> a room of the White House to the display of craftworks by the women of the Blue Ridge Mountains.

One of Mrs. Wilson's more public projects was her work [to improve the condition of the poor neighborhoods of Washington, D.C.]. The first lady took congressmen on tours of the city's bleakest areas and initiated legislation [aimed at {eliminating the slums}].

Sentence Writing

Your sentences may vary, but make sure that your verbals are not actually the main verbs of your clauses. You should be able to double underline your real verbs, as they are here.

1. I enjoy [speaking Italian].

2. [Typing on a small keyboard] hurts my wrists.

3. [Driving to the beach from here] takes about three hours.

4. I spent the day [reading the final chapters of my textbook].

5. I love [to ski in the winter].

6. We were invited [to go out to dinner].

7. I always like [to chat with you].

8. [To cook like a real gourmet] takes practice.

9. [Impressed by my grades], my parents bought me a new car.

10. [Taken in small doses], aspirin helps prevent heart attacks.

CORRECTING MISPLACED OR DANGLING MODIFIERS (PP. 134–137)

Corrections are *italicized*. Yours may differ slightly.

Exercise 1

1. After *I watched* TV for half an hour, the pasta was ready.

2. I found a dollar *as I jogged* around the block.

3. *Sitting in their chairs, the children* ate the cupcakes.

4. One year *after I became manager*, the company closed the store.

5. The sentence is correct.

6. My *mom smiled as she handed me* a bouquet of flowers for my birthday.

7. The usher slipped *on someone's program and fell.*

8. *Through the window,* they gave directions to the driver.

9. The sentence is correct.

10. I bought a new shirt *that has* silver buttons.

Exercise 2

1. The sentence is correct.

2. *Taking careful notes,* the applicants listened to each of the employers.

3. The sentence is correct.

4. *After I gave the waiter my order in a low voice,* he asked me to speak louder.

5. The sentence is correct.

6. We received an invitation to their party; *it arrived in a pink envelope.*

7. *Since our car had a full tank of gas,* we were able to drive our car all the way to San Francisco.

8. *After we set the table,* our guests started eating.

9. I wrote a note *that said* I would return shortly, *and I taped it to the door.*

10. *Wearing gloves and safety goggles,* the student workers built a nice wall.

Exercise 3

1. I saw a parking ticket *clamped down on my windshield.*

2. The sentence is correct.

3. Using red ink, *teachers can mark mistakes* more clearly.

4. *Reading their policy very carefully,* they noticed a loophole.

5. *As they entered the arena,* she kicked her friend by accident.

6. The *frowning* teacher handed the tests back to the students.

7. *As I talked with the other students,* class finally started.

8. We bought a *cat with a fluffy tail* for our friend.

9. *Dressed in farmer outfits,* the pre-schoolers planted seedlings.

10. At the age of sixteen, *a person can easily obtain* a driving permit.

Exercise 4

1. *After the teacher called roll,* the students placed their homework on his desk.

2. The sentence is correct.

3. *With open arms*, the actors accepted the flowers.

4. The sentence is correct.

5. The coach warned the players to wait until the end of the game *to celebrate*.

6. I sent her a picture of us; *I mailed it in a big envelope*.

7. *Going through her coat pockets*, she found an old handkerchief.

8. The sentence is correct.

9. The sentence is correct.

10. After shouting "Happy Birthday!" *everyone was* completely quiet.

Exercise 5

1. One day *after I turned forty*, my new car broke down on the freeway.

2. *My brother lets his dog hang out the window of the car because the dog likes the rush of fresh air on his face.*

3. The sentence is correct.

4. Studying in the writing lab, *I eliminated* my comma problems.

5. The sentence is correct.

6. *We saw a pair of squirrels chasing each other up and down a tree.*

7. The sentence is correct.

8. The sentence is correct.

9. Lifting the heavy television, *she became red in the face*.

10. The sentence is correct.

Proofreading Exercise

Corrections are *italicized*. Yours may differ slightly.

I love parades, so last year my family and I traveled to Pasadena, California, to see one of the biggest parades of all—the Tournament of Roses Parade on New Year's Day. It turned out to be even more wonderful than I expected.

Although we arrived one day early, the city was already crowded with people. Lots of families were setting up campsites on Colorado Boulevard. We didn't want to miss one float in the parade, so we found our own spot and made ourselves at home. When the parade began, I had as much fun watching the spectators as the parade itself. I saw children *sitting on their fathers' shoulders* and pointing at the breathtaking horses and floats. *The floats were decorated completely with flowers or plant material.* I couldn't believe how beautiful they were and how good they smelled.

The crowd was overwhelmed by the sights and sounds of the parade. Everyone especially enjoyed hearing the school bands, *marching and playing their instruments with perfect precision.* They must have practiced for the whole year to be that good.

My experience didn't end with the parade, however. After the last float had passed by, I found a twenty dollar bill *as I walked down Colorado Boulevard. I framed it as a souvenir of my trip to the Rose Parade, and now it hangs on my wall at home.*

FOLLOWING SENTENCE PATTERNS (PP. 141–145)

Exercise 1

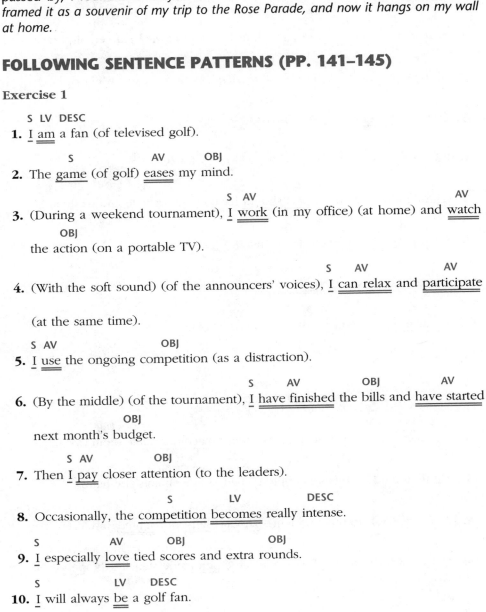

1. S LV DESC
   I am a fan (of televised golf).

2. S AV OBJ
   The game (of golf) eases my mind.

3. (During a weekend tournament), S AV I work (in my office) (at home) and AV watch
   OBJ
   the action (on a portable TV).

4. (With the soft sound) (of the announcers' voices), S AV I can relax and AV participate
   (at the same time).

5. S AV OBJ
   I use the ongoing competition (as a distraction).

6. (By the middle) (of the tournament), S AV OBJ I have finished the bills and AV have started
   OBJ
   next month's budget.

7. S AV OBJ
   Then I pay closer attention (to the leaders).

8. S LV DESC
   Occasionally, the competition becomes really intense.

9. S AV OBJ OBJ
   I especially love tied scores and extra rounds.

10. S LV DESC
    I will always be a golf fan.

Exercise 2

     S   AV
1. People often travel (with their dogs, cats, or other pets).

       S   AV   OBJ
2. Veterinarians offer some suggestions (about traveling) (with pets).

             S   LV   DESC
3. First, a pet should be old enough to travel. [*To travel* is a verbal phrase.]

      S   AV
4. All pets should travel (in special carriers) (with food and water dishes).

          S   AV
5. Ordinary water (in a pet's dish) spills easily.

        S   AV
6. But ice cubes (in the water dish) will melt slowly.

              S   AV   OBJ   OBJ
7. (During long car rides), pets should have enough shade and fresh air.

        S   AV
8. Small pets can ride (with passengers).

          S   AV   OBJ
9. However, a loose pet could cause an accident.

       S   LV DESC   DESC
10. Sedatives (for pets) are risky but sometimes necessary.

Exercise 3

    S AV
1. We live (in a world) (with photocopiers, scanners, and fax machines).

     S AV OBJ   S   AV   OBJ
2. If we need copies (of documents), these machines make them (for us).

               S   AV   OBJ
3. (Up until the late 1800s), people copied all documents (by hand).

                S   AV   OBJ
4. (As a solution) (to this problem), Thomas Edison invented an electric pen.

            S   AV   OBJ   S   LV
5. (Unlike ordinary pens), Edison's electric pen made stencils; the pen itself was

  DESC
inkless.

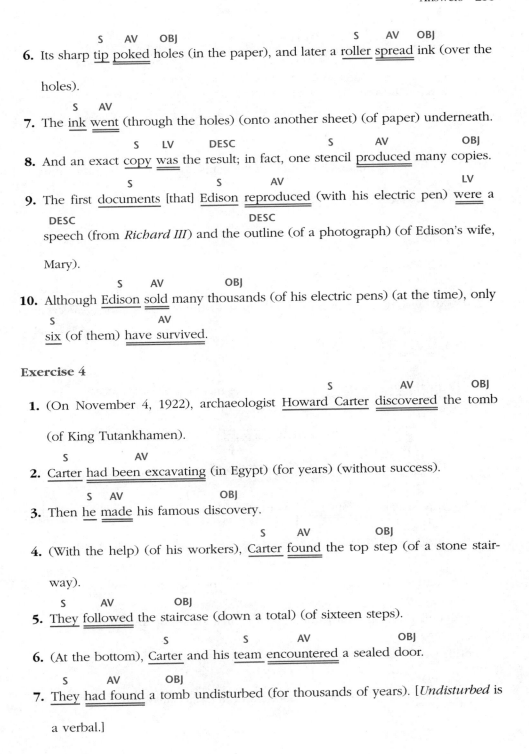

             S   AV   OBJ   S   AV   OBJ

6. Its sharp tip poked holes (in the paper), and later a roller spread ink (over the

holes).

          S   AV

7. The ink went (through the holes) (onto another sheet) (of paper) underneath.

           S   LV   DESC   S   AV   OBJ

8. And an exact copy was the result; in fact, one stencil produced many copies.

           S   S   AV   LV

9. The first documents [that] Edison reproduced (with his electric pen) were a

    DESC   DESC

speech (from *Richard III*) and the outline (of a photograph) (of Edison's wife,

Mary).

            S   AV   OBJ

10. Although Edison sold many thousands (of his electric pens) (at the time), only

    S   AV

six (of them) have survived.

Exercise 4

                           S   AV   OBJ

1. (On November 4, 1922), archaeologist Howard Carter discovered the tomb

(of King Tutankhamen).

    S   AV

2. Carter had been excavating (in Egypt) (for years) (without success).

    S   AV   OBJ

3. Then he made his famous discovery.

                  S   AV   OBJ

4. (With the help) (of his workers), Carter found the top step (of a stone stair-

way).

    S   AV   OBJ

5. They followed the staircase (down a total) (of sixteen steps).

          S   S   AV   OBJ

6. (At the bottom), Carter and his team encountered a sealed door.

    S   AV   OBJ

7. They had found a tomb undisturbed (for thousands of years). [*Undisturbed* is

a verbal.]

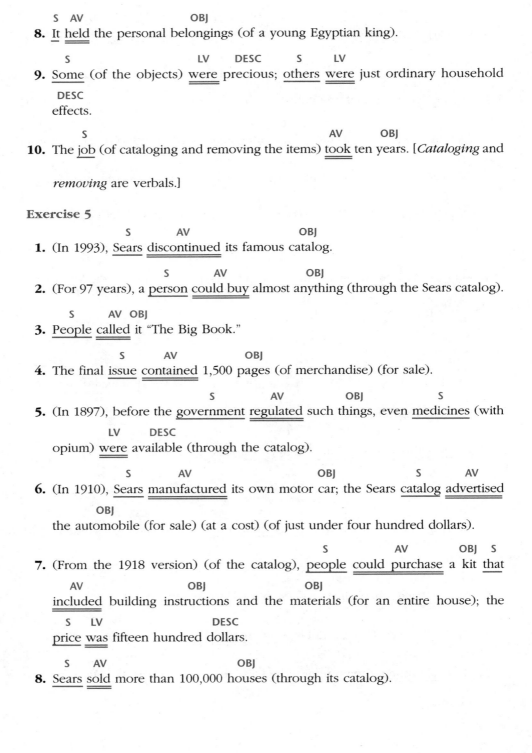

 S   AV   OBJ
8. It held the personal belongings (of a young Egyptian king).

      S   LV   DESC   S   LV
9. Some (of the objects) were precious; others were just ordinary household
   DESC
effects.

       S   AV   OBJ
10. The job (of cataloging and removing the items) took ten years. [*Cataloging* and

removing are verbals.]

Exercise 5

           S   AV   OBJ
1. (In 1993), Sears discontinued its famous catalog.

              S   AV   OBJ
2. (For 97 years), a person could buy almost anything (through the Sears catalog).

    S   AV OBJ
3. People called it "The Big Book."

            S   AV   OBJ
4. The final issue contained 1,500 pages (of merchandise) (for sale).

                     S   AV   OBJ   S
5. (In 1897), before the government regulated such things, even medicines (with
            LV   DESC
opium) were available (through the catalog).

            S   AV   OBJ   S   AV
6. (In 1910), Sears manufactured its own motor car; the Sears catalog advertised
            OBJ
the automobile (for sale) (at a cost) (of just under four hundred dollars).

                                     S   AV   OBJ   S
7. (From the 1918 version) (of the catalog), people could purchase a kit that
       AV   OBJ   OBJ
included building instructions and the materials (for an entire house); the
   S   LV   DESC
price was fifteen hundred dollars.

       S   AV   OBJ
8. Sears sold more than 100,000 houses (through its catalog).

                       S   AV   OBJ

9. (Before 1992), all <u>customers</u> <u>used</u> mail order forms, not phone calls, to place

their orders. [*To place their orders* is a verbal phrase.]

                S   AV   S   AV

10. When the <u>merchandise</u> <u>arrived</u> (at the catalog center), <u>customers</u> <u>went</u> and

  AV OBJ   S   AV   OBJ

<u>picked</u> it up; (for most) (of its history), the <u>catalog</u> <u>offered</u> no delivery service.

Paragraph Exercise

Franklin Delano Roosevelt
1882–1945
Thirty-Second President 1933–1945

                 S   AV   AV

Four times <u>Americans</u> <u>went</u> (to the polls) and <u>elected</u> Franklin Delano

OBJ   S

Roosevelt (as their president). An inspirational and controversial leader, <u>Roosevelt</u>

AV   OBJ

<u>steered</u> Americans (through the dark, troubled days) (of the Great Depression and

World War II).

              S   AV

Franklin <u>Roosevelt</u> <u>grew</u> up (in the luxurious family home) (in Hyde Park,

                AV   OBJ

New York), and <u>spent</u> summers (on beautiful Campobello Island). . . . (In his

                    S   AV   OBJ

twelve years as president), <u>Roosevelt</u> <u>oversaw</u> an unprecedented expansion (of

the federal government). . . .

                 S

Roosevelt's <u>wife</u>, Eleanor, a niece (of former president Theodore Roosevelt)

                                LV

and a distant cousin (to Franklin), <u>was</u>, (like her husband), a popular and

               DESC   S   LV   DESC

controversial figure. <u>She</u> <u>was</u> an outspoken advocate (of civil and human rights)

              AV   OBJ

and (as first lady) <u>took</u> an active role (in American public life).

AVOIDING CLICHÉS, AWKWARD PHRASING, AND WORDINESS (PP. 149–154)

Your answers may differ from these possible revisions.

Exercise 1

1. I compare prices before I buy.

2. I often try three or four stores.

3. I look for the lowest price.

4. I have saved a hundred dollars on one item this way.

5. Omit this sentence.

6. Prices may vary significantly on a single item.

7. But knowing when to buy is not easy.

8. Once I waited for a computer sale that never happened.

9. However, I am happy when I do find a bargain.

10. Looking for good prices is an American pastime.

Exercise 2

1. I received a surprise in class today.

2. I got an unfamiliar grade on a quiz.

3. It was an A.

4. I couldn't believe it.

5. I remembered that the quiz had seemed easy.

6. After doing the homework and seeing the tutor, I had really prepared for it.

7. Mr. Talbot noticed that my perfect score surprised me.

8. I had not done well on previous quizzes.

9. I told him about my extra study efforts.

10. He asked me to share them with my fellow students to help them do better next time.

Exercise 3

1. The blossoms in Fresno County, California, are very beautiful.

2. Each spring, the orchards and fields burst into bloom.

3. Vehicles drive along a route called the Blossom Trail.

4. Flowers cover the landscape for over sixty miles.

5. The apple blossoms have white petals.

6. And bright orange poppies cover the hillsides.

7. The apricot, peach, and nectarine trees bloom in pink and red.

8. The purples and blues of lupines, clover, and other wildflowers complete the spectrum.

9. The best time to see the blooms is the end of February or the beginning of March.

10. Then the Blossom Trail is in full bloom.

Exercise 4

1. Old-fashioned places are hard to find these days.

2. Knott's Berry Farm, near Disneyland, is really old-fashioned.

3. Knott's was a real berry farm in 1920 when Walter and Cordelia Knott started selling dinners in a Western-style ghost-town hotel brought from Arizona.

4. People can ride an old passenger train and get robbed by Knott's Berry Farm bandits.

5. The Knott's merry-go-round, with its hand-carved animals, was made in 1902 by Gustav Dentzel, a famous carousel maker.

6. An old schoolhouse, like those in Western movies, became part of Ghost Town after Walter and Cordelia's grandchildren went to school there.

7. Knott's blacksmiths make horseshoes and demonstrate their skills for visitors.

8. And Native American craftspeople make pots, jewelry, and canoes.

9. Finally, the park offers roller coasters for people who like to scream.

10. Knott's Berry Farm is the only amusement park in the country still owned and operated by the family that started it almost eighty years ago.

Exercise 5

1. The other day I stayed home from school because I was sick.

2. I told my teacher I needed one day of rest, but I almost didn't get it.

3. I had forgotten that Mondays were gardeners' days.

4. These gardeners use power leaf blowers and tree trimmers.

5. Due to the noise, I couldn't sleep.

6. I tried watching television.

7. The daytime shows were worse than the noise.

8. Once the gardeners finished in the afternoon, I fell asleep.

9. Omit this sentence.

10. After sixteen hours of sleep, I felt better and went happily back to school the next day.

Proofreading Exercise

Here is one possible revision.

The *Oxford English Dictionary*, the *OED*, is one of the most important reference works ever written. I'm reading a biography of its first editor, Dr. James Murray, and a man who contributed thousands of definitions and examples to the *OED*. Murray later discovered that this contributor lived in an insane asylum and was guilty of murder. Simon Winchester tells their story in *The Professor and the Madman*.

The eeriest part of the double biography involves how one of the men lost his sanity. William Minor had been a doctor during the civil war and was used to helping people. But as part of his military duties, Dr. Minor was commanded to punish a soldier who had tried to desert the army. Dr. Minor had to brand the deserter's face with a big letter "D." Hurting someone this way may have driven Dr. Minor crazy. Later he become paranoid and killed an innocent man. In the book, Simon Winchester explains that Dr. Minor used his incredible intellect and academic ability to write definitions for the *Oxford English Dictionary* as a way to ease his conscience.

Whenever I use the *OED* in the future, I'll wonder if the word was defined by Dr. Minor. His story proves the old saying, "Truth is stranger than fiction."

CORRECTING FOR PARALLEL STRUCTURE (PP. 156–161)

Your answers may differ from these possible revisions.

Exercise 1

1. Do you know who invented the hot dog and how it got its name?

2. The sentence is correct.

3. The sentence is correct.

4. Tasty hot German sausages were becoming very popular, but they were hard to eat.

5. Stevens had the idea of serving them in a roll of bread and putting hot mustard on them.

6. At the Giants' stadium, these treats were called "red hots," and they were sold by wandering vendors during the game.

7. The sentence is correct.

8. The sentence is correct.

9. Dorgan was spoofing the fact that both "red hots" and Dachshunds were cylindrical in shape, red in color, and German in origin.

10. Now you know more about the man who helped invent the hot dog and the man who gave it its name.

Exercise 2

1. The sentence is correct.

2. Three presidents died on the Fourth of July, and one president was born on the Fourth of July.

3. The ones who died on July 4th were John Adams, Thomas Jefferson, and James Monroe; the one who was born on July 4th was Calvin Coolidge.

4. The sentence is correct.

5. The person who was the youngest to be elected president was John F. Kennedy at 43, but the person who was the youngest to become president was Theodore Roosevelt at 42 (due to McKinley's assassination).

6. Gerald Ford was never elected vice president or president; he came to both positions through the resignations of Spiro Agnew and Richard Nixon, respectively.

7. The various careers of these men prior to becoming president included farming, editing, teaching, acting, tailoring, practicing law or business, and serving in the military.

8. The sentence is correct.

9. Franklin D. Roosevelt's family tree linked him to eleven other presidents either by blood or by marriage.

10. FDR holds two other distinctions in presidential history: he was the first to be on TV, and he served the longest term in office (twelve years).

Exercise 3

1. The sentence is correct.

2. It doesn't look or act like other robots.

3. Its "head" contains a microphone for ears, a small screen for a face, and a video camera for eyes.

4. The sentence is correct.

5. The sentence is correct.

6. The difference between this and other robots is that the PRoP, as it's called, becomes an extension of anyone who controls it through the Internet.

7. A person in one city will be able to log on to the PRoP in another city and wander around—seeing what it sees, speaking to people it meets, and hearing what it hears.

8. The sentence is correct.

9. The inventors of the PRoP believe that research labs and businesses will be most interested in the PRoPs at first.

10. But in the future, PRoPs could make it possible to take a vacation or play a game of chess with a faraway friend without ever leaving your desk.

Exercise 4

1. The sentence is correct.

2. The sentence is correct.

3. These are the Latin root words meaning "thousand" and "year."

4. The sentence is correct.

5. Some companies with *millennium* in their names have chosen to take out letters or to make it plural.

6. There is the Millenium Hotel and the Millenia car model.

7. The sentence is correct.

8. We worry not only about how to spell *millennium* but also about how to keep it fresh.

9. A company relies on two things above all: customer loyalty and name recognition.

10. How will customers recognize the name of a company that uses the word *millennium* but chooses to spell it differently?

Exercise 5

1. I've been learning to cook lately, but I keep making the same mistakes.

2. I always add too much salt or too much sugar.

3. The sentence is correct.

4. If I use too much salt, I could add a little sugar.

5. If soups or stews have too much salt, I could add a slice of raw potato.

6. If the salt is still too overpowering, I could double the dish's ingredients and not add any salt to the new batch.

7. Then, if there's too much food, I could put half in the freezer for later.

8. If I use too much sugar when baking, I could add a little salt.

9. If vegetables and entrees are too sweet, I could add some vinegar.

10. The sentence is correct.

Proofreading Exercise

Your revisions within the paragraph may differ. This paragraph is just one possibility.

Carry A. Nation was an American woman who lived from 1846 to 1911. She is most famous for two things: her name, which helped inspire her to be an activist, and her habit of wrecking any saloon in sight. Carry Nation hated alcohol and any place that sold it. She was a powerful woman who was almost six feet tall. During her adult life, she went on a mission to destroy saloons across the country one at a time. Her crusade began in Wichita. She used a hatchet to smash windows, chop up furniture, crack mirrors, and break as many liquor bottles in a saloon as possible. Carry A. Nation repeated this offense from east to west. Whenever she landed in jail, this enterprising American sold toy replicas of her hatchet and gave speeches to raise money for her bail. Carry Nation took action based on her beliefs. She caused trouble for some people but helped other people. She donated funds to the poor and founded a shelter for drunkard's wives.

USING PRONOUNS (PP. 166–169)

Exercise 1

1. I

2. she

3. she and I

4. I

5. she and I

6. she

7. I

8. her and me

9. she

10. her

Exercise 2

1. its
2. its
3. their
4. their
5. their
6. its
7. his
8. Everyone in the class sold books back to the bookstore.
9. their
10. Either the workers or the boss will win the dispute.

Exercise 3

1. me
2. She and he
3. I
4. their
5. their
6. I
7. Each of the new teachers has *a* set of books.
8. their
9. Everyone at the polling place had *an* opinion and expressed it with *a* vote.
10. he

Exercise 4

1. I finished printing my term paper, turned off my computer, and put *my paper* in my backpack.
2. Sandra told her mother, "Your car has a new dent in it."
3. *They felt better* because they bought their textbooks early.
4. Jeffrey's brother *said, "You can take my laptop to school."*
5. *My shirt* shrunk when I put it in the dryer.
6. The student told his counselor, *"You don't understand me."*
7. While we were counting the money from our garage sale, *the money* blew away.
8. *When our dog runs away, we get angry.*
9. Robert asked his friend, *"Why wasn't I invited to the party?"*
10. The sentence is correct.

Exercise 5

1. The Hascoms bought some new bushes, but *the bushes* were too short.

2. The sentence is correct.

3. I signed the credit card slip, put my card back in my wallet, and handed *the slip* to the cashier.

4. When students work in groups, *students* get a lot of work done.

5. As he took the lenses out of the frames, the *lenses* (or the *frames*) broke.

6. Whenever I put gas in my car, I get a headache from the smell of *gasoline*.

7. Coupons help people save money on certain items.

8. The sentence is correct.

9. *The teacher asked Pearl* to copy her notes for another student. (or *Pearl was asked to copy the teacher's* notes for another student.)

10. The sentence is correct.

Proofreading Exercise

Corrections are *italicized*.

I told my friend Audrey a rumor at work the other day, and as soon as I did, I knew I would regret *telling her*. I forgot that Audrey is not as mature as *I*. Right before I told her the rumor, I said, "Now this is just between you and *me*, and you're not going to tell anyone, right?" She assured me that the only person she would talk to about it was *I*. I made the mistake of believing her. Later I saw *her* and another coworker laughing confidentially. The rumor was out, and I knew that the one responsible was *I*. Audrey and I are still coworkers, but *she* and I are no longer friends.

AVOIDING SHIFTS IN PERSON (P. 170–171)

Proofreading Exercises

Your revisions may differ depending on whether you choose to begin in first, second, or third person.

1. You have probably seen images of astronauts floating in their space capsules, eating food from little silver freeze-dried cube-shaped pouches, and sipping Tang out of special straws made to function in the weightlessness of space. Now you can buy that same food and eat it yourself on earth. NASA has gone online with a site called thespacestore.com, and all you have to do is point and click and get these space munchies delivered to your door. If you want NASA souvenirs, you can purchase them at the same site.

2. Those of us who drive need to be more aware of pedestrians. We can't always gauge what people walking down the street will do. We might think that all pedestrians will keep walking forward in a crosswalk, but they might decide to turn back if they forgot something. We could run into them if that happens. We could affect other people's lives in an instant. We all should slow down and be more considerate of others.

3. This paragraph is correct.

REVIEW OF SENTENCE STRUCTURE ERRORS (PP. 172–174)

Your corrections may differ slightly.

1. B. wordy (It tastes better than smooth peanut butter.)

2. A. cliché (Writing essays is difficult for me.)

3. B. shift in person (I like riding my bike because *I* don't have to wait for it to pick *me* up.)

4. B. pronoun error (A recruiter . . . gave my friend and *me* an application.)

5. B. run-on sentence (. . . full of details; I cannot understand . . .)

6. A. pronoun reference error (Everyone in the class looked amazed.)

7. B. run-on sentence (. . . four classes this semester. I should have taken . . .)

8. A. not parallel (. . . so that they are relaxing, rejuvenating, and fun.)

9. B. subject/verb agreement error (Each of the kittens *is* the same size.)

10. A. cliché (You have helped me a lot.)

11. B. subject/verb agreement (One of its pieces *is* missing . . .)

12. A. fragment (Our train was late due to snowy weather.)

13. A. subject/verb agreement error (A flock of birds *flies* . . .)

14. B. shift in person (Contestants must understand that *they* can't always win.)

15. A. misplaced modifier (Keeping his eyes tightly closed, *the little boy received his vaccination.*)

Proofreading Exercise

Corrections are *italicized*. Yours may differ.

Let's Get Technical

In my child development classes, I'm learning about ways to keep girls interested in technology. Studies *show* that girls and boys begin their school years equally interested in technology. After elementary school, *girls lose interest*. Because boys keep up with computers and other technology throughout their educations, *boys* get ahead in these fields. Experts have come up with some suggestions for teachers and parents to help *girls stay involved in technology*.

Girls need opportunities to experiment with computers. Girls spend time on computers, but they usually just do their *assignments; then* they log off. Since computer games and programs are often aimed at *boys, parents* and teachers need to buy computer products that will challenge girls not only in literature and art, but also in math, science, and *business*.

Another suggestion is to put computers in places where girls can socialize. One reason many boys stay interested in technology is that *they can do it on their own*. Girls tend to be more interested in working with others and *sharing* activities. When computer terminals are placed close to one another, girls work at them longer.

Finally, parents and teachers need to *provide positive role models. They need to teach girls* about successful women in the fields of business, *science*, and technology. And the earlier *girls get interested* in these fields, the better.

PUNCTUATION AND CAPITAL LETTERS

PERIOD, QUESTION MARK, EXCLAMATION POINT, SEMICOLON, COLON, DASH (PP. 177–181)

Your answers may vary slightly, especially in the use of optional pieces of punctuation (the exclamation point and the dash).

Exercise 1

1. My friend Kristine and I arrived early for work yesterday; it was a very important day.

2. We had worked late the night before perfecting our presentation.

3. The boss had given us an opportunity to train our colleagues in the use of a new computer program.

4. I wondered how the other workers would react when they heard that we had been chosen to teach them.

5. Would they be pleased or annoyed?

6. Kristine and I worked hard on the visual aid to accompany our workshop: a slide show of sample screens from the program.

7. Kristine thought our workshop should end with a test; however, I didn't think that was a good idea.

8. I knew that our fellow employees—at least *some* of them—would not want us to test them.

9. By the time we ended our presentation, we both realized that I had been right.

10. Now our co-workers see us as a couple of experts—not a couple of know-it-alls.

Exercise 2

1. Have you ever heard of Vinnie Ream?

2. This young woman—a very controversial figure in Washington, D.C.—began her career as a sculptor in 1863 at the age of sixteen.

3. Miss Ream was a student of the famous sculptor Clark Mills; he is perhaps best-known for his statue of Andrew Jackson located across from the White House.

4. Vinnie Ream started to work with Mills in his studio in the basement of the Capitol building; soon members of Congress were volunteering to sit for Miss Ream, and she sculpted busts of them.

5. Her fame and notoriety grew in the late 1860s; that's when she was awarded a ten-thousand-dollar commission to create a life-size statue of Abraham Lincoln.

6. Vinnie Ream had known Lincoln; in fact, before his assassination, President Lincoln would allow Miss Ream to sit in his office within the White House and work on a bust of him as he carried out the business of running the country.

7. Ream's intimate observation of Lincoln at work affected her design of Lincoln's posture and facial expression for her statue of him.

8. Vinnie Ream's relationships and the works she produced were not accepted by everyone; Ream's youth and physical beauty led to much of this harsh criticism.

9. Some people questioned her motives; others even questioned her abilities.

10. Ream prospered in spite of the jealous accusations of others and often demonstrated her sculpting abilities in public to prove that she did her own work.

Exercise 3

1. Ralph Waldo Emerson gave us this famous bit of advice: "Build a better mousetrap, and the world will beat a path to your door."

2. People have not stopped inventing mousetraps; in fact, there are more U.S. patents for mousetraps than for any device—over four thousand of them! (or .)

3. Some are simple; some are complicated, and some are just weird.

4. Nearly fifty new patents for machines to kill mice are awarded every year—perhaps thanks to Mr. Emerson's advice.

5. The most enduring mousetrap was designed by John Mast; it is the one most of us picture when we think of a mousetrap: a piece of wood with a spring-loaded bar that snaps down on the mouse just as it takes the bait.

6. John Mast's creation received Patent #744,379 in 1903; since then no other patented mousetrap has done a better job.

7. There is a long list of technologies that other inventions have used to trap mice: electricity, sonar, lasers, super glues, etc.

8. One patented mousetrap was built in the shape of a multilevel house with several stairways; however, its elaborate design made it impractical and expensive.

9. In 1878, one person invented a mousetrap for travelers; it was a box that was supposed to hold men's removable collars and at night catch mice, but it was not a success.

10. Who would want to put an article of clothing back into a box used to trap a mouse?

Exercise 4

1. People in Australia have been asking themselves a question: why are some dolphins carrying big sponges around on their heads?

2. First it was just one dolphin; now several dolphins are doing it.

3. Marine biologists all over the world have been trying to understand this unusual sponge-carrying behavior.

4. They wonder about whether the sponges decrease the dolphins' ability to maneuver under water.

5. If they do, then why would the dolphins sacrifice this ability?

6. The dolphins might be using the sponges for a very important reason: to help them find food.

7. Some scientists think that the sponges may protect the dolphins' beaks in some way.

8. The sponges might indicate position in the social order; that's another explanation.

9. Or the dolphins could be imitating each other—a kind of dolphin "fad," in other words.

10. Only one group of experts knows whether these sponges are hunting tools or just fashion statements: (or;) that is the dolphins themselves.

Exercise 5

1. I just read an article that connected two things that I would never have thought went together: the Old West, with its miners and saloon life, and Shakespeare, with his poetry and politics.

2. People who had traveled out West on the Oregon Trail brought their Shakespeare books and shared them with a willing audience: the unruly population of the mining camps and tiny towns of the West.

3. Mountain men like Jim Bridger paid others who could read to act out Shakespeare's plays; then he memorized the speeches and performed them for others.

4. Theaters staged productions of the tragedies of *Hamlet*, *Othello*, and *Romeo and Juliet* to the delight of the Western crowds; however, if they weren't pleased with an actor, theatergoers threw vegetables—as large pumpkins at times—to get the actor off the stage.

5. Crowds likewise rewarded good acting, which was lively and not overly refined; spectators in gold mining camps threw nuggets and bags of gold on stage if they liked a performance.

6. Oral storytelling had always been popular in the West; therefore, people of the time embraced Shakespeare's language without thinking of it as intellectual or sophisticated.

7. In the mid-1800s, people across the country had strong opinions about how Shakespeare should be performed; there was a riot at one New York City theater concerning a particularly snobby performance of *Macbeth*.

8. The fight moved from the theater into the streets; more than twenty people were killed, and a hundred were injured.

9. The casting of characters in Western performances included everything from all-male casts in the mining camps to a female Juliet performing without a real Romeo; a stuffed dummy played his part.

10. There was even a little girl named Anna Maria Quinn—just six years old—who played *Hamlet* at the Metropolitan Theatre in San Francisco in 1854.

Proofreading Exercise

Your punctuation choices may differ slightly.

I wonder why the swimming pool on campus doesn't have a covered area for spectators. I'm certain that the pool area is an uncomfortable place for people to be—unless they're in the pool. I have friends on the swim team; therefore, I know what I'm talking about. Those of us who watch the swim team at practice or competitions have to squint, wear loads of sunblock, and drink gallons of water just to cope with the heat and glare. Why doesn't the school install a canopy over the spectator benches? I have even considered taking up a collection from the other pool visitors, buying a canopy, and installing it myself.

COMMA RULES 1, 2, AND 3 (PP. 184-188)

Exercise 1

1. I've been reading Helen Keller's book *The Story of My Life,* and I have learned a lot more about her.

2. I originally thought that Keller was born deaf and blind, but I was wrong.

3. When she was just under two years old, Keller became ill with a terrible fever.

4. The sentence is correct.

5. Not long after the doctor shared his fears with her family, Keller recovered from her fever.

6. Unfortunately, this sudden illness left Keller without the ability to see, to hear, or to speak.

7. The only tools that Keller had left were her sense of touch, her active mind, and her own curiosity.

8. With her teacher Anne Sullivan's constant assistance, Keller eventually learned to read, to write, and to speak.

9. The sentence is correct.

10. In my opinion, Helen Keller was an amazing person, and her story inspires me to do my best.

Exercise 2

1. Throughout human history, people have imagined, designed, and patented a lot of silly contraptions.

2. I've just read about two of the silliest: one of them is a self-cooling rocking chair, and the other is a locket to hold a person's used chewing gum.

3. The "Air-Cooled Rocking-Chair" was patented on July 6, 1869, and the person sitting in the chair is the one who cools it.

4. Beneath the seat of the chair, the designer installed a bellows like those used to blow air into a fireplace.

5. Along the back of the chair, the patent calls for a flexible tube to rise above the sitting person's head.

6. As the person rocks on the seat, the bellows sends blasts of air through the tube and over his head.

7. I don't think that I would like that, do you?

8. The "Chewing-Gum Preserver" was patented on January 1, 1889, to allow the gum chewer to carry used chewing gum in a safe, sanitary, and responsible way.

9. In the drawing that accompanies the description of this invention, it looks a lot like a pocket watch.

10. The chewing-gum locket could be worn on a chain, or it could be carried in a pocket.

Exercise 3

1. Whenever I ask my friend Karen a computer-related question, I end up regretting it.

2. Once she gets started, Karen is unable to stop talking about computers.

3. When I needed her help the last time, my printer wasn't working.

4. Instead of just solving the problem, Karen went on and on about print settings and font choices that I could be using.

5. When she gets like this, her face lights up, and I feel bad for not wanting to hear the latest news on software upgrades, e-mail programs, and hardware improvements.

6. I feel guilty, but I know that I am the normal one.

7. I even pointed her problem out to her by asking, "You can't control yourself, can you?"

8. The sentence is correct.

9. Karen always solves my problem, so I should be grateful.

10. When I ask for Karen's help in the future, I plan to listen and try to learn something.

Exercise 4

1. Scientists have been studying the human face, and they have been able to identify five thousand distinct facial expressions.

2. The sentence is correct.

3. Winking is action number forty-six, and we do it with the facial muscle that surrounds the eye.

4. People around the world make the same basic expressions when they are happy, surprised, sad, disgusted, afraid, or angry.

5. These six categories of facial expressions are universally understood, but different societies have different rules about showing their emotions.

6. The smile is one of the most powerful expressions, for it changes the way we feel.

7. If we give someone a real smile showing genuine happiness, then our brains react by producing a feeling of pleasure.

8. If we give more of a polite imitation smile, then our brains show no change.

9. The sentence is correct.

10. A smile also wins the long-distance record for facial expressions, for it can be seen from as far away as several hundred feet.

Exercise 5

1. Gold is amazing, isn't it?

2. Unlike metals that change their appearance after contact with water, oil, and other substances, gold maintains its shine and brilliant color under almost any circumstances.

3. When a miner named James Marshall found gold in the dark soil of California in 1848, the gold rush began.

4. The piece of gold that Marshall discovered was only about the size of a child's fingernail, but it meant that there was more to be found.

5. Before the gold rush, San Francisco was a small town called Yerba Buena.

6. The sentence is correct.

7. Gold is actually present all over the world, but the biggest nugget to be found so far came from a location on the Potomac River.

8. This chunk of gold is as big as a yam, and it is on display at the National Museum of Natural History.

9. Some people have become rich directly because of gold, and some have become rich indirectly because of gold.

10. For example, if it had not been for California's gold rush, Levi Strauss would not have had any customers, and the world would not have blue jeans.

Proofreading Exercise

When you belong to a large family, holidays are a mixed blessing. They are certainly times to see one another, but how do you choose where to go and whom to see? For example, I have four sets of relatives living in different areas, and they all want to get together for Thanksgiving. If I accept one group's invitation, I disappoint the others. If I turn them all down and stay home with my immediate family, I make all of my other relatives mad. I guess I will just have to invite the whole clan to spend Thanksgiving at my house, won't I?

Sentence Writing

Here are some possible combinations. Yours may differ.

> I drive to school alone everyday, but I would consider carpooling.
>
> When my car alarm goes off, I don't even look out the window anymore.
>
> Although Melanie and Kurt are currently software developers, they used to be dancers, and now they both want to get back in shape.
>
> Because I was born, got married, and graduated from college on the fifth of May, I have a special fondness for that date.

COMMA RULES 4, 5, AND 6 (PP. 191–195)

Exercise 1

1. The sentence is correct.

2. The sentence is correct.

3. Cats become confused when their owners react angrily, not happily, to these "presents."

4. Desmond Morris, renowned animal expert, explains this misunderstood behavior in his book *Catwatching*.

5. The sentence is correct.

6. The sentence is correct.

7. In the absence of kittens, these cats treat their owners as the next best thing, kitten replacements.

8. The first step in the process of teaching "kittens" how to hunt, and the one cat owners hate most, is sharing the results of the hunt with them.

9. The owners' reaction, which usually involves yelling and disappointment, should include praise and lots of petting.

10. The sentence is correct.

Exercise 2

1. Paula, who left at intermission, missed the best part of the play.

2. The sentence is correct.

3. The sentence is correct.

4. Our teacher posted the results of the midterm, which we took last week.

5. The sentence is correct.

6. Mr. Simon, the math teacher, looks a lot like Mr. Simon, the English teacher.

7. My clothes dryer, which has an automatic shut-off switch, is safer than yours, which doesn't.

8. The sentence is correct.

9. The sentence is correct.

10. John and Brenda, who ask a lot of questions, usually do well on their exams.

Exercise 3

1. This year's photo directory, I believe, turned out better than last year's.

2. The sentence is correct.

3. There were, I think, still a few problems.

4. The sentence is correct.

5. The sentence is correct.

6. My supervisor, whose picture is at the top of our page, is wearing his name tag, but he's not listed at the bottom.

7. Ms. Tracy, the photographer who took the pictures, needed to help people with their poses.

8. The sentence is correct.

9. And no one, it seems, had time to look in a mirror.

10. The sentence is correct.

Exercise 4

1. We hope, of course, that people will continue to vote in elections.

2. The sentence is correct.

3. The sentence is correct.

4. The Fosters, who usually volunteer their house as a polling place, may have to install new equipment.

5. You may leave the sentence alone, or you may use commas around *therefore*.

6. You may leave the sentence alone, or you may use a comma after *Therefore*.

7. The voting booth, a small cubicle where each person casts a vote, will probably become more high-tech.

8. The sentence is correct.

9. The sentence is correct.

10. No one, we trust, will attempt to influence our thoughts there.

Exercise 5

1. Jim Henson, who created the Muppets, began his television career in the mid-1950s.

2. He was, it seems, eager to be on TV, and there was an opening for someone who worked with puppets.

3. Henson and a buddy of his quickly fabricated a few puppets, including one called Pierre the French Rat, and they got the job.

4. Henson's next project, *Sam and Friends*, also starred puppets.

5. *Sam and Friends* was a live broadcast lasting only five minutes; however, it was on two times a day and ran for six years.

6. Kermit the Frog, the character which we now associate with *Sesame Street*, was part of the cast of *Sam and Friends*.

7. Henson provided the voice and animated the movements of Kermit and a few others from the beginning, and he worked with Frank Oz, who helped round out the cast of Muppet characters.

8. In 1969, the Muppets moved to *Sesame Street*; however, they graduated to their own prime time program, *The Muppet Show*, in the late 1970s.

9. The sentence is correct.

10. The sentence is correct.

Proofreading Exercise

Two types of punctuation, internal punctuation and end punctuation, can be used in writing. Internal punctuation is used within the sentence, and end punctuation is used at the end of a sentence. Commas, the most important pieces of internal punctuation, are used to separate or enclose information within sentences. Semicolons, the next most important, also have two main functions. Their primary function, separating two independent clauses, is also the most widely known. A lesser-known need for semicolons, to separate items in a list already containing commas, occurs rarely in college writing. Colons and dashes, likewise, have special uses within sentences. And of the three pieces of end punctuation—periods, question marks, and exclamation points—the period, which signals the end of the majority of English sentences, is obviously the most common.

Sentence Writing

Here are some possible combinations. Yours may differ.

> I have seen *Mrs. Miniver*, a great old movie, many times.
>
> I have seen the great old movie *Mrs. Miniver* many times.

> I think you could make more money at a different job.
>
> You could, I think, make more money at a different job.

> My friend Carla, a natural born writer, never takes notes but gets the highest grades in the class.
>
> My writer friend Carla never takes notes and gets the highest grades in the class.

REVIEW OF THE COMMA (P. 196)

I am writing you this note, Irene, to ask you to do me a favor. [4] When you get home from work tonight, would you take the ham out of the freezer? [3] I plan to get started on the beans, the cole slaw, and the potato salad as soon as I walk in the door after work. [2] I will be so busy, however, that I might forget to thaw out the ham. [5] It's the first time I've cooked all the food for the picnic by myself, and I want everything to be perfect. [1] The big enamel roasting pan, which is in the back of the cupboard under the sink, will be the best place to keep the ham as it thaws. [6] Thanks for your help.

QUOTATION MARKS AND UNDERLINING/ITALICS (PP. 198–202)

Exercise 1

1. The Brady Bunch is still a popular television series.

2. "The greater part of our happiness or misery depends on our dispositions," said Martha Washington, "not on our circumstances."

3. "Do I have to do all of the housework by myself?" my roommate asked.

4. Last night we watched the movie Wag the Dog on DVD.

5. Oscar Wilde wrote the play The Importance of Being Earnest, the novel The Picture of Dorian Gray, the poem "The Ballad of Reading Gaol," and the children's story "The Selfish Giant."

6. "No one can make you feel inferior without your consent," Eleanor Roosevelt once said.

7. "The class period can't be over!" said the student, "I haven't even started my concluding paragraph yet."

8. I found my cousin in the library reading the latest issue of <u>Smithsonian</u> magazine.

9. We were asked to read Amy Tan's essay "Fish Cheeks" for Wednesday's class.

10. The movie version of <u>The Joy Luck Club</u> was just as sad as the book.

Exercise 2

1. "The Raven" is a poem by Edgar Allan Poe.

2. "Once you complete your test," the teacher said, "please bring it up to my desk."

3. I have a subscription to several magazines, including <u>The New Yorker.</u>

4. "Everything exists in limited quantities," Pablo Picasso perceived, "even happiness."

5. "How many times," she asked, "are you going to mention the price we paid for dinner?"

6. After Babe Ruth's death, his wife remarked, "I don't even have an autographed ball. You don't ask your husband for an autographed ball. He'd probably think you were nuts."

7. Sophocles, the Greek playwright, wrote the tragedy <u>Oedipus Rex</u> in the fifth century BC.

8. "When you go by on a train, everything looks beautiful. But if you stop," Edward Hopper explained, "it becomes drab."

9. There is a Mexican proverb that says, "Whoever sells land sells his mother."

10. When Fiorello La Guardia, who was just over five feet tall, was asked what it felt like to be short, he answered, "Like a dime among pennies."

Exercise 3

1. In his book <u>Catwatching,</u> Desmond Morris has this to say about their preferences: "Cats hate doors."

2. Phil Hartman was the voice of Troy McClure and many other memorable characters on the animated TV series <u>The Simpsons.</u>

3. "Hold fast to your dreams," wrote Langston Hughes, "for if dreams die, then life is like a broken winged bird that cannot fly."

4. Langston Hughes wrote of his childhood in a short essay entitled "Salvation"; it is part of his larger autobiography <u>The Big Sea</u>.

5. Joan Didion describes her relationship with migraine headaches in her essay "In Bed."

6. "Where can I buy some poster board?" he asked.

7. "There is a school-supply store around the corner," his friend replied, "but I don't think that it's open this late."

8. Sylvia asked the other students if they had seen the Alfred Hitchcock movie called <u>The Birds</u>.

9. "I don't remember," James answered.

10. "It's not something you could ever forget!" she yelled.

Exercise 4

1. Kurt Vonnegut, in his short story "Harrison Bergeron," describes his main character's appearance as "Halloween and hardware."

2. "Now he belongs to the ages!" cried Edwin M. Stanton after Abraham Lincoln's assassination.

3. In her book <u>The Mysterious Affair at Styles</u>, Agatha Christie wrote that "Every murderer is probably somebody's old friend."

4. "Swear not by the moon," says Juliet to Romeo.

5. John F. Kennedy told the U.S. Congress, "The human mind is our fundamental resource."

6. Abraham Lincoln stated that "Public opinion in this country is everything."

7. "Writers are always selling somebody out," Joan Didion observed.

8. The expression "All animals are equal, but some animals are more equal than others" can be found in George Orwell's novel <u>Animal Farm</u>.

9. A Swahili proverb warns that "To the person who seizes two things, one always slips from his grasp!"

10. Groucho Marx once remarked, "I wouldn't want to belong to any club that would accept me as a member."

Exercise 5

1. Ovid reminded us that "We can learn even from our enemies."

2. "We know what a person thinks not when he tells us what he thinks," said Isaac Bashevis Singer, "but by his actions."

3. The Spanish proverb "El pez muere por la boca" translated means "The fish dies because it opens its mouth."

4. "Ask yourself whether you are happy, and you cease to be so," John Stuart Mill wrote.

5. A Russian proverb states, "Without a shepherd, sheep are not a flock."

6. William Faulkner felt that "Some things you must always be unable to bear."

7. St. Jerome had the following insight: "The friendship that can cease has never been real."

8. Oscar Wilde found that "In this world there are only two tragedies. One is not getting what one wants, and the other is getting it."

9. Henry Ford warned, "You can't build a reputation on what you're going to do."

10. "Choose a job you love," Confucius suggested, "and you will never have to work a day in your life."

Proofreading Exercise

I admire the way that Helen Keller describes her feelings in her autobiography, The Story of My Life. Being totally blind and deaf, Keller tries to explain how she can experience something like moonlight. She writes, "I cannot, it is true, see the moon climb up the sky behind the pines and steal softly across the heavens." "But," she continues, "I know she is there, and . . . I feel the shimmer of her garments as she passes." Keller could *feel* light rather than see it. She explains that, when a certain combination of air and light strike her, "A luminous warmth seems to enfold me. . . . It is like the kiss of warm lips on my face."

CAPITAL LETTERS (PP. 204–208)

Exercise 1

1. Many consider *The Diary of Anne Frank* to be one of the most important books of the twentieth century.

2. Anne Frank wrote her famous diary during the Nazi occupation of Holland in World War II.

3. The building in Amsterdam where the Frank family and several others hid during the two years before their capture is now a museum and has been recently renovated.

4. Visitors to the Anne Frank House can stand before her desk and see pictures of movie stars like Greta Garbo on her wall.

5. They can climb the strairs hidden behind a bookcase that led to the annex where Anne lived with her mother, Edith; her father, Otto; and her sister, Margot.

6. One of the others hiding with the Franks was Peter van Pels, who was roughly the same age as Anne.

7. Anne writes of her relationship with Peter in her diary.

8. Visitors to the museum can enter the room where Peter gave Anne her first kiss just a few months before the Nazis discovered their hiding place in 1944.

9. Anne's family and Peter's were both sent to concentration camps in Germany.

10. Only Anne's father lived to see the Anne Frank House open as a museum for the first time on May 3, 1960.

Exercise 2

1. Dad and I have both decided to take college classes next fall.

2. Fortunately, in Los Angeles we live near several colleges and universities.

3. Classes at the community colleges usually begin in late August or early September.

4. Within twenty minutes, we could drive to Los Angeles Valley College, Los Angeles City College, Glendale Community College, or Pasadena City College.

5. I want to take credit classes, and my dad wants to sign up for community education classes.

6. For instance, I will enroll in the academic courses necessary to transfer to a university.

7. These include English, math, science, and history classes.

8. My father, on the other hand, wants to take noncredit classes with titles like "Learn to Play Keyboards," "Web Pages Made Easy," and "Be Your Own Real Estate Agent."

9. Dad already has a great job, so he can take classes just for fun.

10. I know that if I want to go to one of the University of California campuses later, I will have to be serious from the start.

Exercise 3

1. I grew up watching *The Wizard of Oz* once a year on TV before video stores like Blockbuster even rented movies to watch at home.

2. I especially remember enjoying it with my brother and sisters when we lived on Topeka Drive.

3. Mom would remind us early in the day to get all of our homework done.

4. "If your homework isn't finished," she'd say, "you can't see the Munchkins!"

5. My favorite part has always been when Dorothy's house drops on one of the wicked witches and her feet shrivel up under the house.

6. The Wicked Witch of the West wants revenge after that, but Dorothy and Toto get help from Glinda, the Good Witch of the North.

7. Glinda tells Dorothy about the Emerald City and the Wizard of Oz.

8. On their way, Toto and Dorothy meet the Scarecrow, the Tin Man, and the Cowardly Lion.

9. Together they conquer the witch and meet Professor Marvel, the real man who has been pretending to be a wizard.

10. The ruby slippers give Dorothy the power to get back to Kansas and to her Aunt Em and Uncle Henry.

Exercise 4

1. Oscar Wilde was an Irish-born writer who lived and wrote in England for much of his life during the late 1800s.

2. He was famous for his refined ideas about art and literature.

3. While still a young man, Wilde traveled to America.

4. Contrary to what many people expected, he was well received in rough mining towns such as Leadville, Colorado.

5. He gave one particularly long speech to the miners who lived in Leadville.

6. Wilde spoke on the following topic: "The Practical Application of the Aesthetic Theory to Exterior and Interior House Decoration, with Observations on Dress and Personal Ornament."

7. During his stay in Leadville, Wilde had gained the miners' respect by visiting them down in the mines and by proving that he could drink as much whiskey as they could without getting drunk.

8. Wilde wrote about one incident that took place in Leadville.

9. Before giving a lecture he called *The Ethics of Art,* Wilde was told that two criminals accused of murder had been found in town.

10. Earlier that evening on the same stage where Wilde was about to give his speech, the two men were convicted and executed by Leadville officials.

Exercise 5

1. The southern writer known as Flannery O'Connor was born with the name Mary Flannery O'Connor.

2. O'Connor lived much of her life in Milledgeville, Georgia.

3. She attended Peabody High School, Georgia State College for Women (currently Georgia College), and the State University of Iowa (currently the University of Iowa).

4. While at college in Georgia, O'Connor edited the campus newspaper, *The Colonnade,* and its literary magazine, *The Corinthian.*

5. When she began publishing her writing, O'Connor left off her first name, Mary.

6. Students in literature classes study O'Connor's short stories, including "Revelation," "Good Country People," "A Good Man Is Hard to Find," and "The Life You Save May Be Your Own."

7. O'Connor's stories received the O. Henry Award many times.

8. And organizations such as the Ford Foundation and the National Institute of Arts and Letters awarded O'Connor with grants to support her writing.

9. She also wrote the novels *Wise Blood* and *The Violent Bear It Away.*

10. In 1962, Notre Dame's St. Mary's College made Flannery O'Connor an honorary Doctor of Letters.

REVIEW OF PUNCTUATION AND CAPITAL LETTERS (P. 209)

1. The Golden Gate Bridge is the most famous landmark in San Francisco.

2. Have you ever read Gary Soto's narrative essay "The Pie"?

3. We traveled to many European cities with our high school band; it was an experience we'll never forget.

4. How much would someone pay for a script from the first Star Wars movie?

5. We received your resumé, Ms. Clark, and will contact you if we have any openings.

6. The participant who guesses the correct number of gumballs will win the gigantic gumball machine.

7. Prof. Mitchell teaches the beginning French class.

8. Whenever I go there, I leave something behind; then I have to drive back and get it.

9. We brought the food, but we forgot the plates, the cutlery, and the plastic cups.

10. Roy Scheider came up with the famous line "We're gonna need a bigger boat" in the movie Jaws.

11. I love to read the cartoons in the newspaper; it's my favorite thing to do on Sundays.

12. Packing for a short trip seems easy; however, it's not.

13. Our English instructor made us memorize the following rhyme about commas: "When in doubt, leave them out."

14. I wonder if I needed to bring my mathematics book with me today.

15. <u>I Love Lucy</u> is the only TV series that my whole family thinks is funny.

COMPREHENSIVE TEST (PP. 210–211)

1. (pro ref) The girls put down the suitcases and walked away.

2. (ww) I hope that my application is *accepted.*

3. (cliché) I don't know why we didn't see the clear solution.

4. (cap) My family took a trip to the San Diego Zoo.

5. (pro) The instructor gave my friend and *me* extra credit for attending the play.

6. (pro agr) Everyone was allowed to revise *the latest* essay.

7. (ro) The countertops were clean, but the floors needed mopping.

8. (dm) *While we were taking a long vacation,* our bus broke down in Wichita.

9. (pro ref) She said, "Ms. Kepler, I lost my notebook."

10. (wordy) The box was empty.

11. (p) I wonder if I will finish my project by the due date.

12. (apos) The *men's* team challenged the *women's* team.

13. (mm) *When she was thirty,* she had her first child.

14. (c/s) The hall has been reserved; however, they haven't chosen a caterer yet.

15. (//) We wore our ribbons as symbols of hope, solidarity, and *commitment.*

16. (shift in time) I start a new journal page whenever I *finish* an entry.

17. (ww) *You're* going to need a new car soon.

18. (frag) Because the party was so loud, the neighbors called the police.

19. (s/v agr) A bouquet of roses *was* delivered to our office today.

20. (pro agr) Each of the dogs at the kennel has *its* own distinct personality.

WRITING

ORGANIZING IDEAS (P. 228)

Exercise 1 Thesis or Fact? (P. 228)

1.	FACT	**6.**	THESIS
2.	THESIS	**7.**	THESIS
3.	THESIS	**8.**	FACT
4.	FACT	**9.**	THESIS
5.	THESIS	**10.**	FACT

Exercise 2 Adding Transitional Expressions (P. 231)

When I moved into my own apartment for the first time last month, I discovered the many hidden expenses of entering "the real world." *First of all*, I had no idea that utility companies needed a security deposit from anyone who hasn't rented before. Each utility required a thirty to fifty dollar deposit. *Therefore*, my start-up costs just for gas, electricity, and phone used up all the money I had saved for furnishings. *Next*, I found out how expensive it was to supply a kitchen with the basic staples of food and cleaning supplies. My initial trip to the grocery store cost $125, and I hadn't even bought my curtains at that point. *Finally*, I was able to budget my money and keep a little aside for any other unexpected expenses of living on my own.

WRITING ABOUT WHAT YOU READ (P. 245)

Assignment 17

100-Word Summary of "Straight Talk"

Times have changed, and words have changed with them. Life has become more expensive and more complicated in the past several decades. With new products and technologies come words used to describe them. Now that we have so many words, we don't value the meanings of the words we use. Words are not like objects. We can give things to people without the things changing. But it is hard to be sure that our words are understood by the people who read our writing. And if we get lazy about the meanings of words, people can take advantage of us.

Index